CLAMP

7

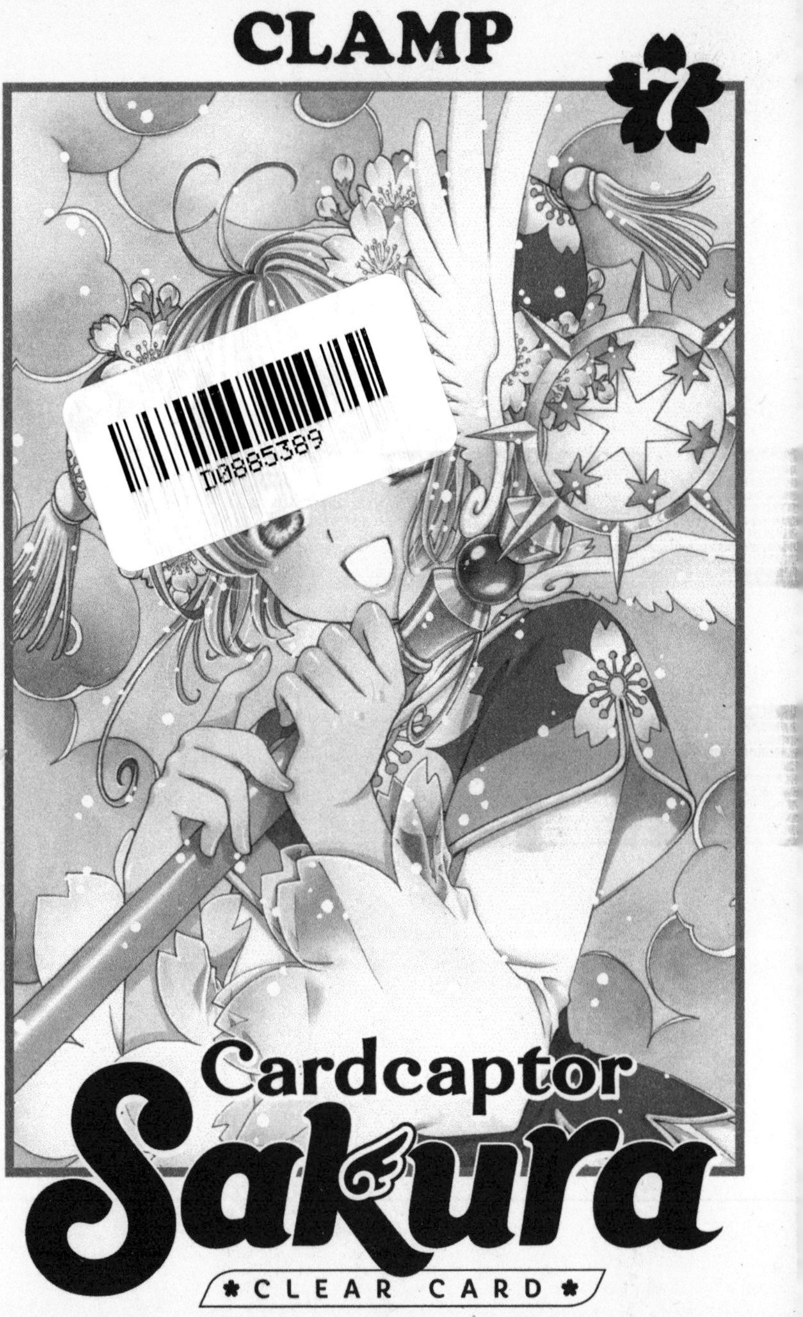

Cardcaptor Sakura

CLEAR CARD

Cardcaptor Sakura

CLEAR CARD

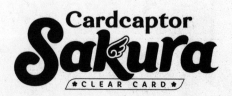

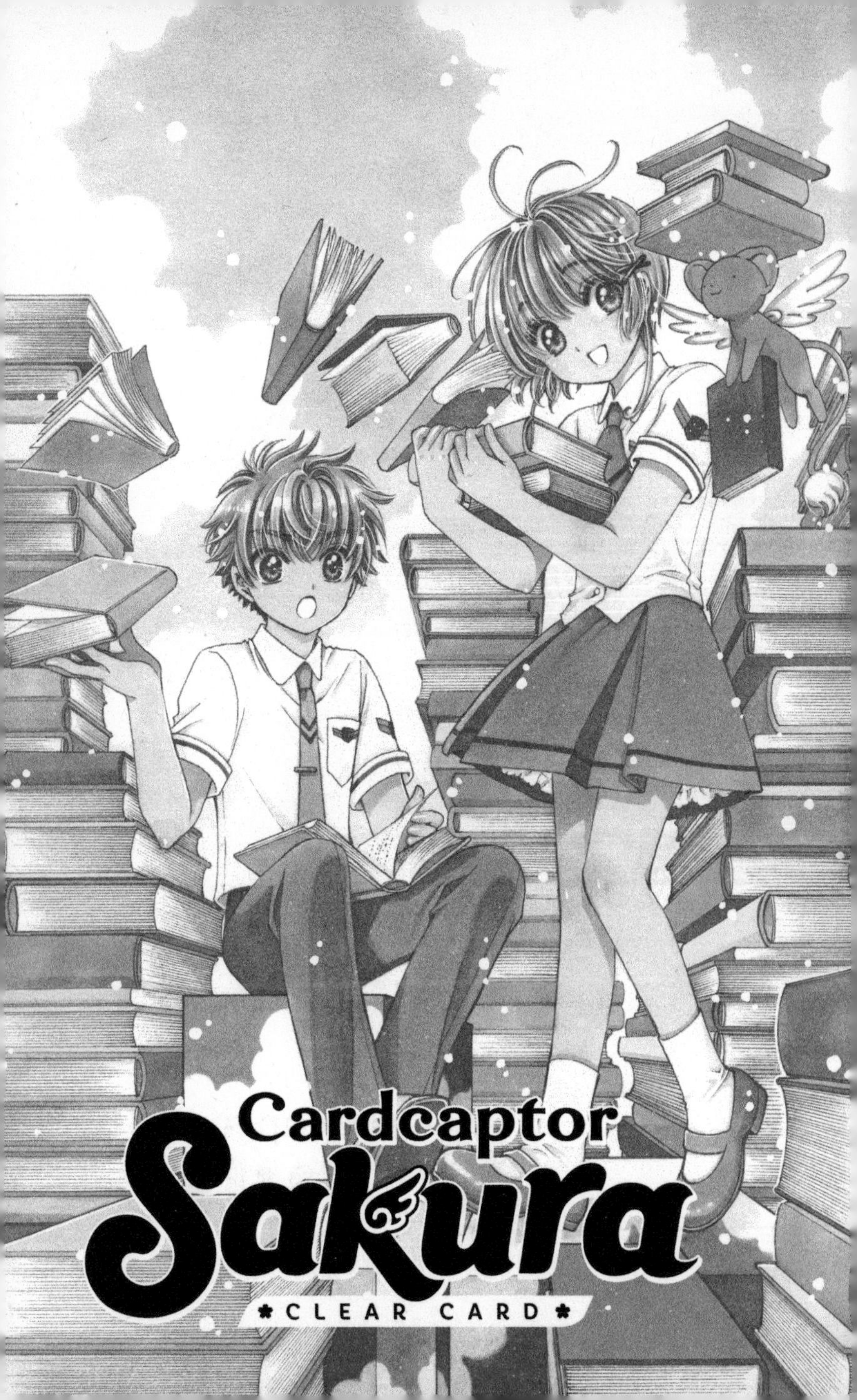
Cardcaptor
Sakura
CLEAR CARD

Cardcaptor
Sakura
CLEAR CARD

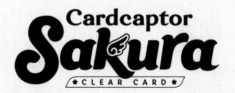

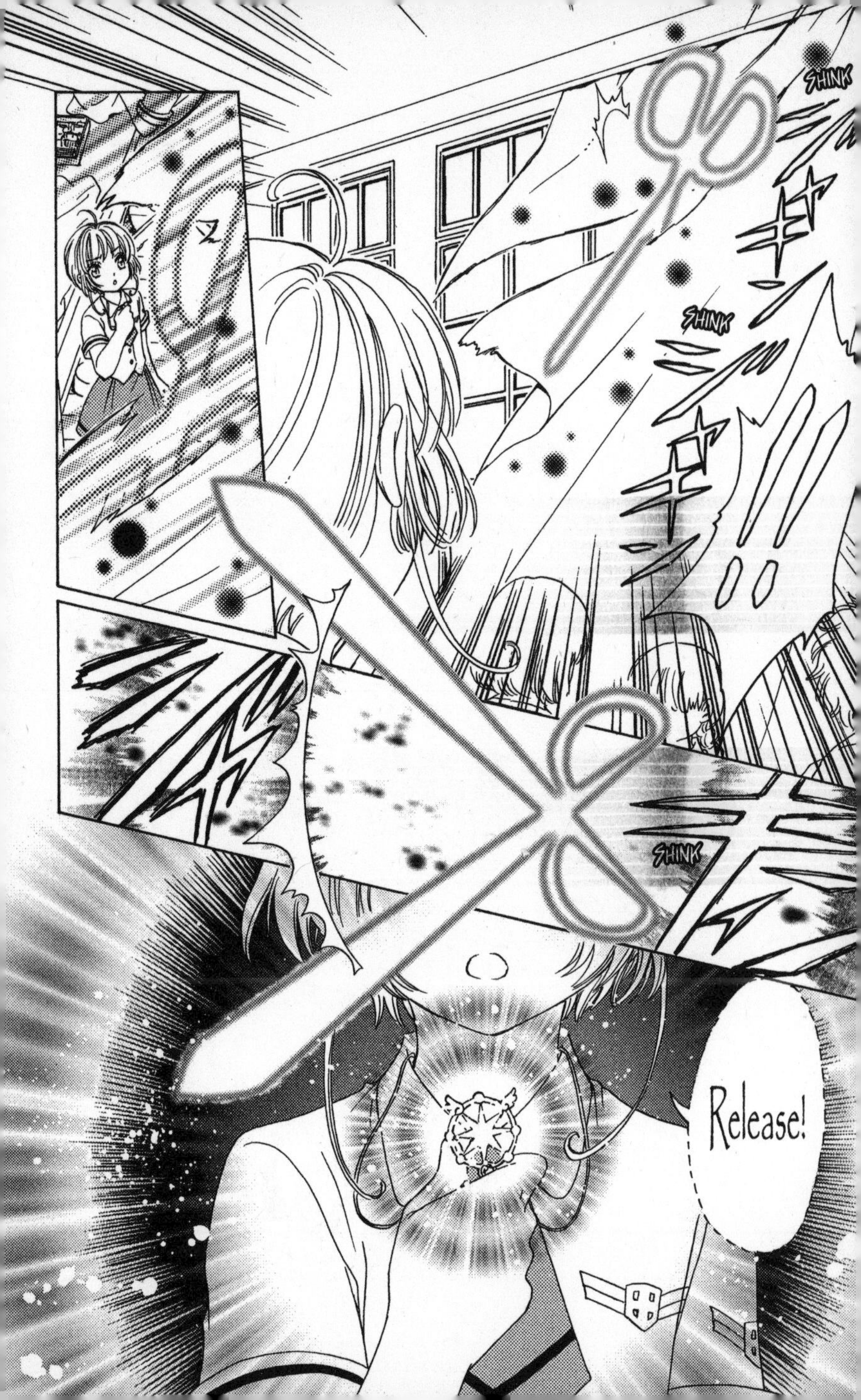
SHINK
SHINK
SHINK
Release!

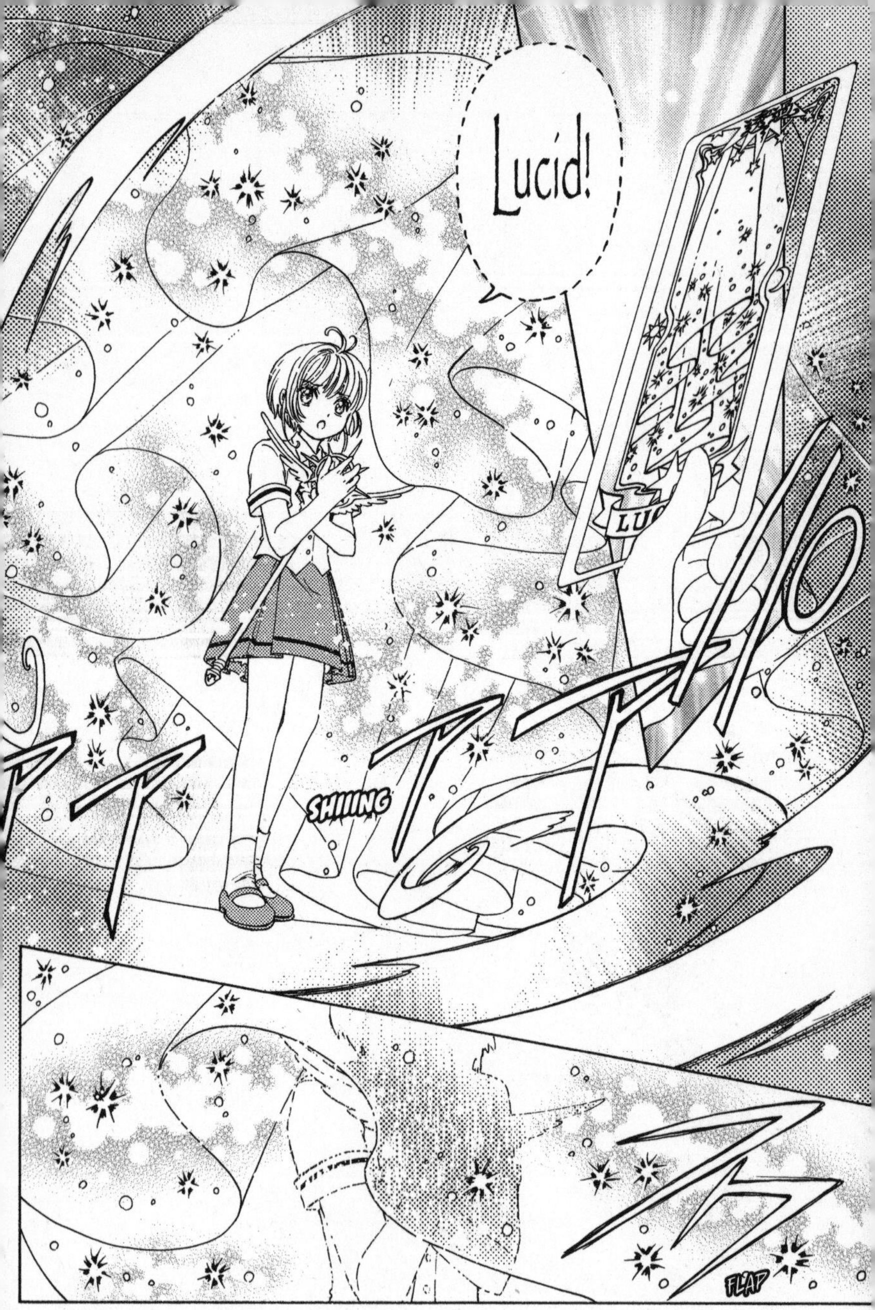
Lucid!
LUC
SHIIING
FLAP

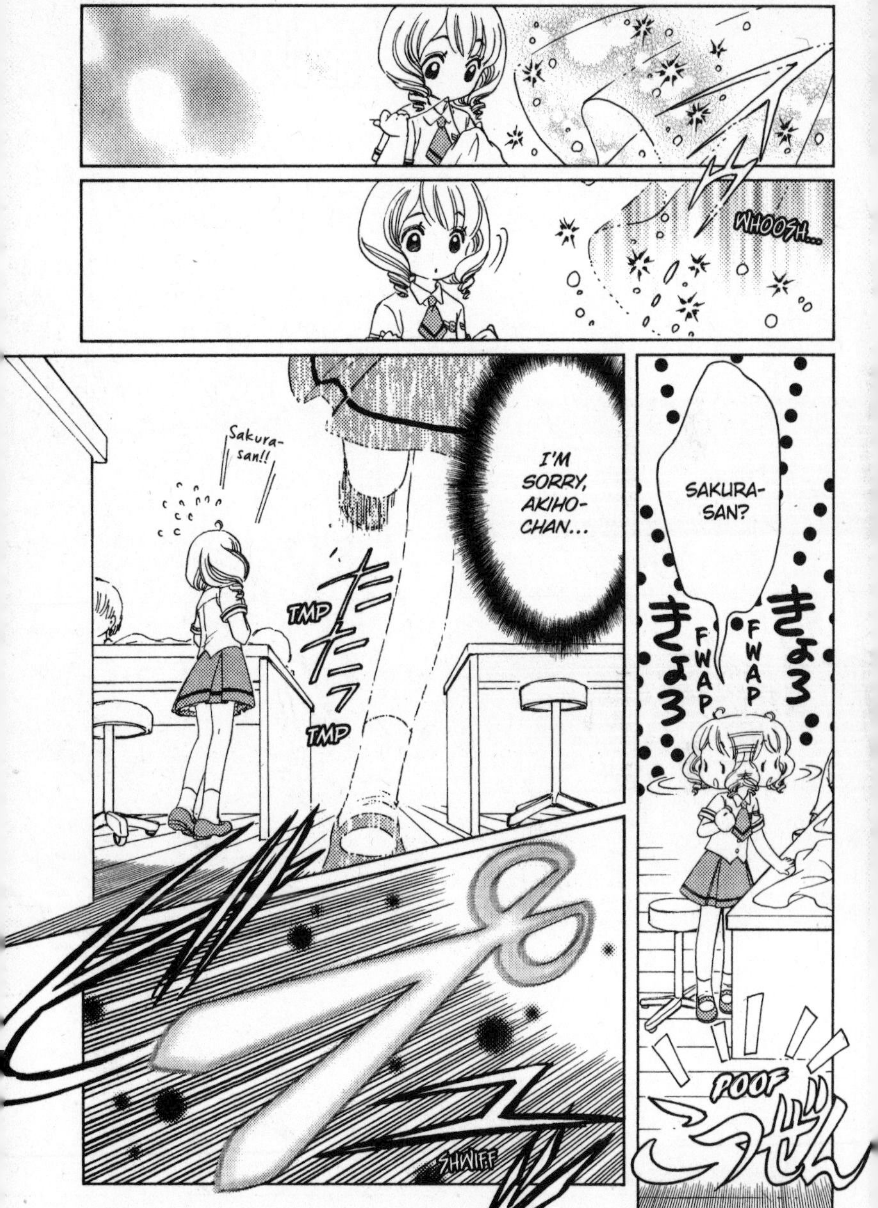
WHOOSH...
SAKURA-SAN?
FWAP
FWAP
きょろ
きょろ
POOF
こつぜん
I'M SORRY, AKIHO-CHAN...
Sakura-san!!
TMP
TMP
SHWIFF

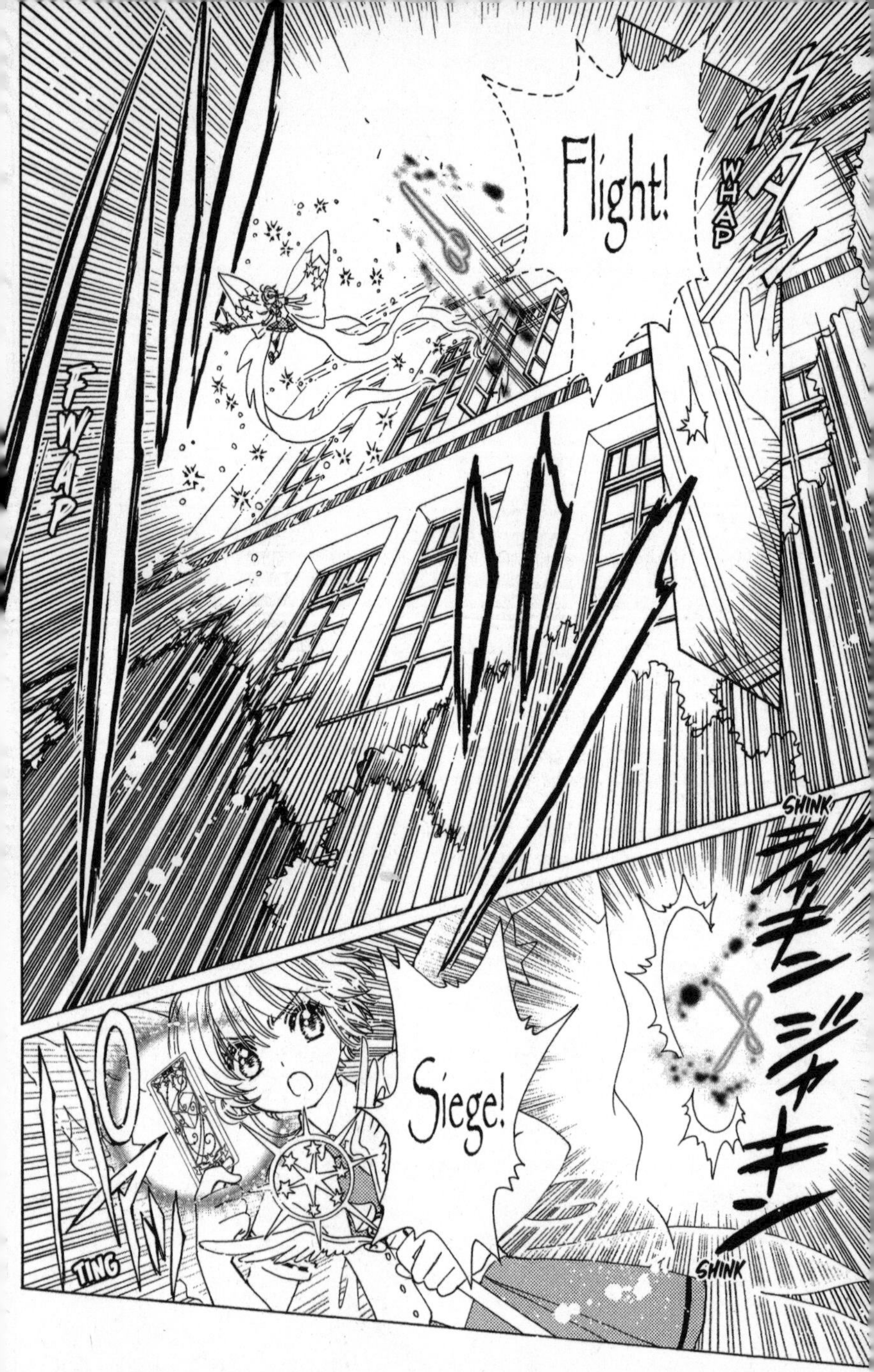
WHAP
Flight!
FWAP
SHINK
SHINK
Siege!
TING

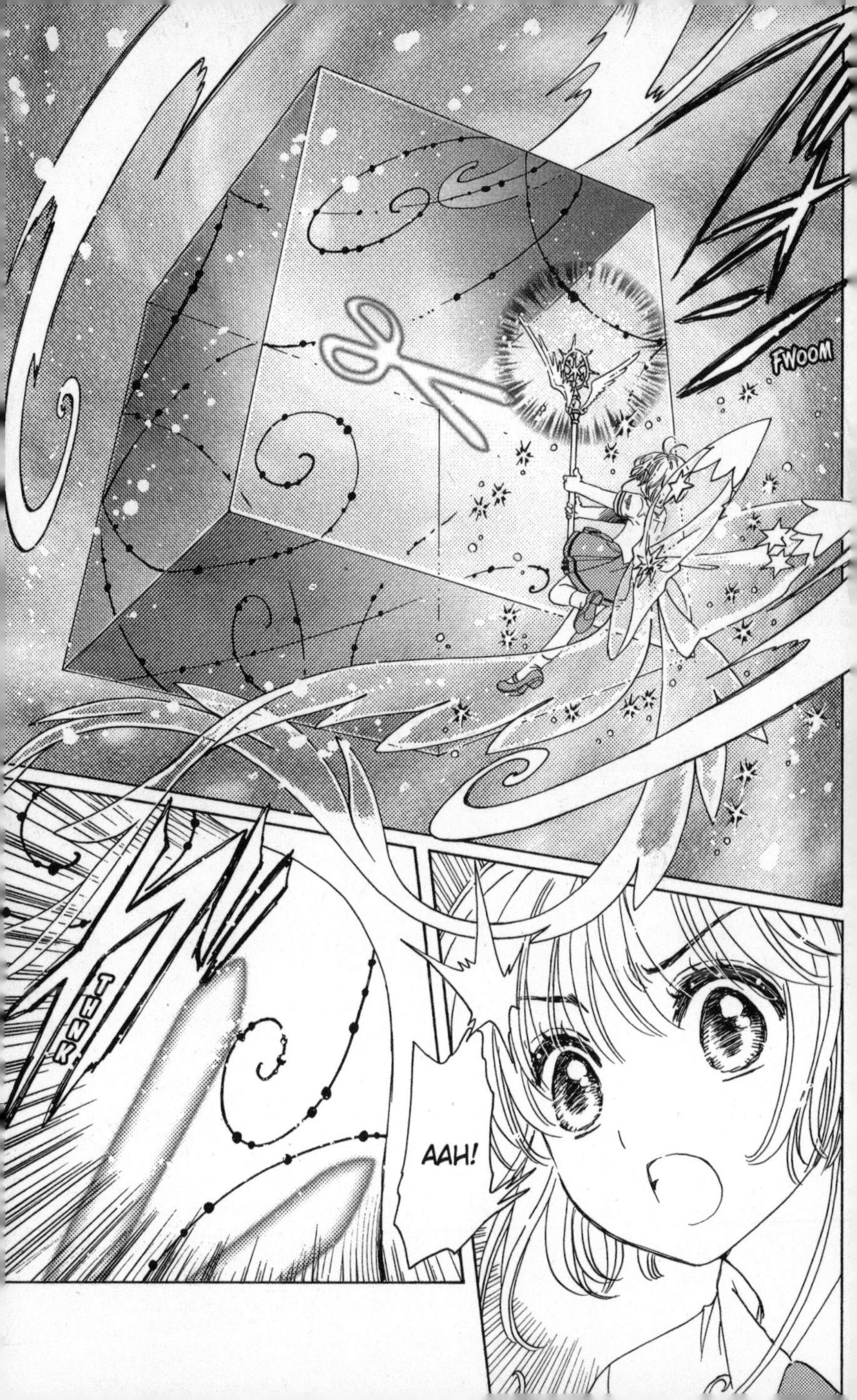
FWOOM
THUNK
AAH!

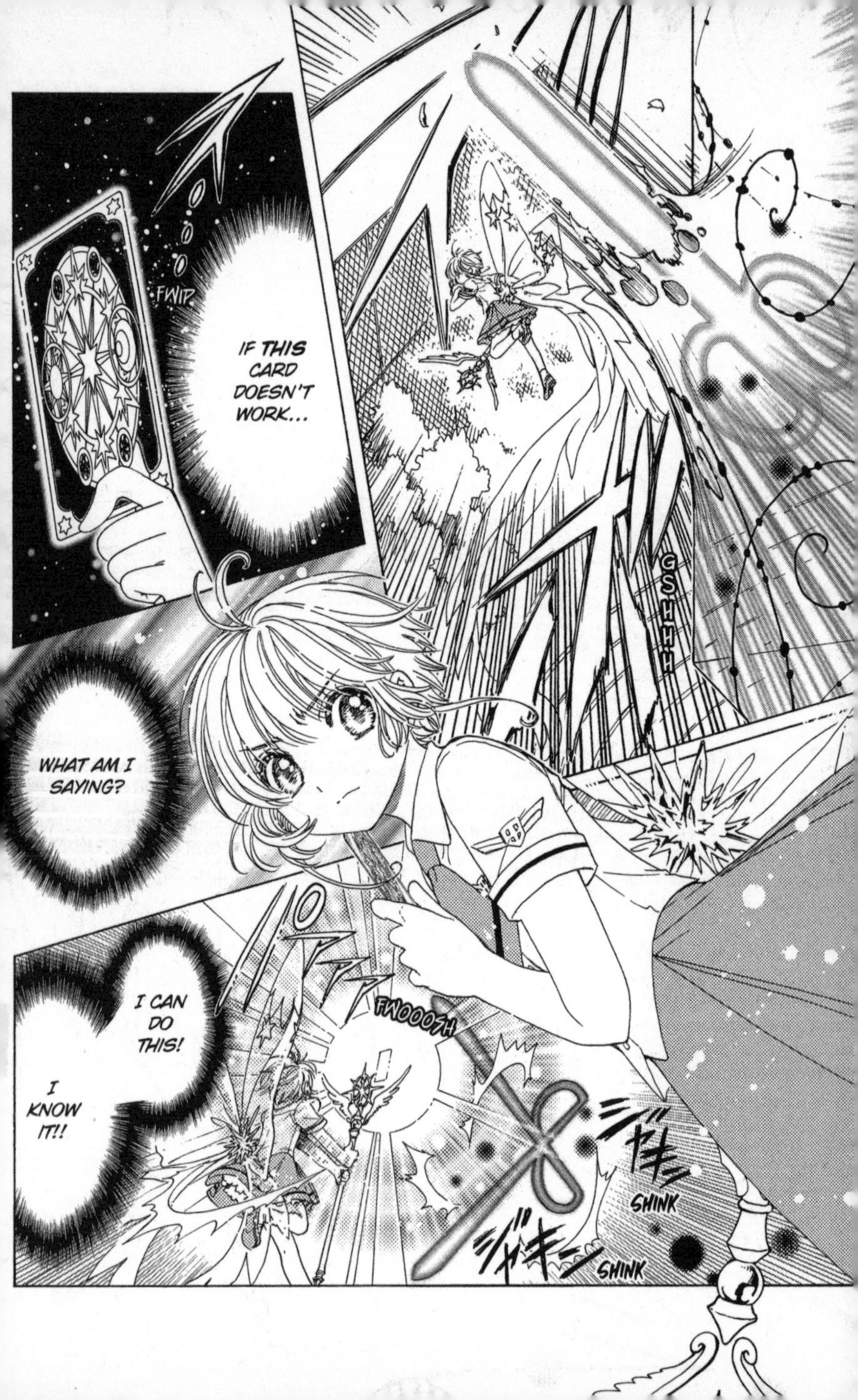
GSHHH
FWIP
IF THIS CARD DOESN'T WORK...
WHAT AM I SAYING?
I CAN DO THIS!
I KNOW IT!!
FWOOOSH
ジャキン
SHINK
ジャキン
SHINK

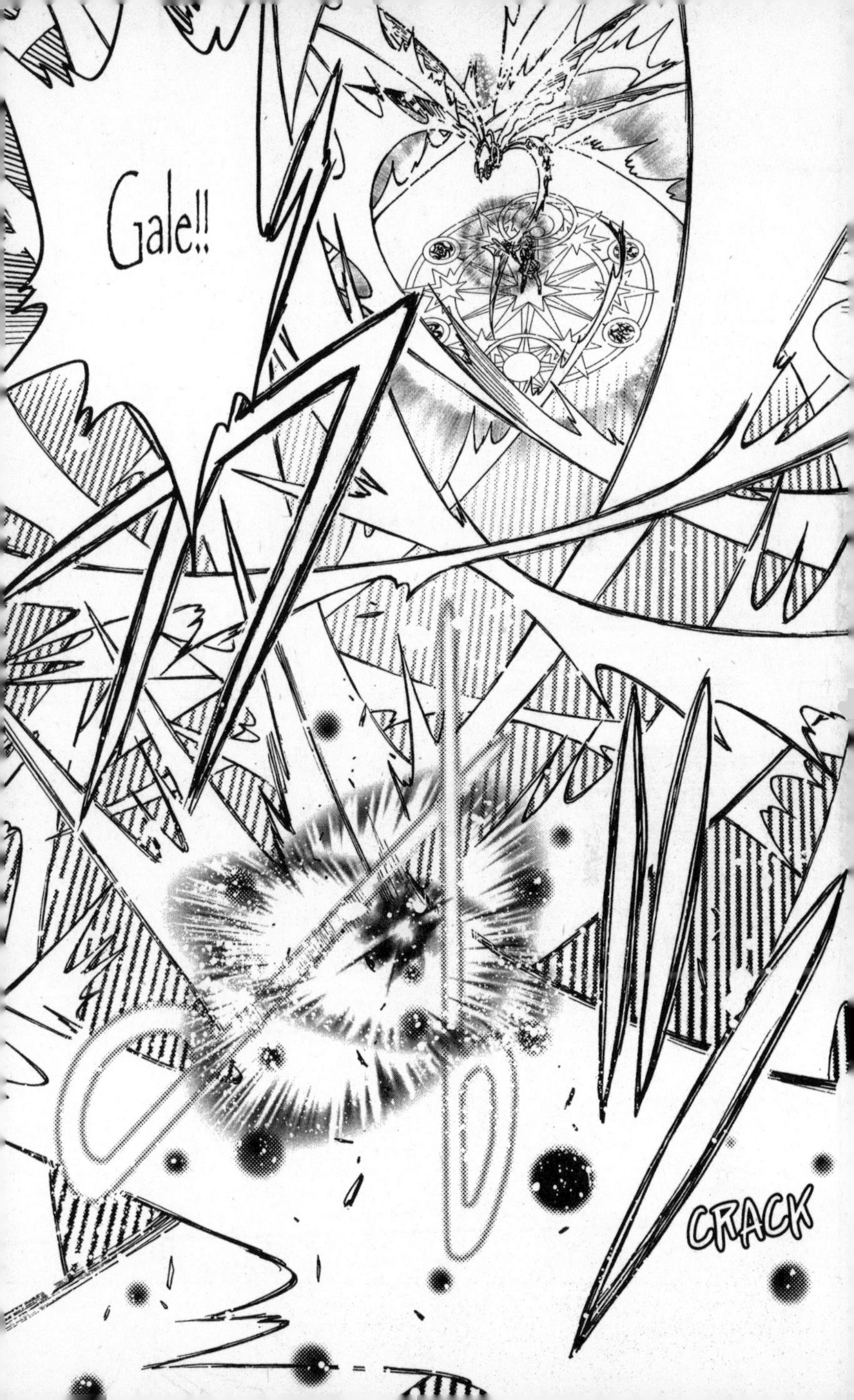
Gale!!
CRACK

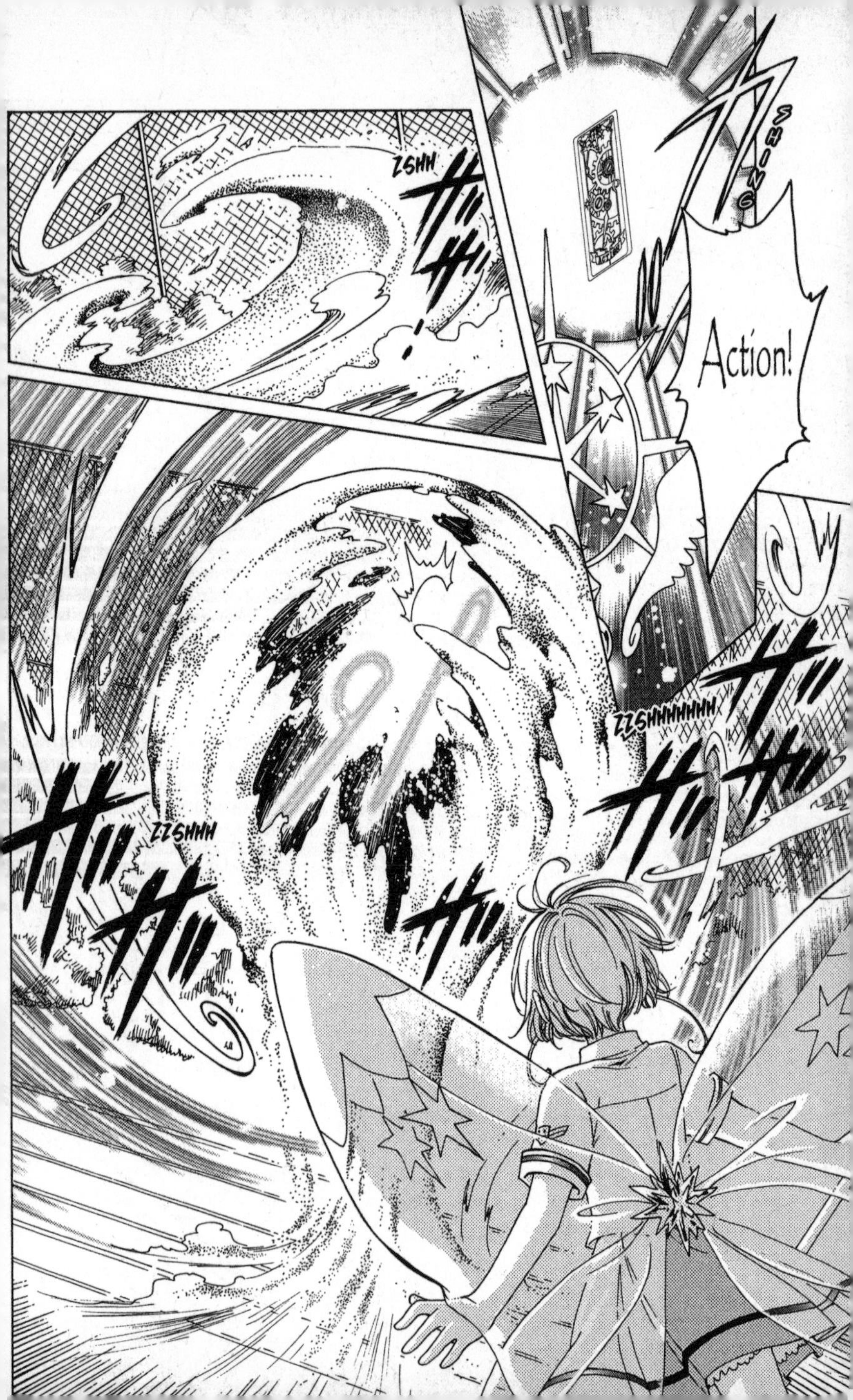
SHING
Action!
ZSHH
ZZSHHHHHHH
ZZSHH

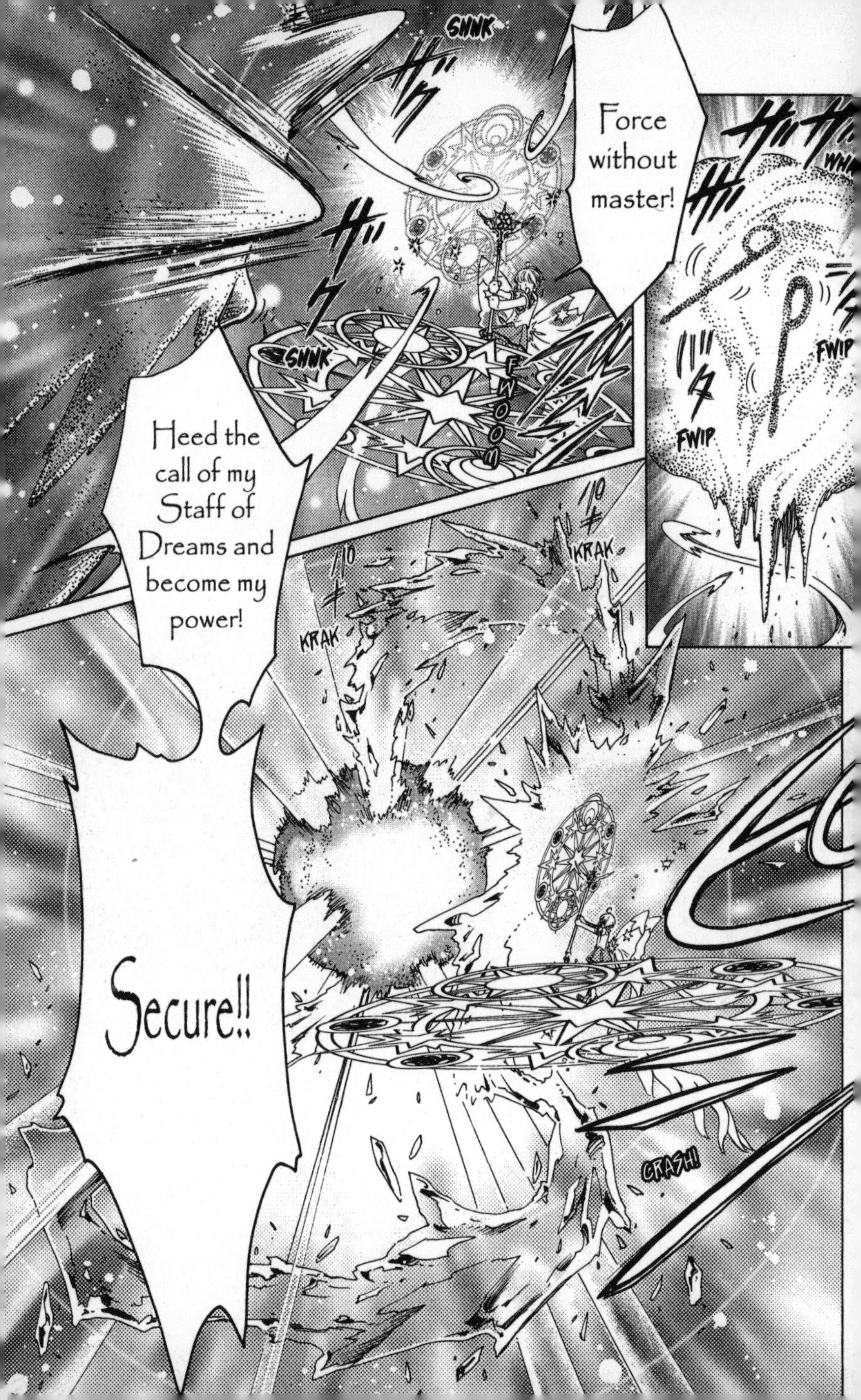
Force without master!
SHNK
SHNK
FWOOM
FWIP
FWIP
Heed the call of my Staff of Dreams and become my power!
KRAK
KRAK
Secure!!
CRASH!

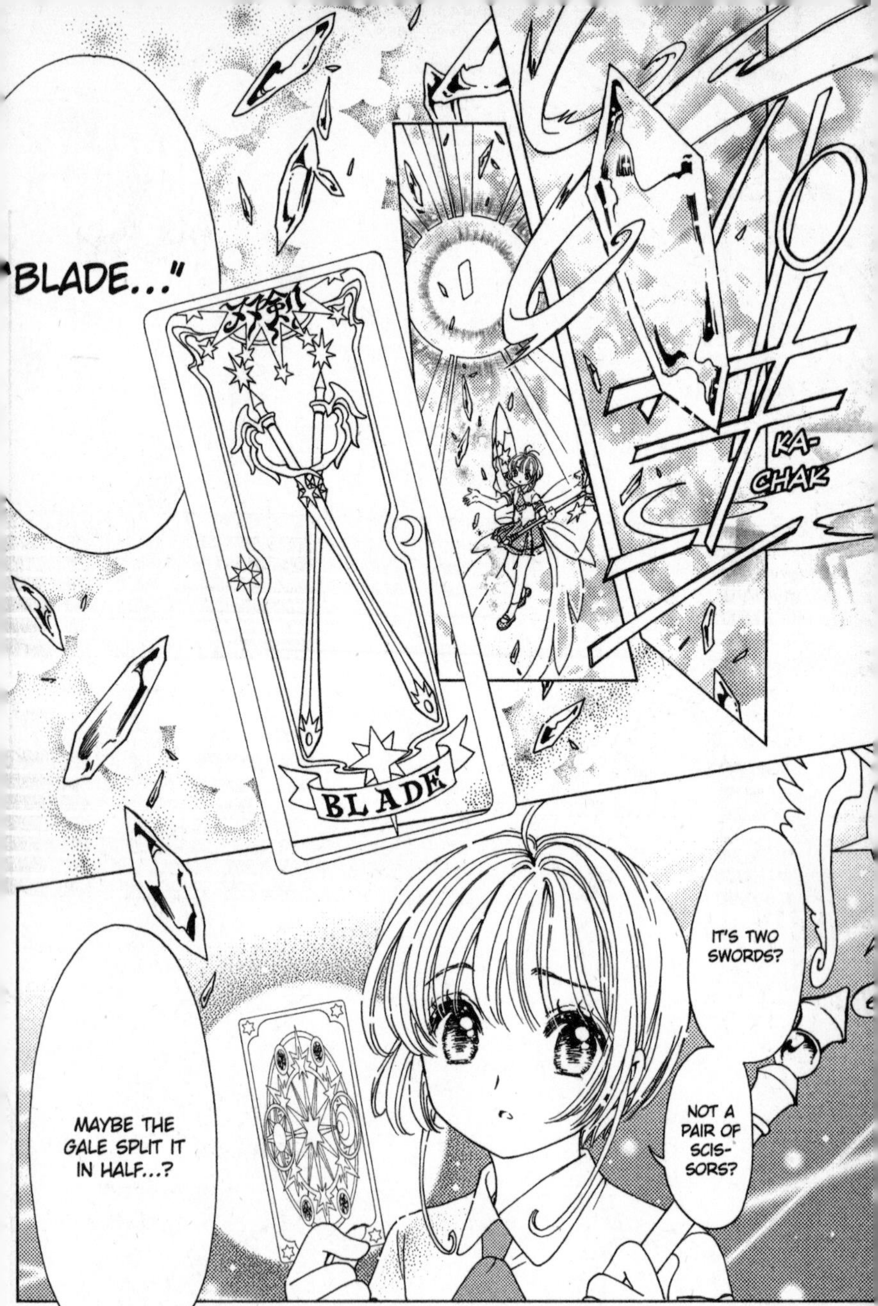
"BLADE..."
BLADE
KA-CHAK
IT'S TWO SWORDS?
NOT A PAIR OF SCIS-SORS?
MAYBE THE GALE SPLIT IT IN HALF...?

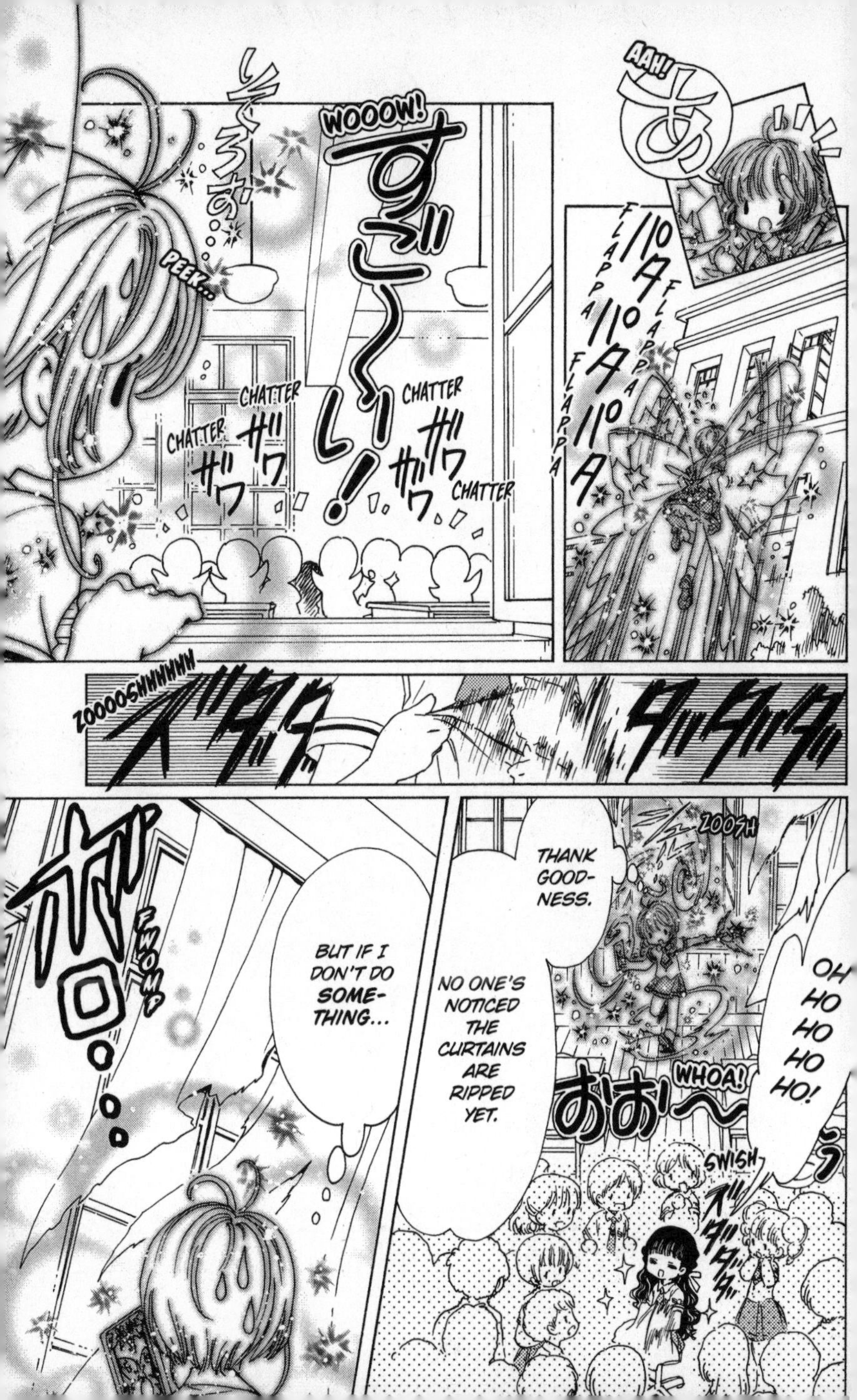
AAH!
FLAPPA FLAPPA FLAPPA
WOOOW!
PEEK...
CHATTER
CHATTER
CHATTER
CHATTER
ZOOOOSHHHHHH
ZOOSH
THANK GOODNESS.
NO ONE'S NOTICED THE CURTAINS ARE RIPPED YET.
OH HO HO HO HO!
WHOA!
SWISH
FWOMP
BUT IF I DON'T DO SOMETHING...

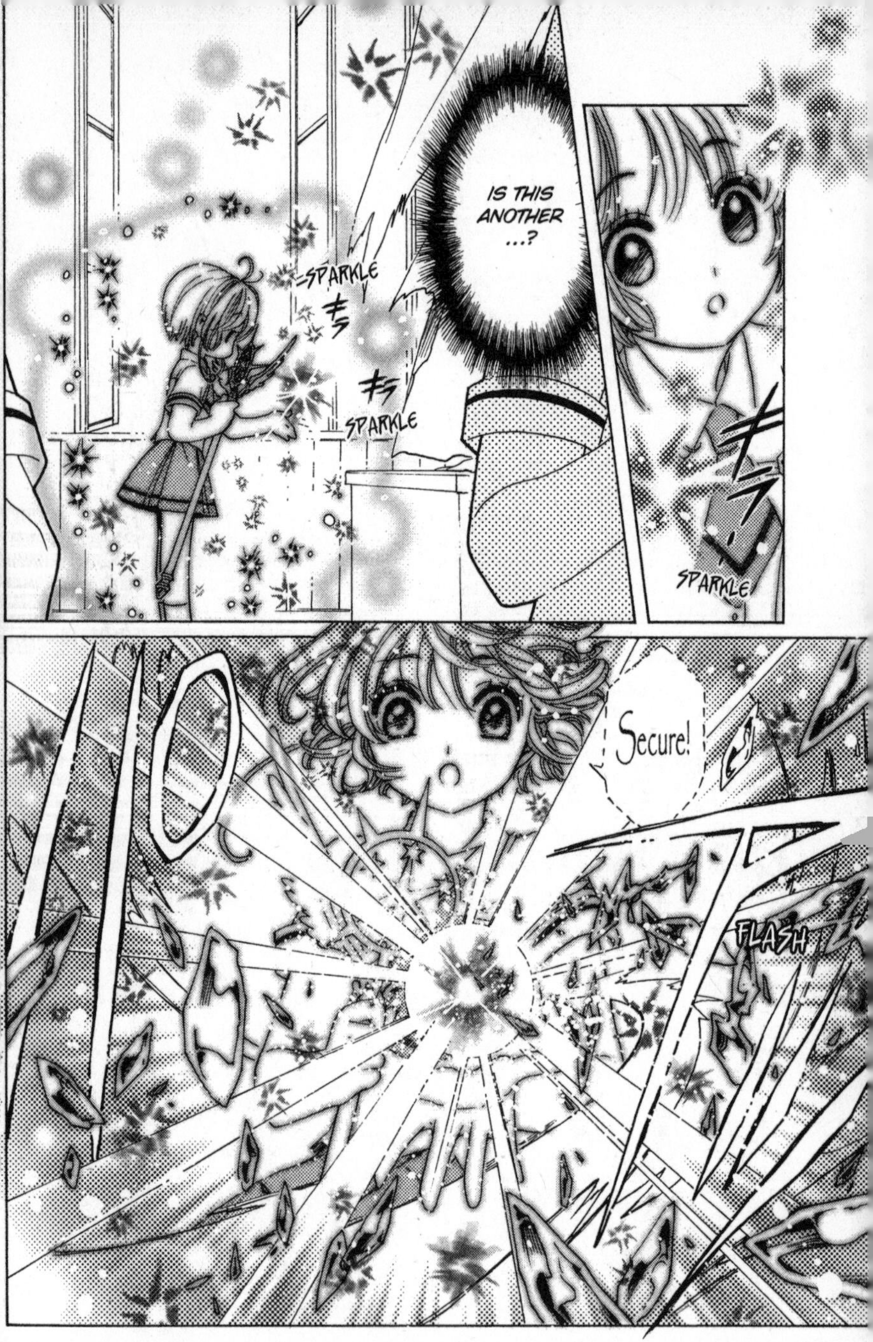
キラ
SPARKLE
IS THIS ANOTHER ...?
SPARKLE
キラ
キラ
SPARKLE
Secure!
FLASH

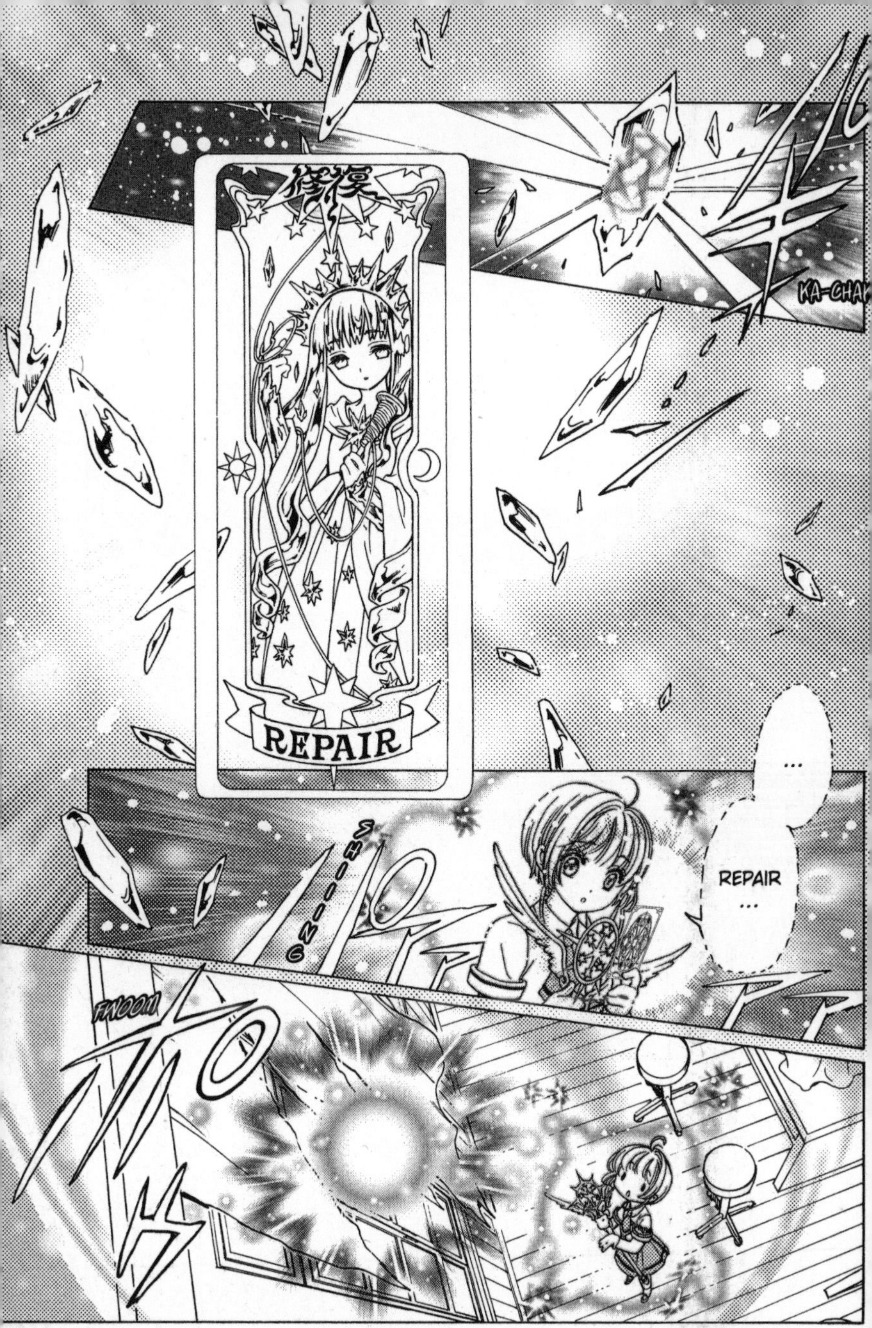
KA-CHA
REPAIR
...
REPAIR
...
SHIIIING
FWOOM

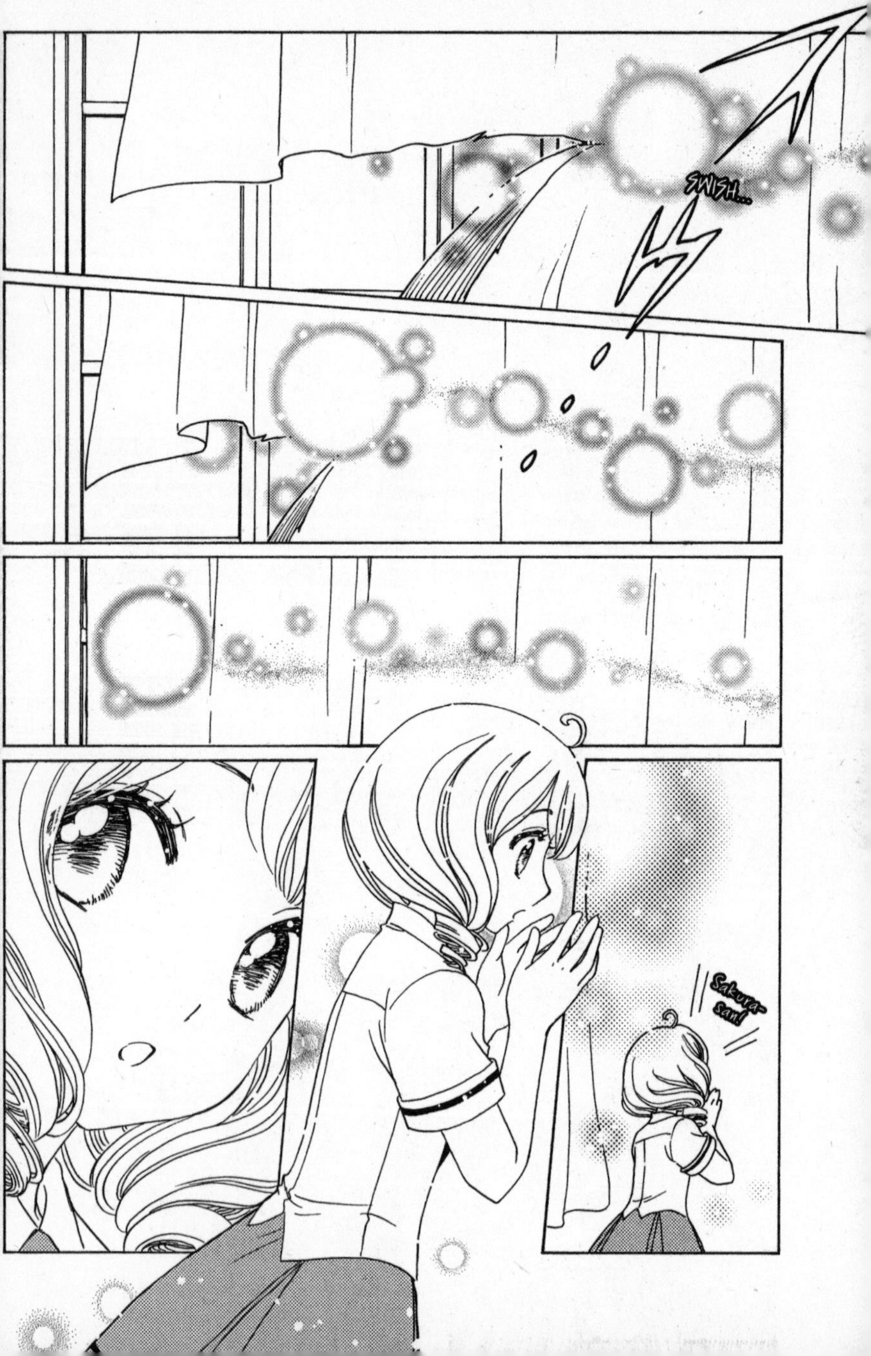
SWISH...
Sakura-san!

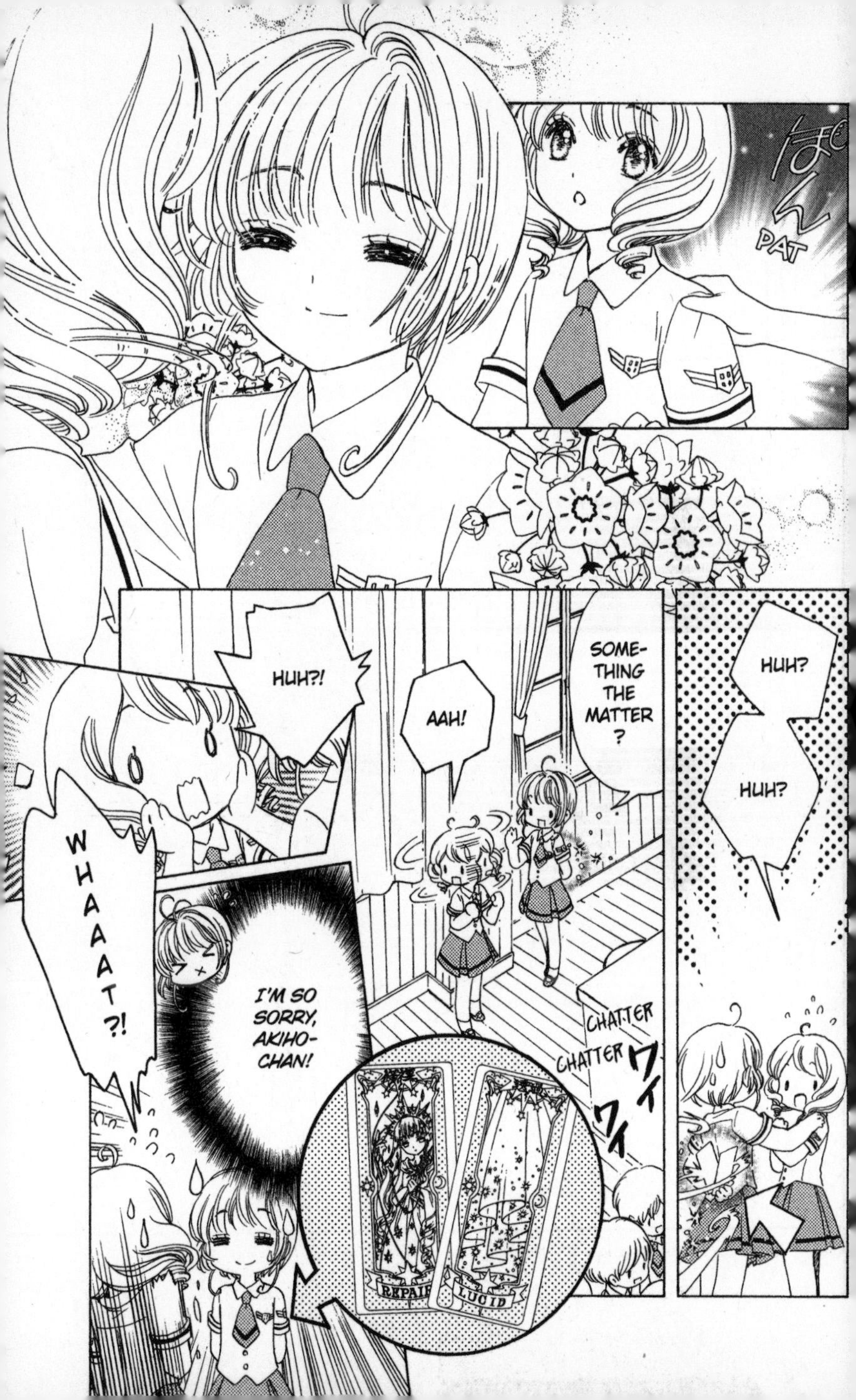
ぽん
PAT
HUH?
HUH?
SOME-THING THE MATTER?
AAH!
CHATTER
CHATTER
ワイワイ
HUH?!
WHAAAAT?!
I'M SO SORRY, AKIHO-CHAN!
REPAIR
LUCID

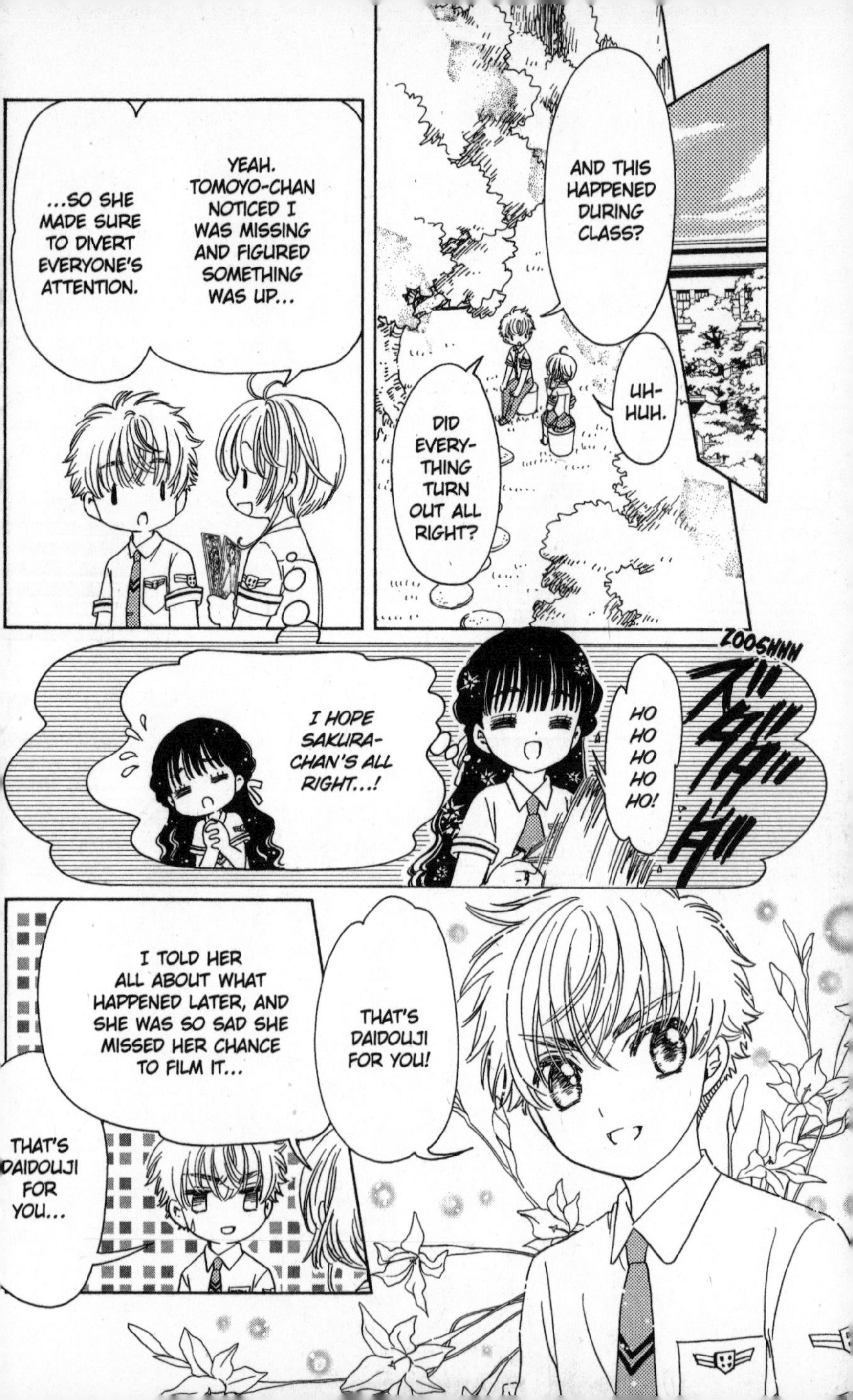
AND THIS HAPPENED DURING CLASS?
UH-HUH.
DID EVERYTHING TURN OUT ALL RIGHT?
YEAH. TOMOYO-CHAN NOTICED I WAS MISSING AND FIGURED SOMETHING WAS UP...
...SO SHE MADE SURE TO DIVERT EVERYONE'S ATTENTION.
ZOOSHHH
HO HO HO HO HO!
I HOPE SAKURA-CHAN'S ALL RIGHT...!
THAT'S DAIDOUJI FOR YOU!
I TOLD HER ALL ABOUT WHAT HAPPENED LATER, AND SHE WAS SO SAD SHE MISSED HER CHANCE TO FILM IT...
THAT'S DAIDOUJI FOR YOU...

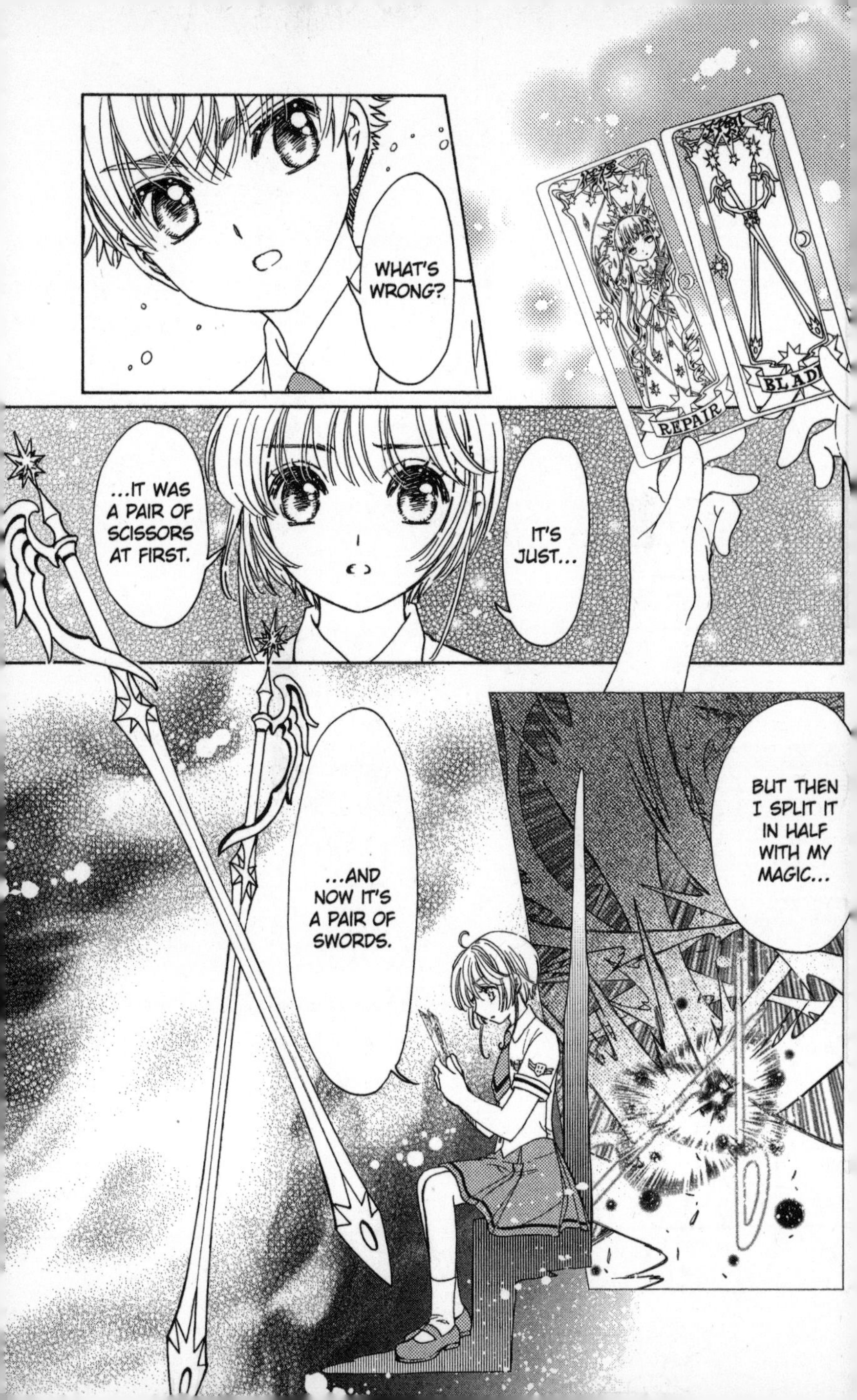
REPAIR
WHAT'S WRONG?
IT'S JUST...
...IT WAS A PAIR OF SCISSORS AT FIRST.
BUT THEN I SPLIT IT IN HALF WITH MY MAGIC...
...AND NOW IT'S A PAIR OF SWORDS.

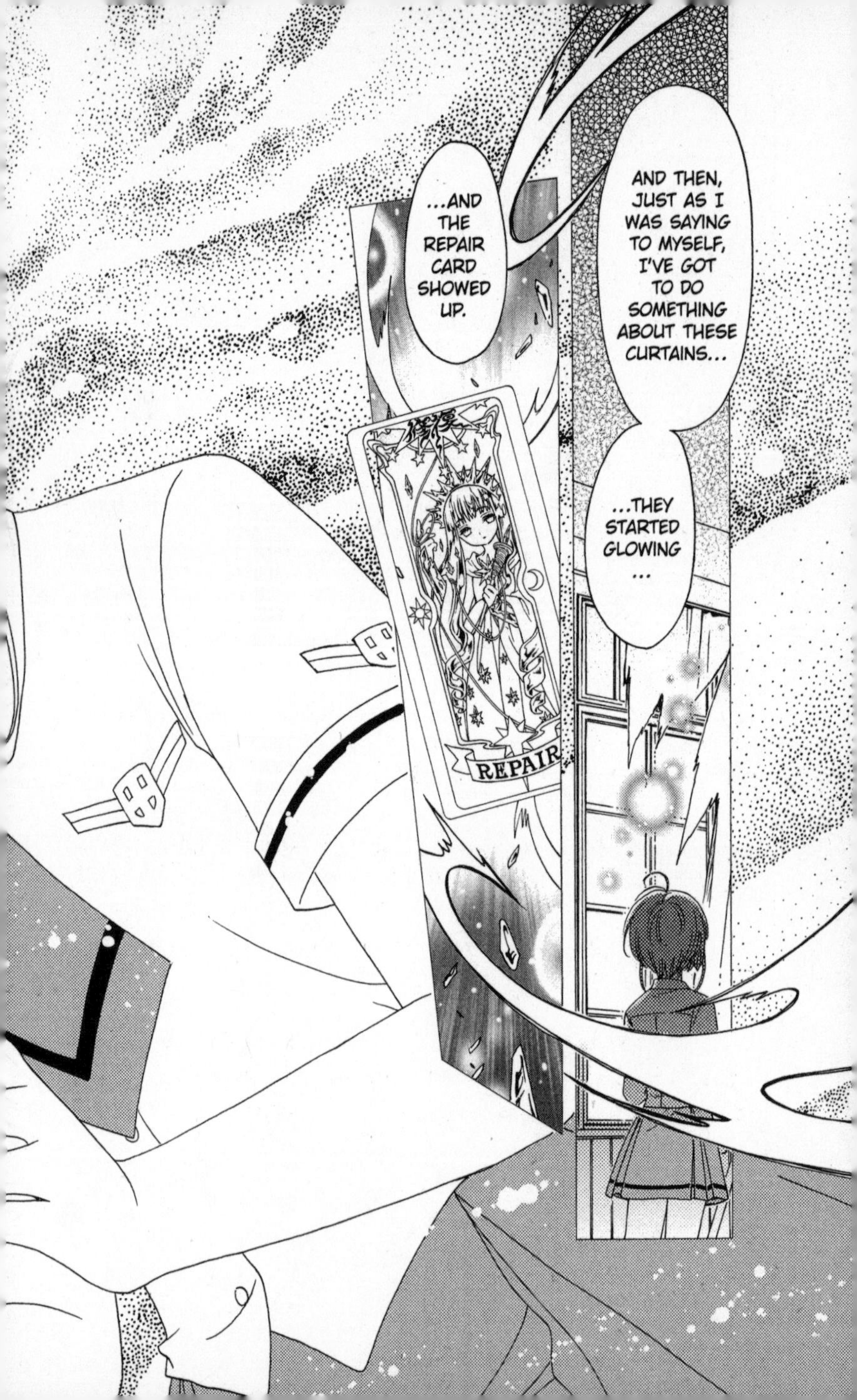
AND THEN, JUST AS I WAS SAYING TO MYSELF, I'VE GOT TO DO SOMETHING ABOUT THESE CURTAINS...
...THEY STARTED GLOWING...
...AND THE REPAIR CARD SHOWED UP.
REPAIR

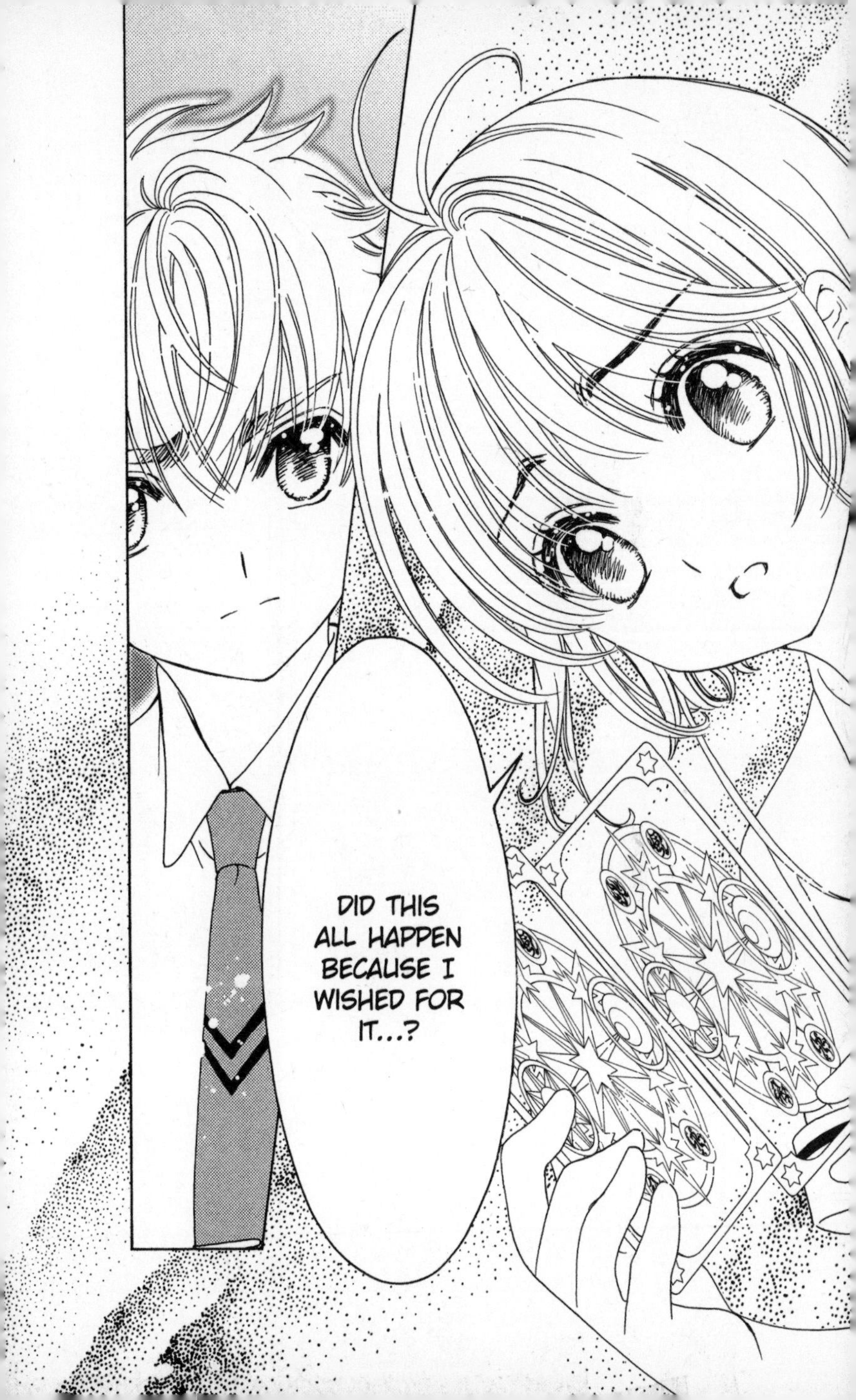
DID THIS ALL HAPPEN BECAUSE I WISHED FOR IT...?

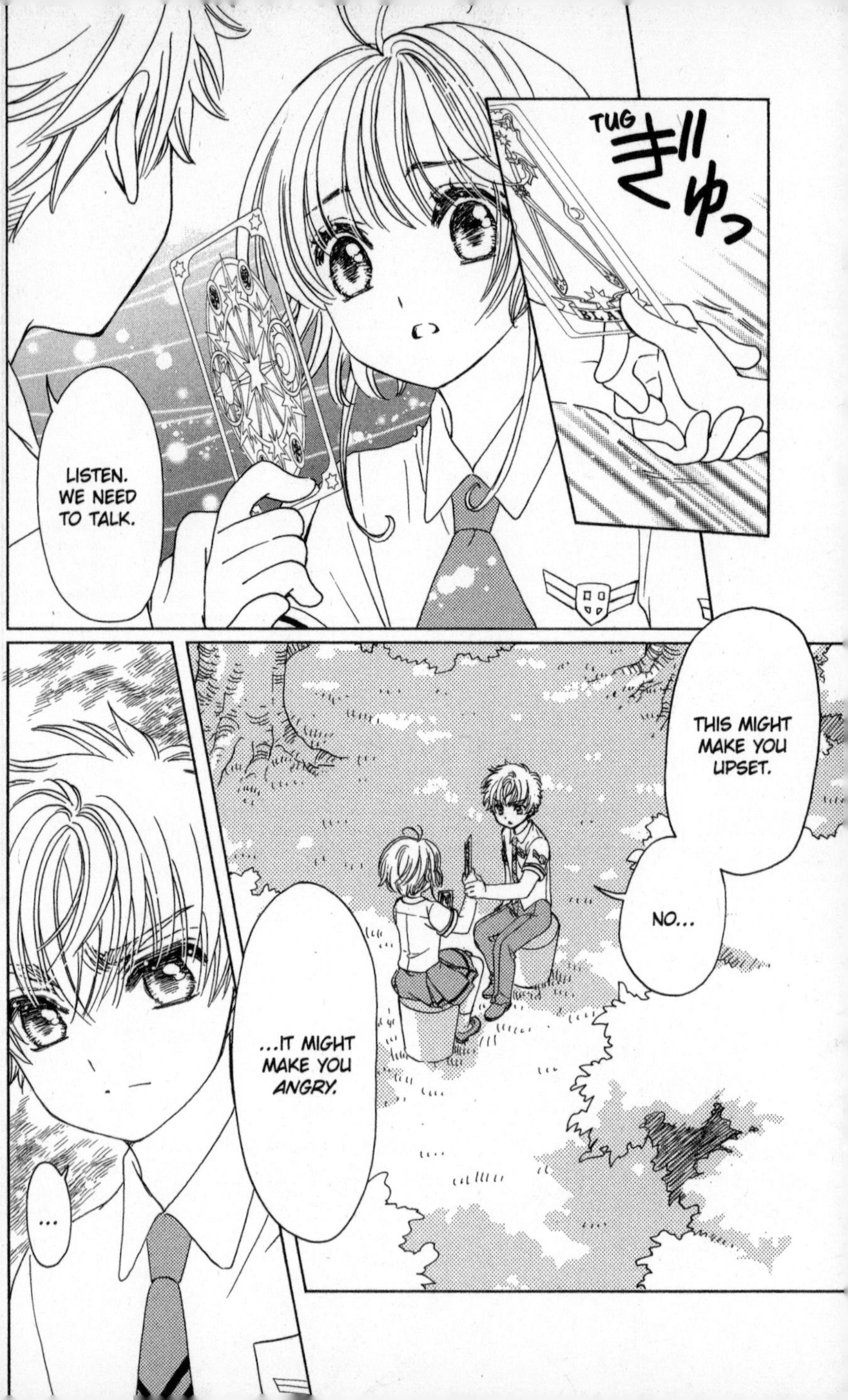
TUG
ぎゅっ
LISTEN. WE NEED TO TALK.
THIS MIGHT MAKE YOU UPSET.
NO...
...IT MIGHT MAKE YOU ANGRY.
...

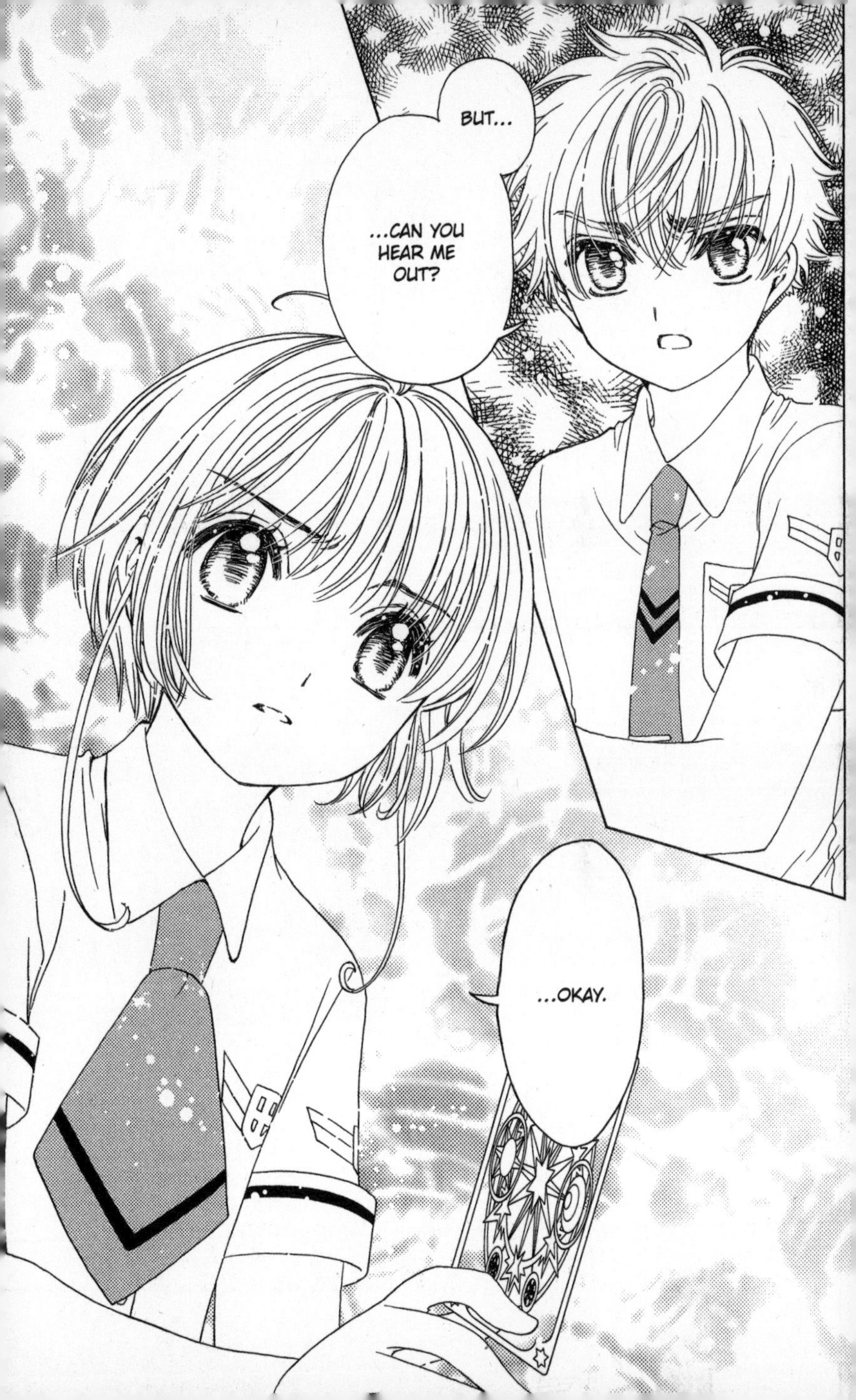
BUT...
...CAN YOU HEAR ME OUT?
...OKAY.

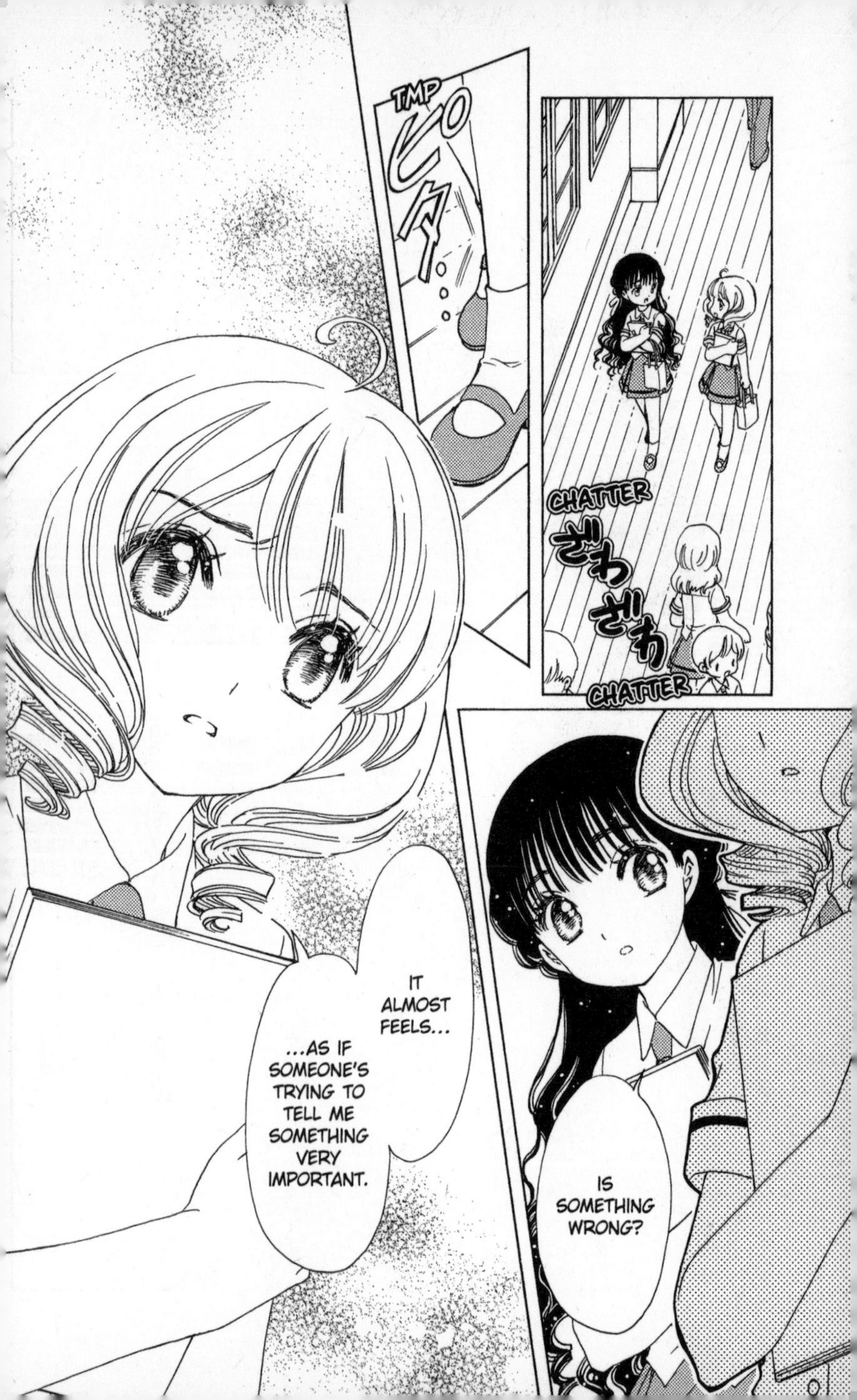
CHATTER
ざわ ざわ
CHATTER
TMP
ピタ
IS SOMETHING WRONG?
IT ALMOST FEELS...
...AS IF SOMEONE'S TRYING TO TELL ME SOMETHING VERY IMPORTANT.

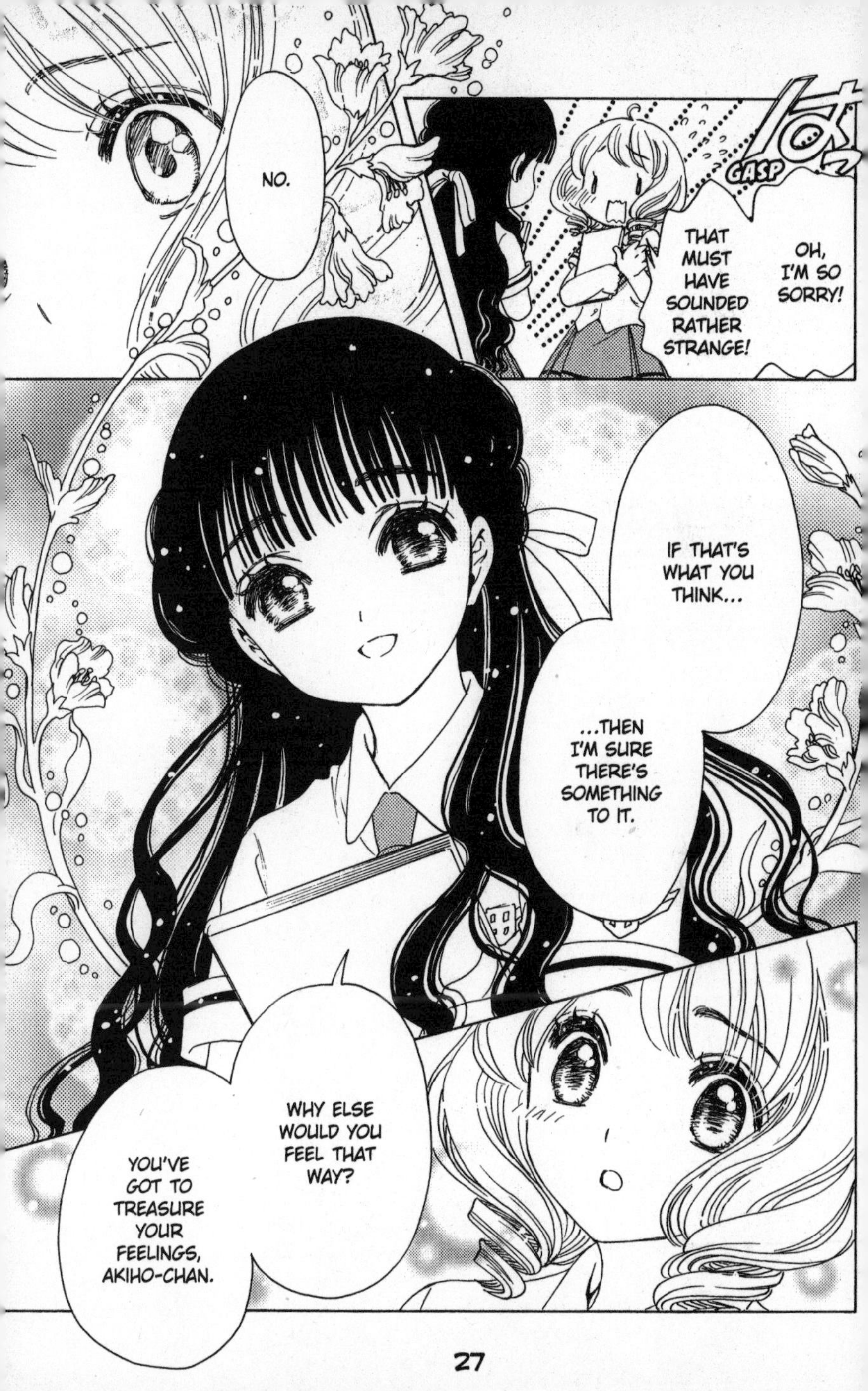
はっ
GASP
OH, I'M SO SORRY!
THAT MUST HAVE SOUNDED RATHER STRANGE!
NO.
IF THAT'S WHAT YOU THINK...
...THEN I'M SURE THERE'S SOMETHING TO IT.
WHY ELSE WOULD YOU FEEL THAT WAY?
YOU'VE GOT TO TREASURE YOUR FEELINGS, AKIHO-CHAN.

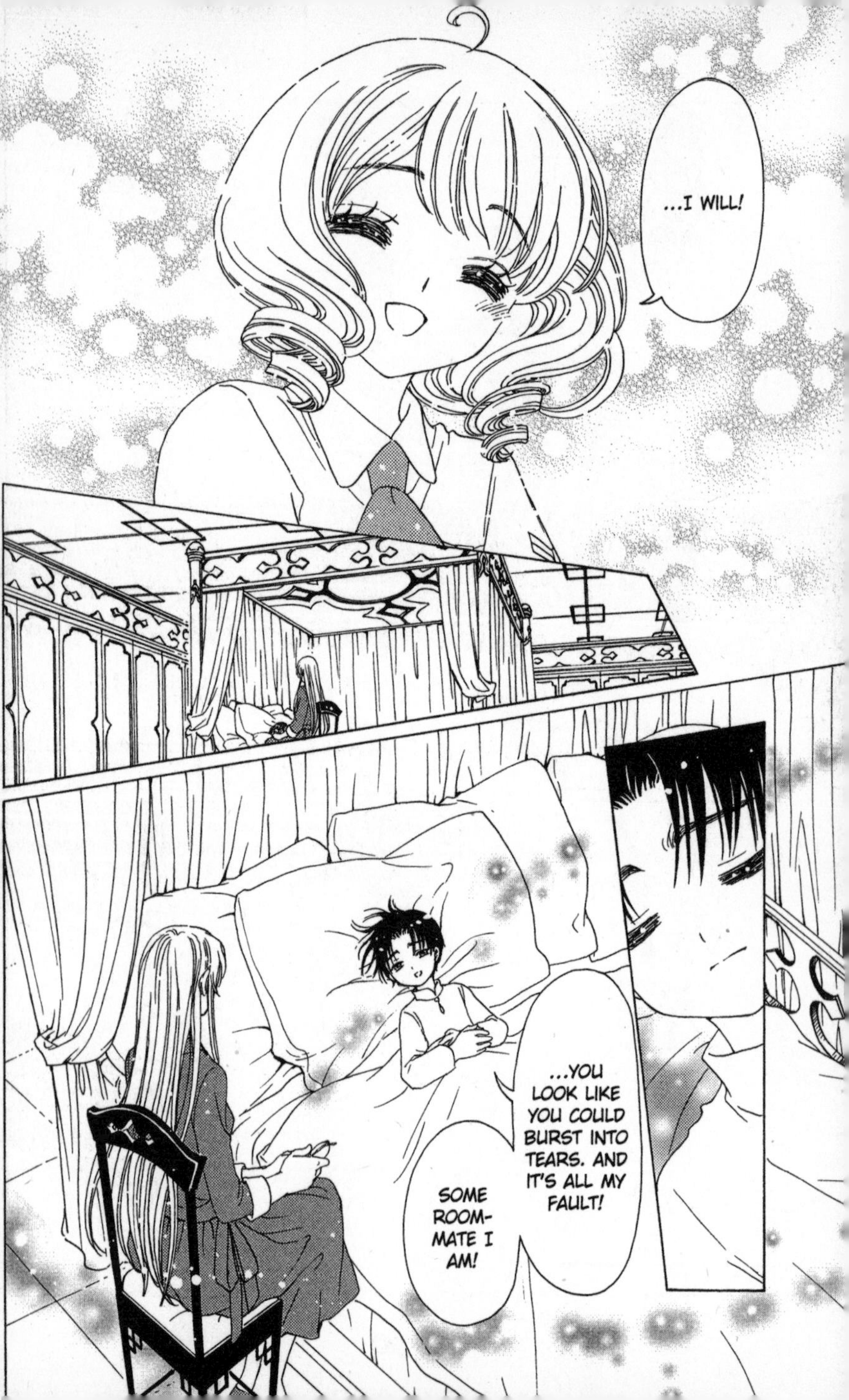
...I WILL!
...YOU LOOK LIKE YOU COULD BURST INTO TEARS. AND IT'S ALL MY FAULT!
SOME ROOM-MATE I AM!

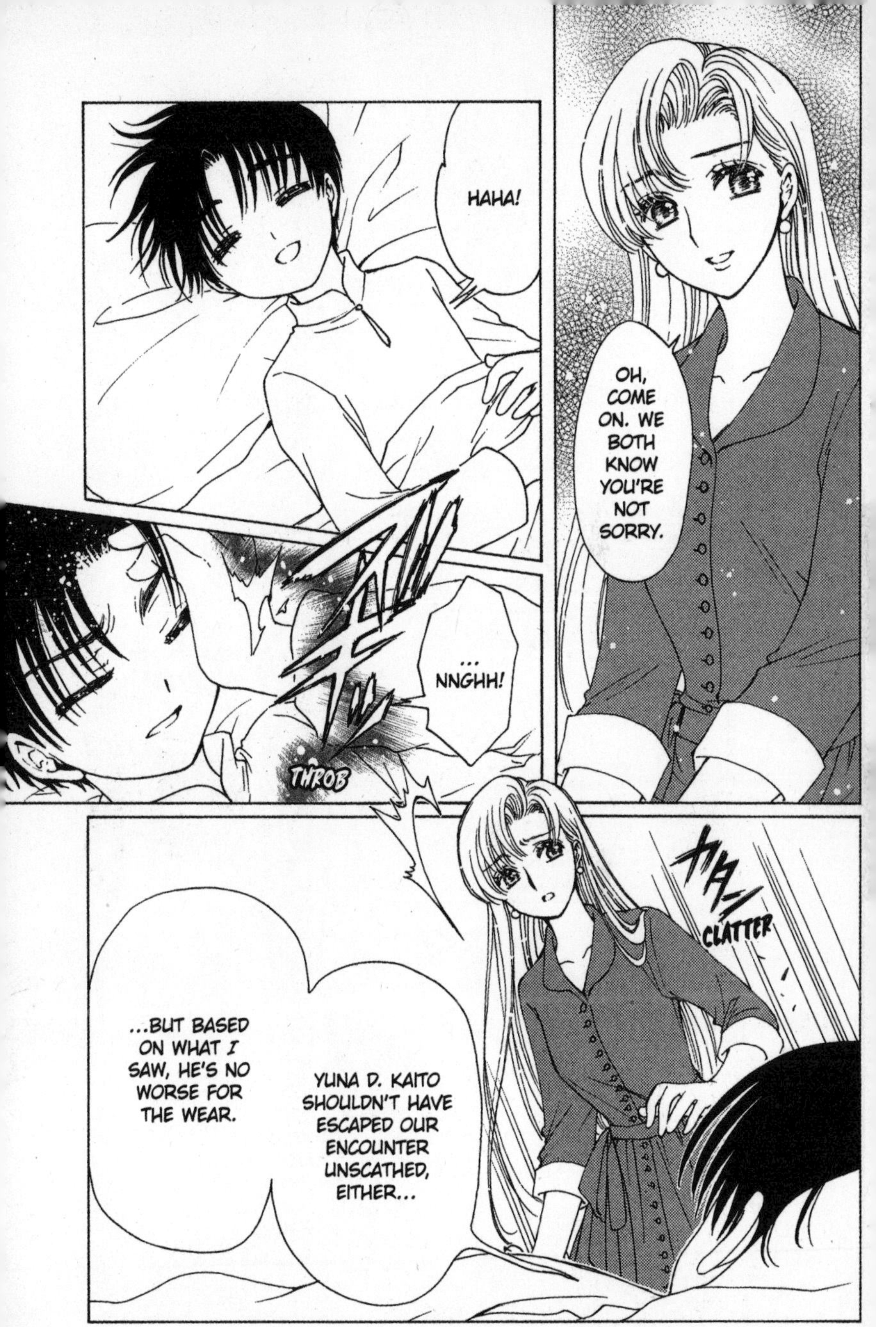
OH, COME ON. WE BOTH KNOW YOU'RE NOT SORRY.
HAHA!
...NNGHH!
THROB
CLATTER
YUNA D. KAITO SHOULDN'T HAVE ESCAPED OUR ENCOUNTER UNSCATHED, EITHER...
...BUT BASED ON WHAT *I* SAW, HE'S NO WORSE FOR THE WEAR.

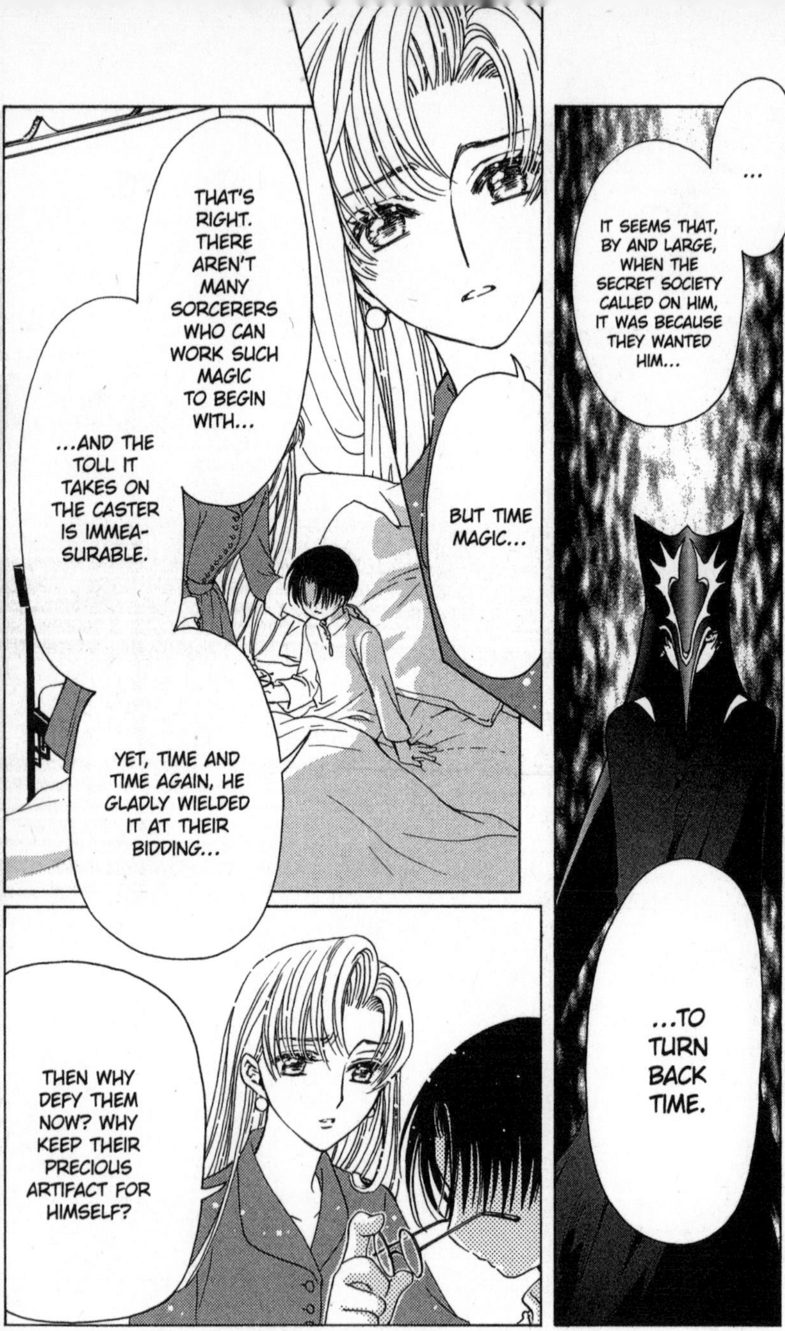
THAT'S RIGHT. THERE AREN'T MANY SORCERERS WHO CAN WORK SUCH MAGIC TO BEGIN WITH...
BUT TIME MAGIC...
...AND THE TOLL IT TAKES ON THE CASTER IS IMMEA-SURABLE.
YET, TIME AND TIME AGAIN, HE GLADLY WIELDED IT AT THEIR BIDDING...
THEN WHY DEFY THEM NOW? WHY KEEP THEIR PRECIOUS ARTIFACT FOR HIMSELF?
...
IT SEEMS THAT, BY AND LARGE, WHEN THE SECRET SOCIETY CALLED ON HIM, IT WAS BECAUSE THEY WANTED HIM...
...TO TURN BACK TIME.

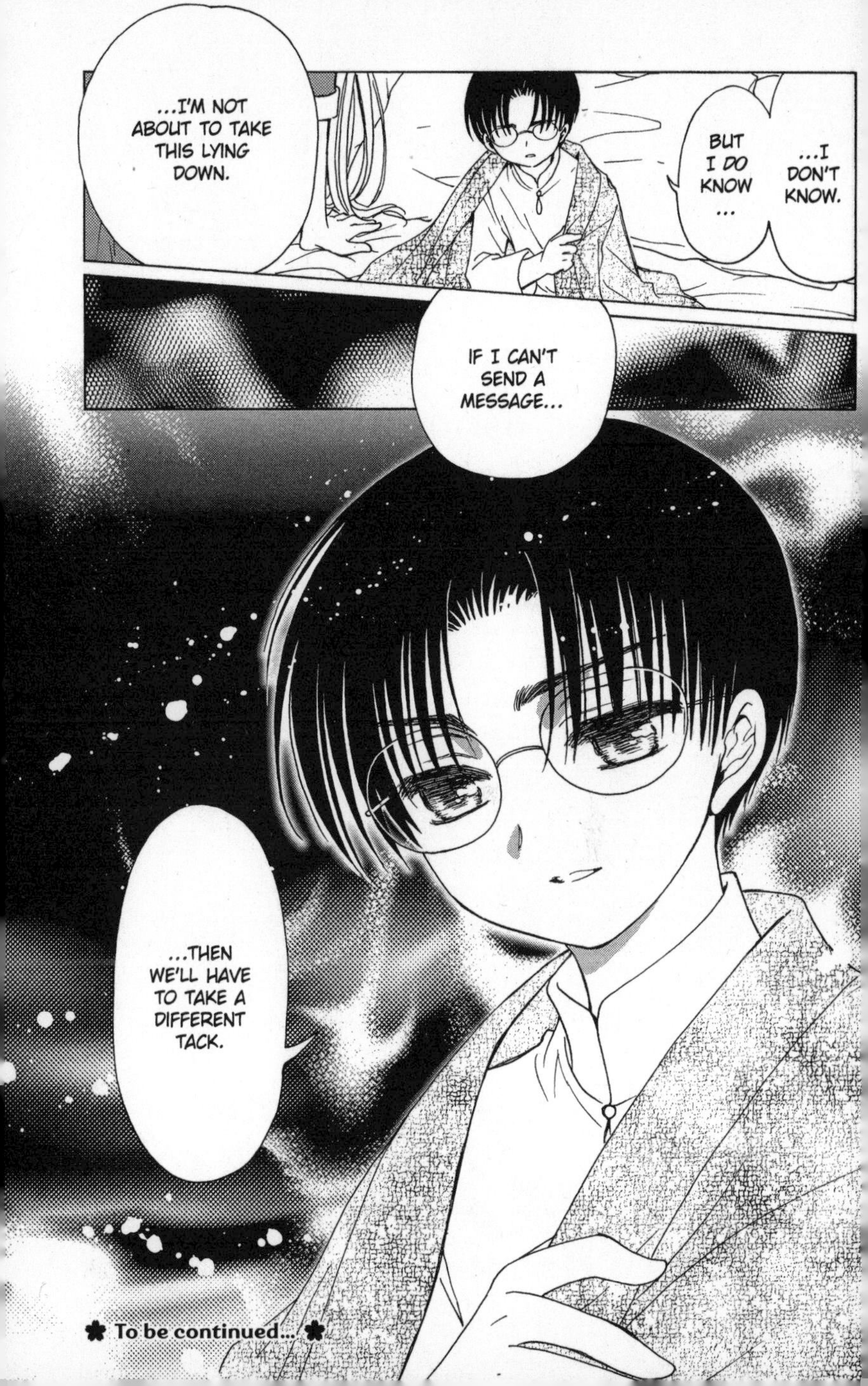
...I DON'T KNOW.
BUT I DO KNOW ...
...I'M NOT ABOUT TO TAKE THIS LYING DOWN.
IF I CAN'T SEND A MESSAGE...
...THEN WE'LL HAVE TO TAKE A DIFFERENT TACK.
To be continued...

Cardcaptor Sakura
CLEAR CARD

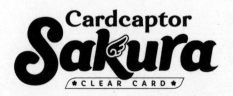

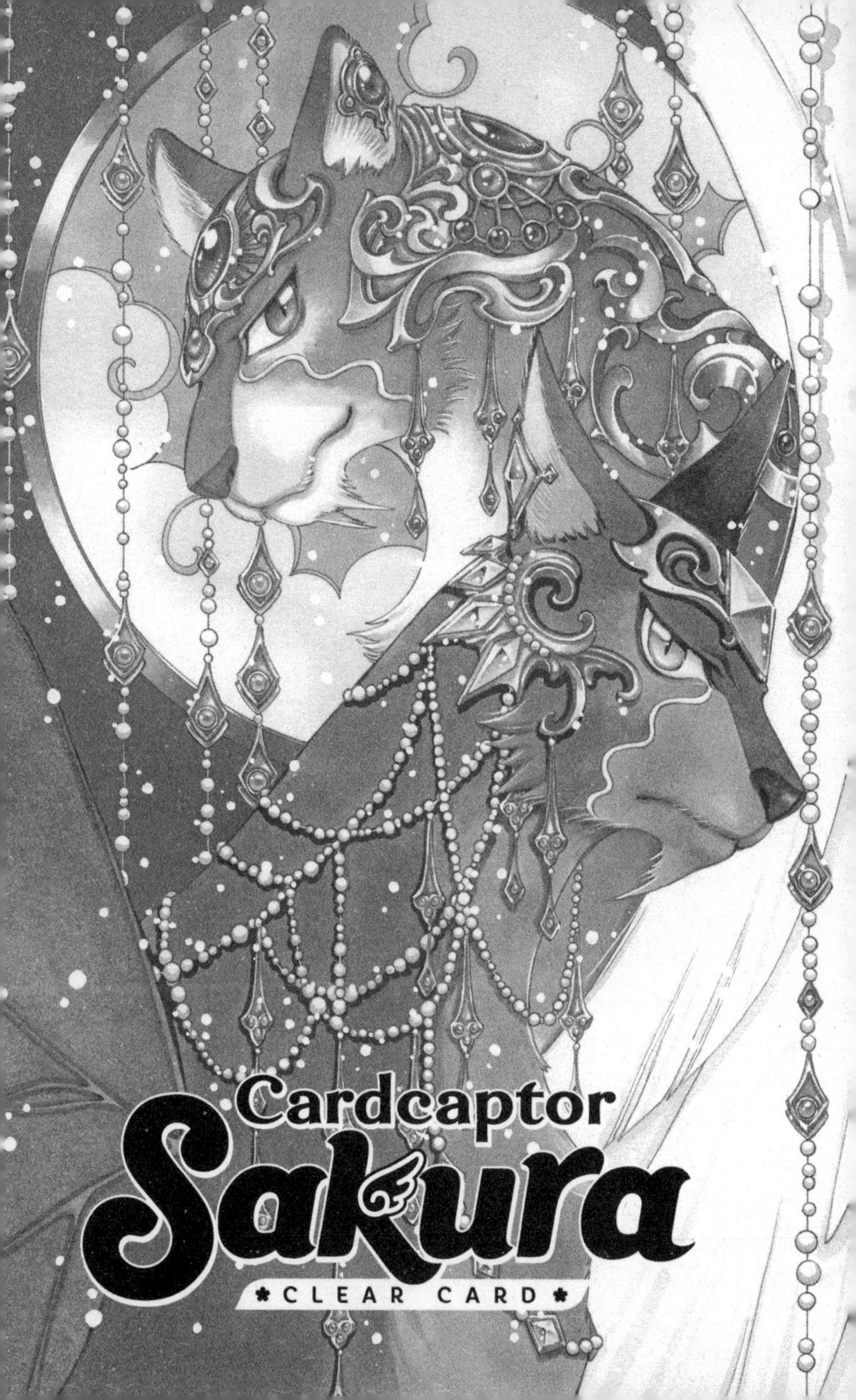
Cardcaptor
Sakura
CLEAR CARD

Cardcaptor Sakura CLEAR CARD

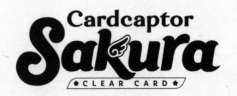

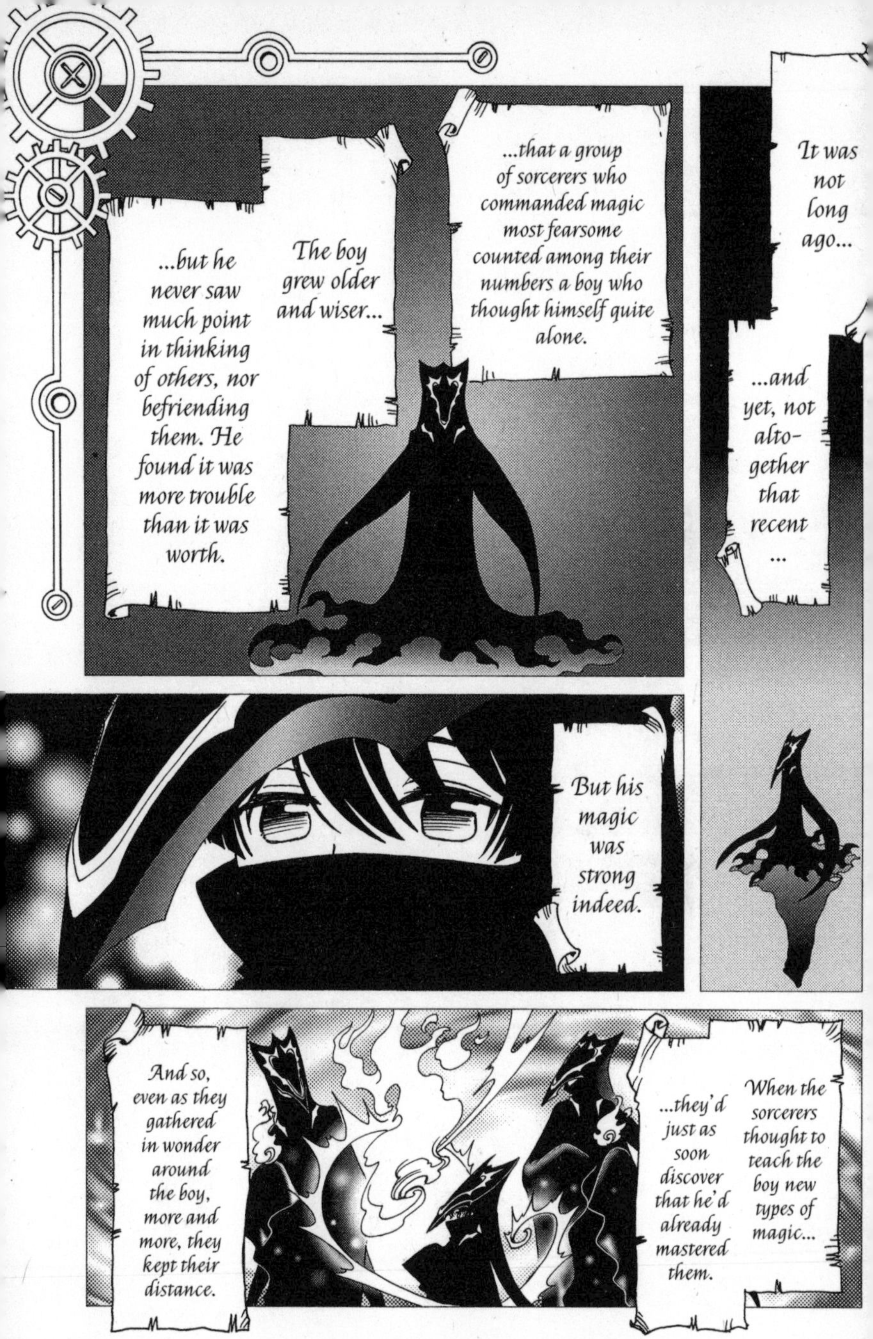
It was not long ago...
...and yet, not altogether that recent...
...that a group of sorcerers who commanded magic most fearsome counted among their numbers a boy who thought himself quite alone.
The boy grew older and wiser...
...but he never saw much point in thinking of others, nor befriending them. He found it was more trouble than it was worth.
But his magic was strong indeed.
When the sorcerers thought to teach the boy new types of magic...
...they'd just as soon discover that he'd already mastered them.
And so, even as they gathered in wonder around the boy, more and more, they kept their distance.

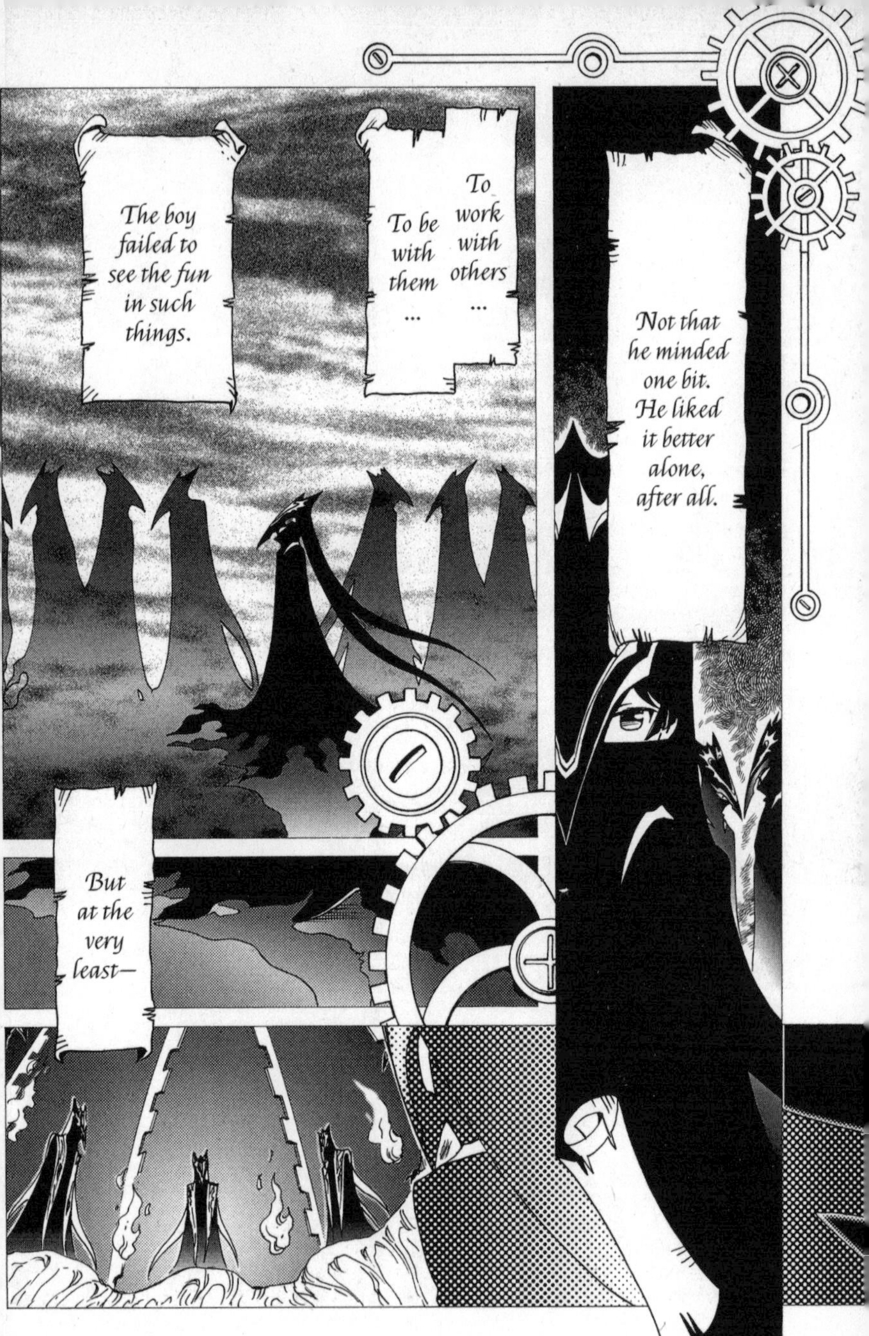
To work with others...
To be with them...
The boy failed to see the fun in such things.
Not that he minded one bit. He liked it better alone, after all.
But at the very least—

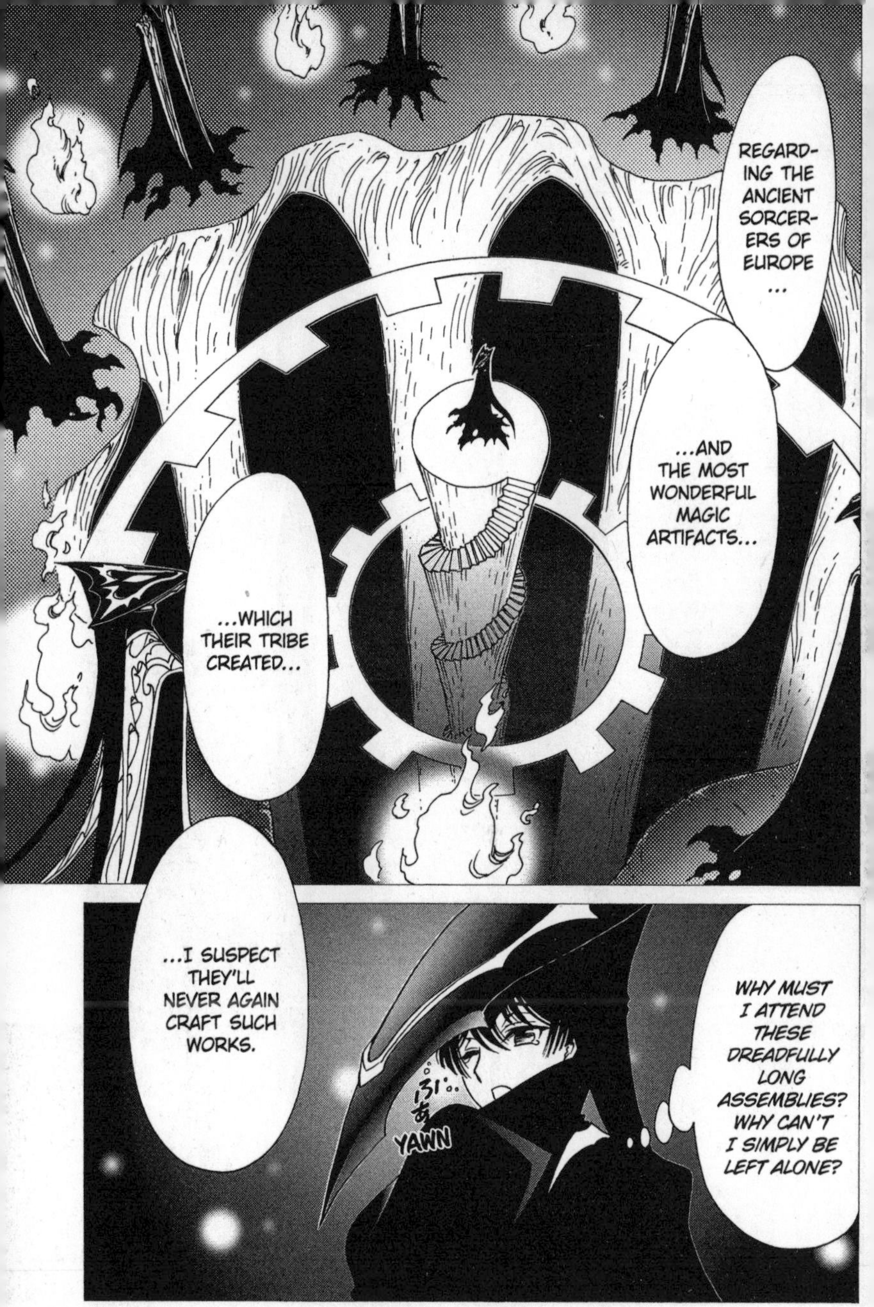
REGARDING THE ANCIENT SORCERERS OF EUROPE...
...AND THE MOST WONDERFUL MAGIC ARTIFACTS...
...WHICH THEIR TRIBE CREATED...
WHY MUST I ATTEND THESE DREADFULLY LONG ASSEMBLIES? WHY CAN'T I SIMPLY BE LEFT ALONE?
ふぁ
YAWN
...I SUSPECT THEY'LL NEVER AGAIN CRAFT SUCH WORKS.

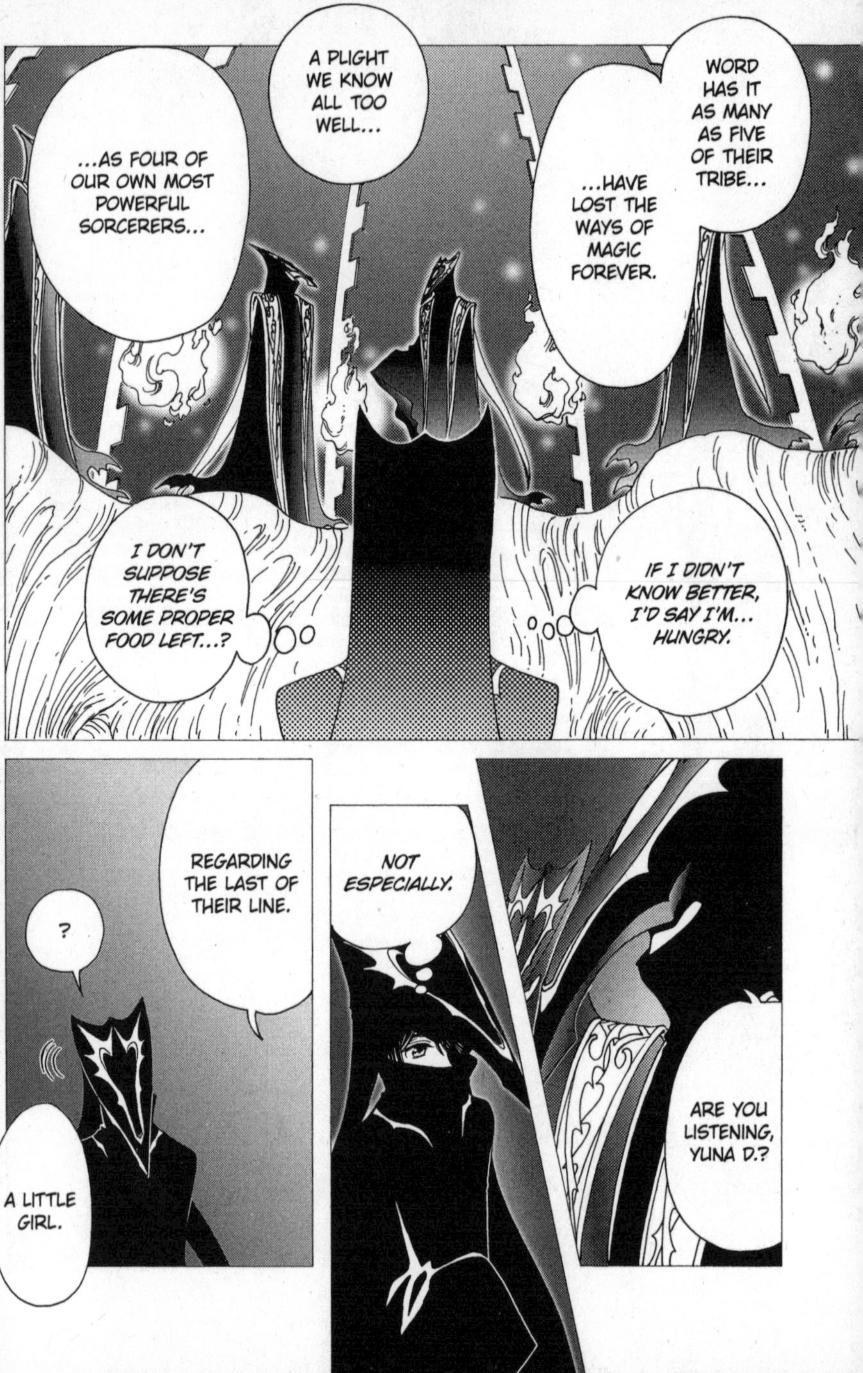
WORD HAS IT AS MANY AS FIVE OF THEIR TRIBE...
...HAVE LOST THE WAYS OF MAGIC FOREVER.
A PLIGHT WE KNOW ALL TOO WELL...
...AS FOUR OF OUR OWN MOST POWERFUL SORCERERS...
IF I DIDN'T KNOW BETTER, I'D SAY I'M... HUNGRY.
I DON'T SUPPOSE THERE'S SOME PROPER FOOD LEFT...?
ARE YOU LISTENING, YUNA D.?
NOT ESPECIALLY.
REGARDING THE LAST OF THEIR LINE.
?
A LITTLE GIRL.

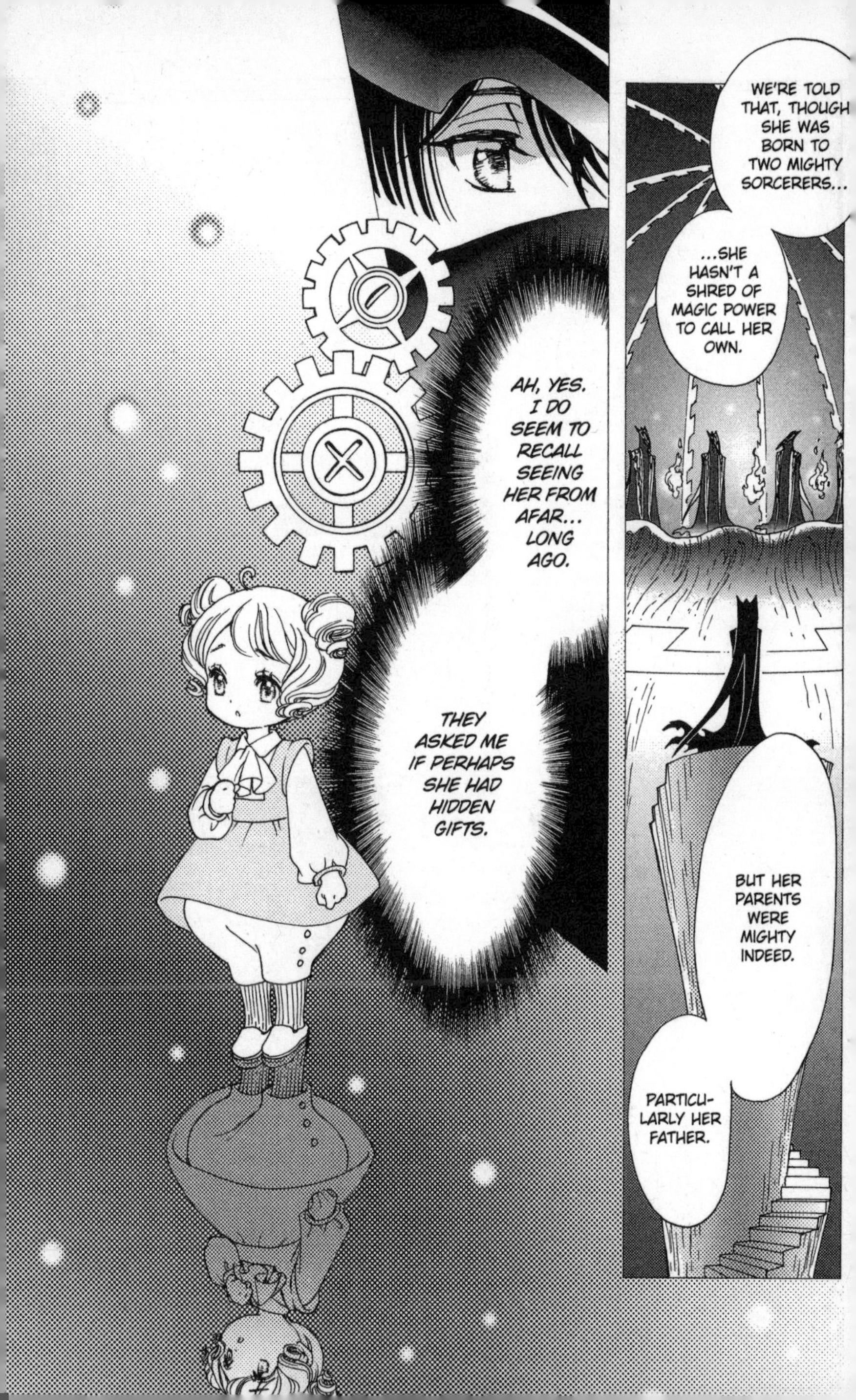
WE'RE TOLD THAT, THOUGH SHE WAS BORN TO TWO MIGHTY SORCERERS...
...SHE HASN'T A SHRED OF MAGIC POWER TO CALL HER OWN.
BUT HER PARENTS WERE MIGHTY INDEED.
PARTICU-LARLY HER FATHER.
AH, YES. I DO SEEM TO RECALL SEEING HER FROM AFAR... LONG AGO.
THEY ASKED ME IF PERHAPS SHE HAD HIDDEN GIFTS.

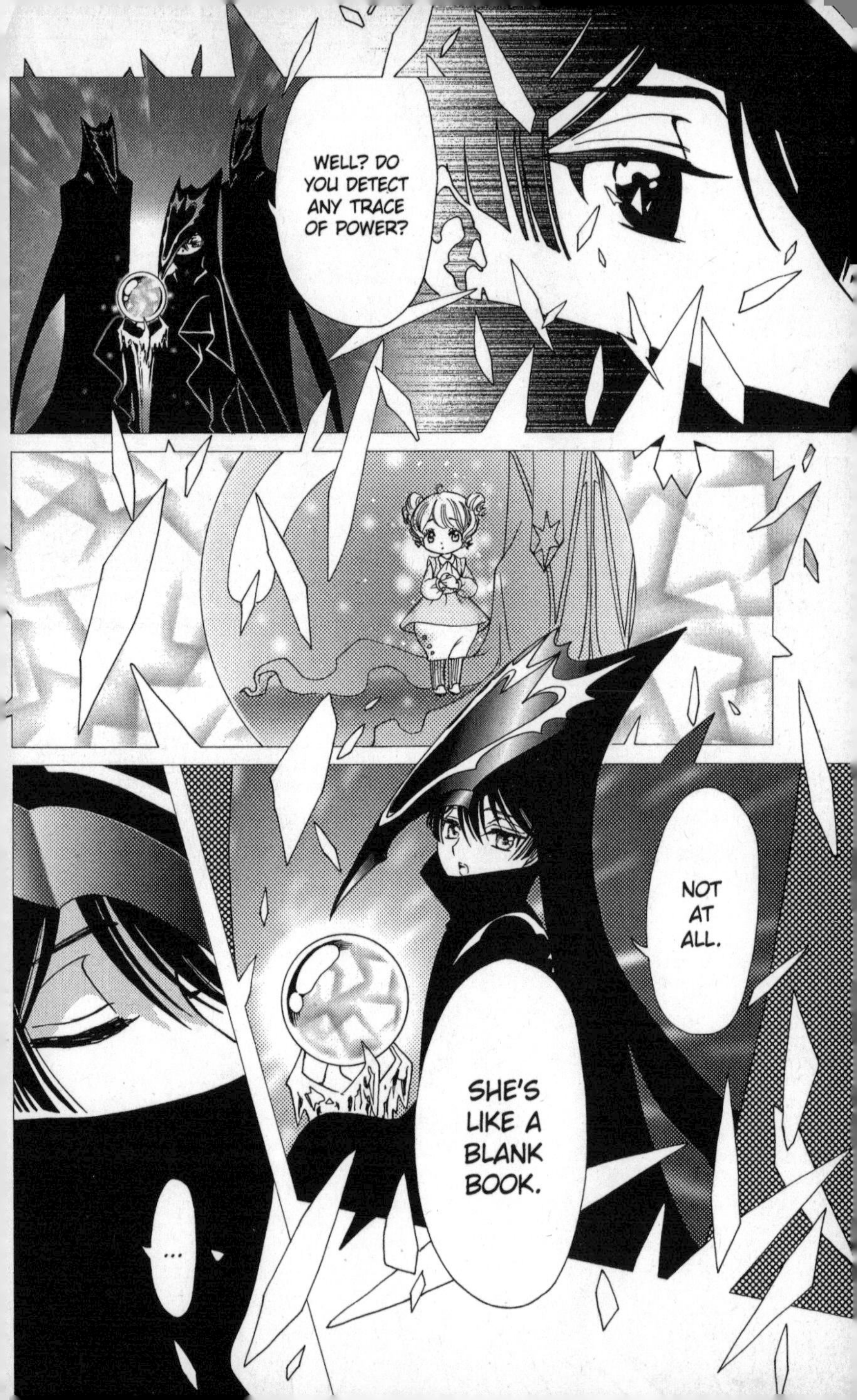
WELL? DO YOU DETECT ANY TRACE OF POWER?
NOT AT ALL.
SHE'S LIKE A BLANK BOOK.
...

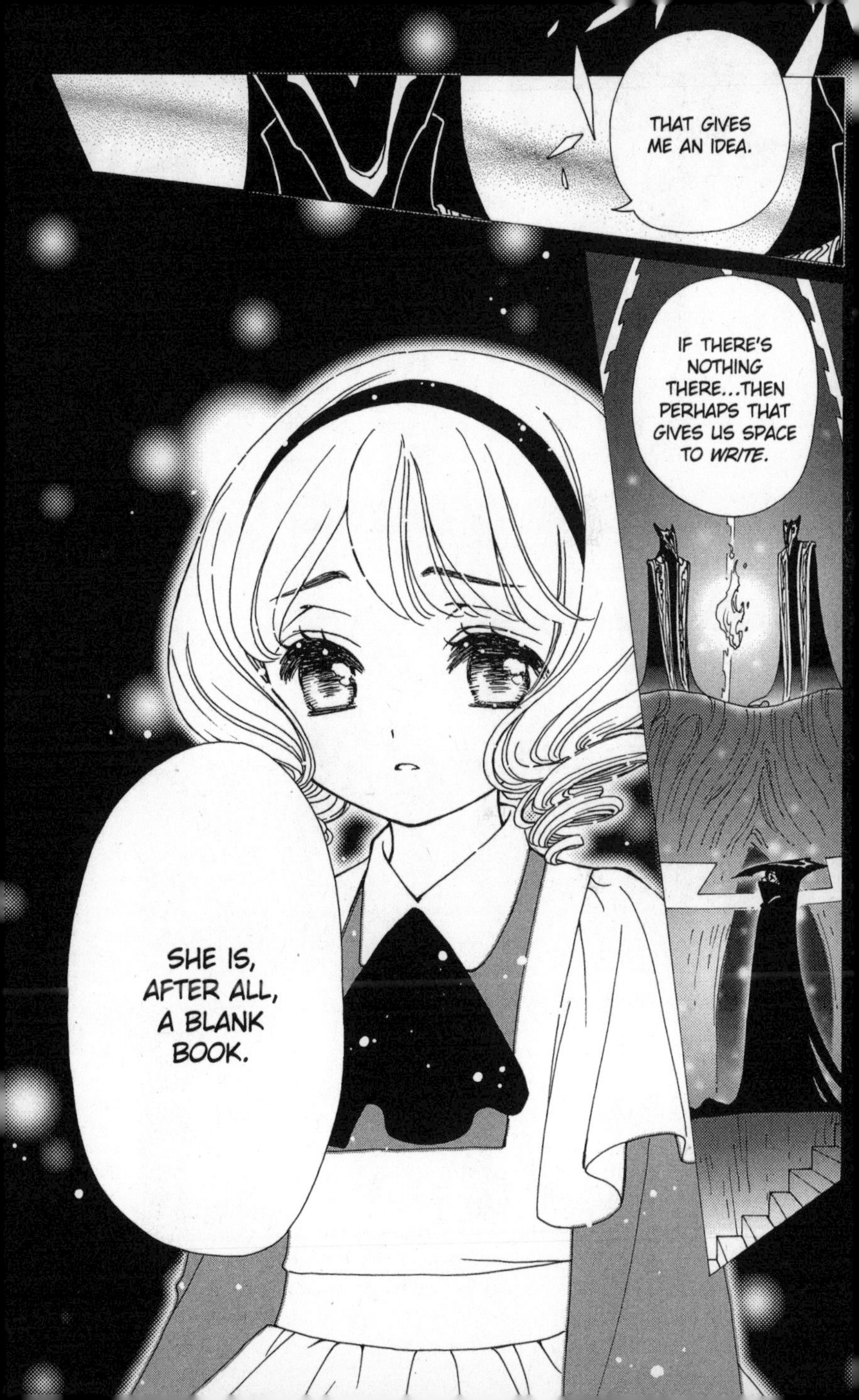
THAT GIVES ME AN IDEA.
IF THERE'S NOTHING THERE...THEN PERHAPS THAT GIVES US SPACE TO *WRITE*.
SHE IS, AFTER ALL, A BLANK BOOK.

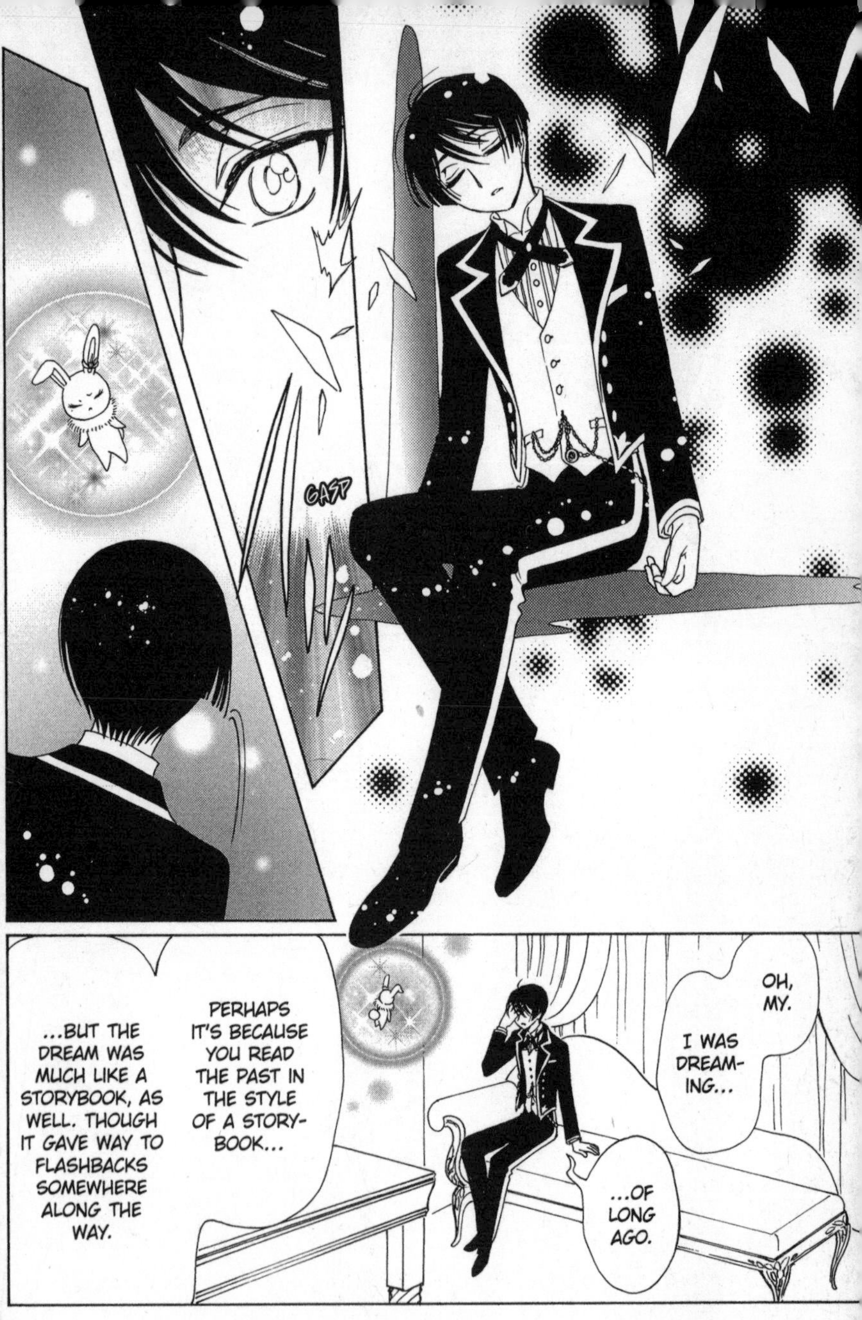
GASP
OH, MY.
I WAS DREAMING...
...OF LONG AGO.
PERHAPS IT'S BECAUSE YOU READ THE PAST IN THE STYLE OF A STORYBOOK...
...BUT THE DREAM WAS MUCH LIKE A STORYBOOK, AS WELL. THOUGH IT GAVE WAY TO FLASHBACKS SOMEWHERE ALONG THE WAY.

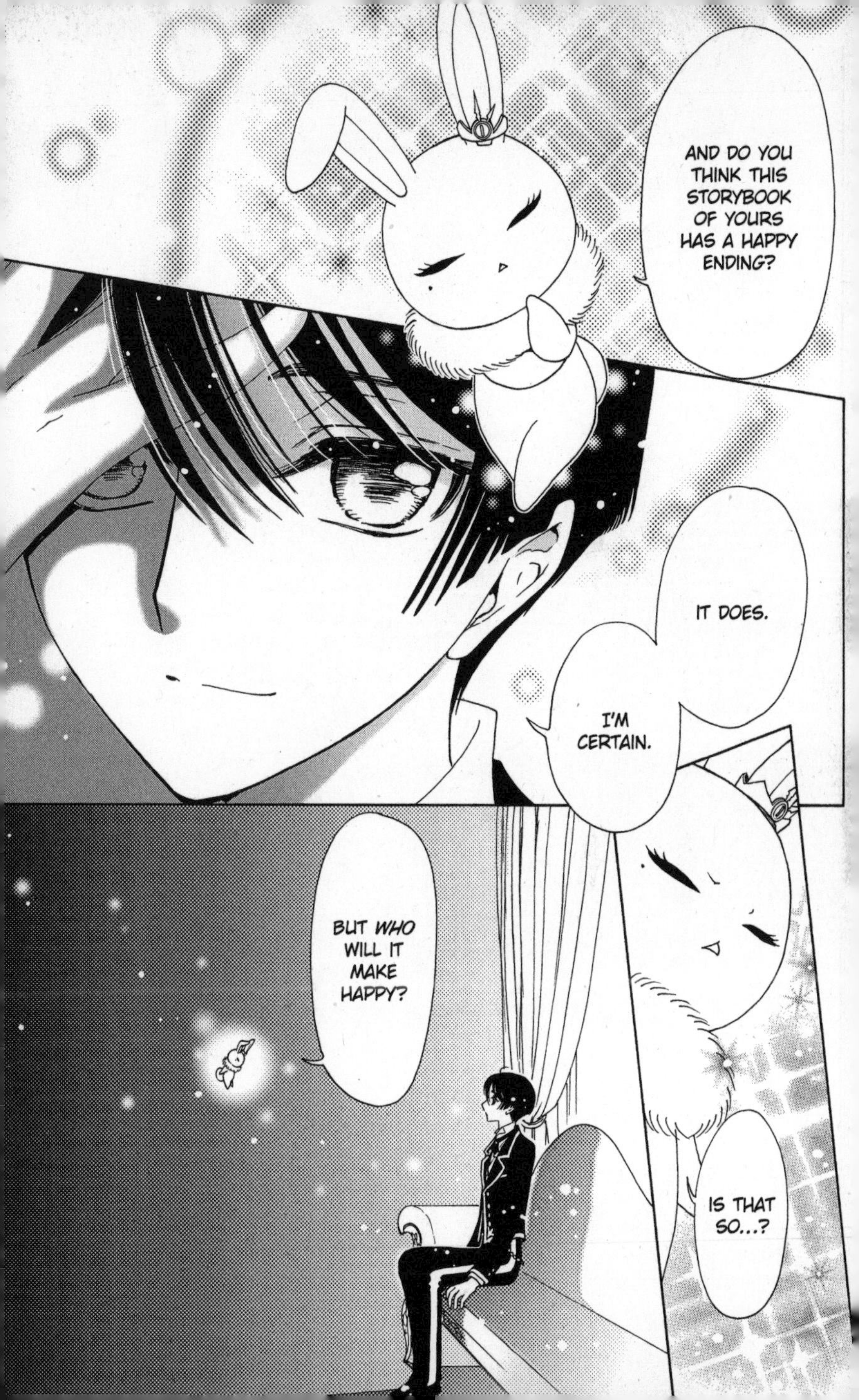
AND DO YOU THINK THIS STORYBOOK OF YOURS HAS A HAPPY ENDING?
IT DOES.
I'M CERTAIN.
IS THAT SO...?
BUT *WHO* WILL IT MAKE HAPPY?

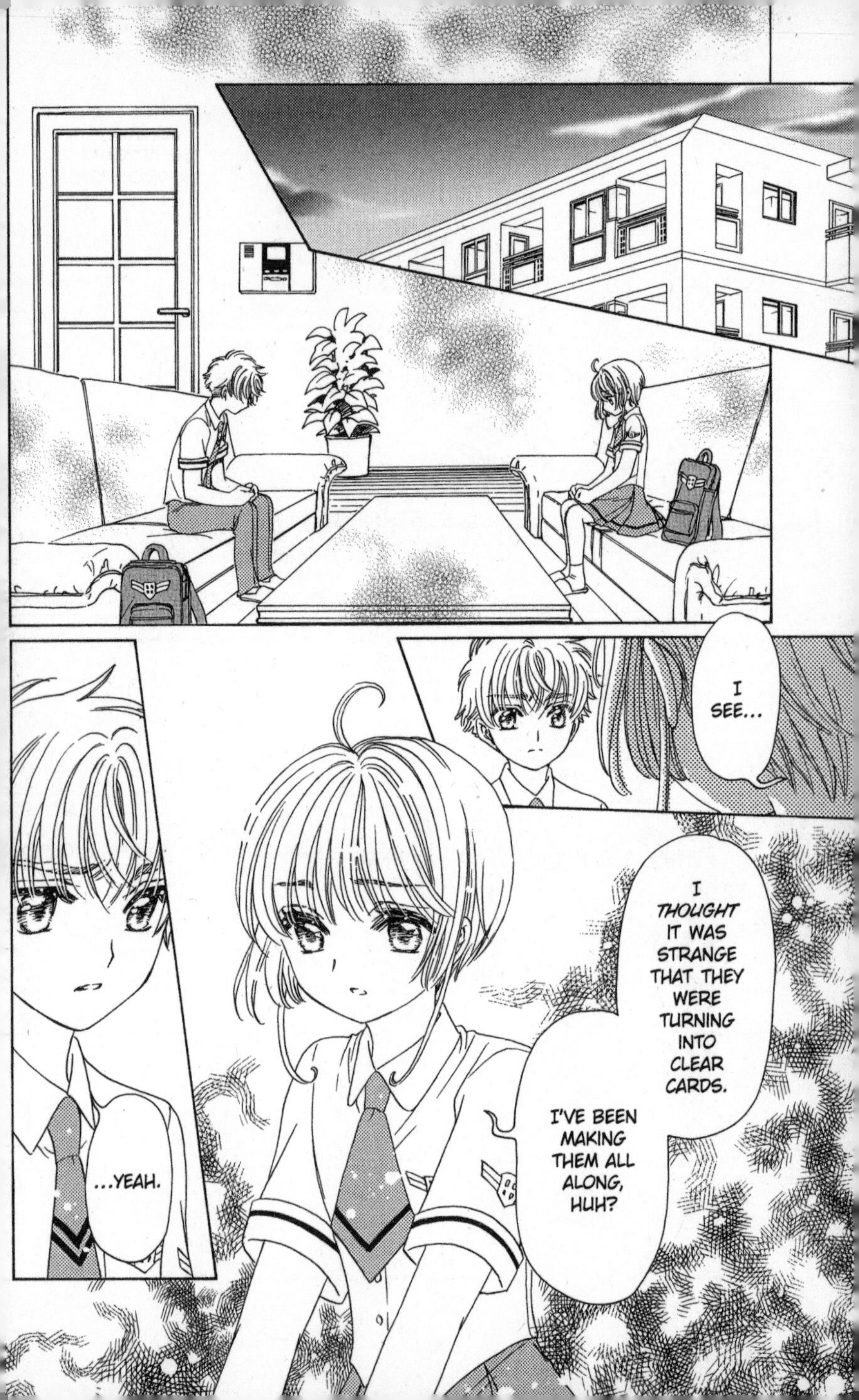
I SEE...
I *THOUGHT* IT WAS STRANGE THAT THEY WERE TURNING INTO CLEAR CARDS.
I'VE BEEN MAKING THEM ALL ALONG, HUH?
...YEAH.

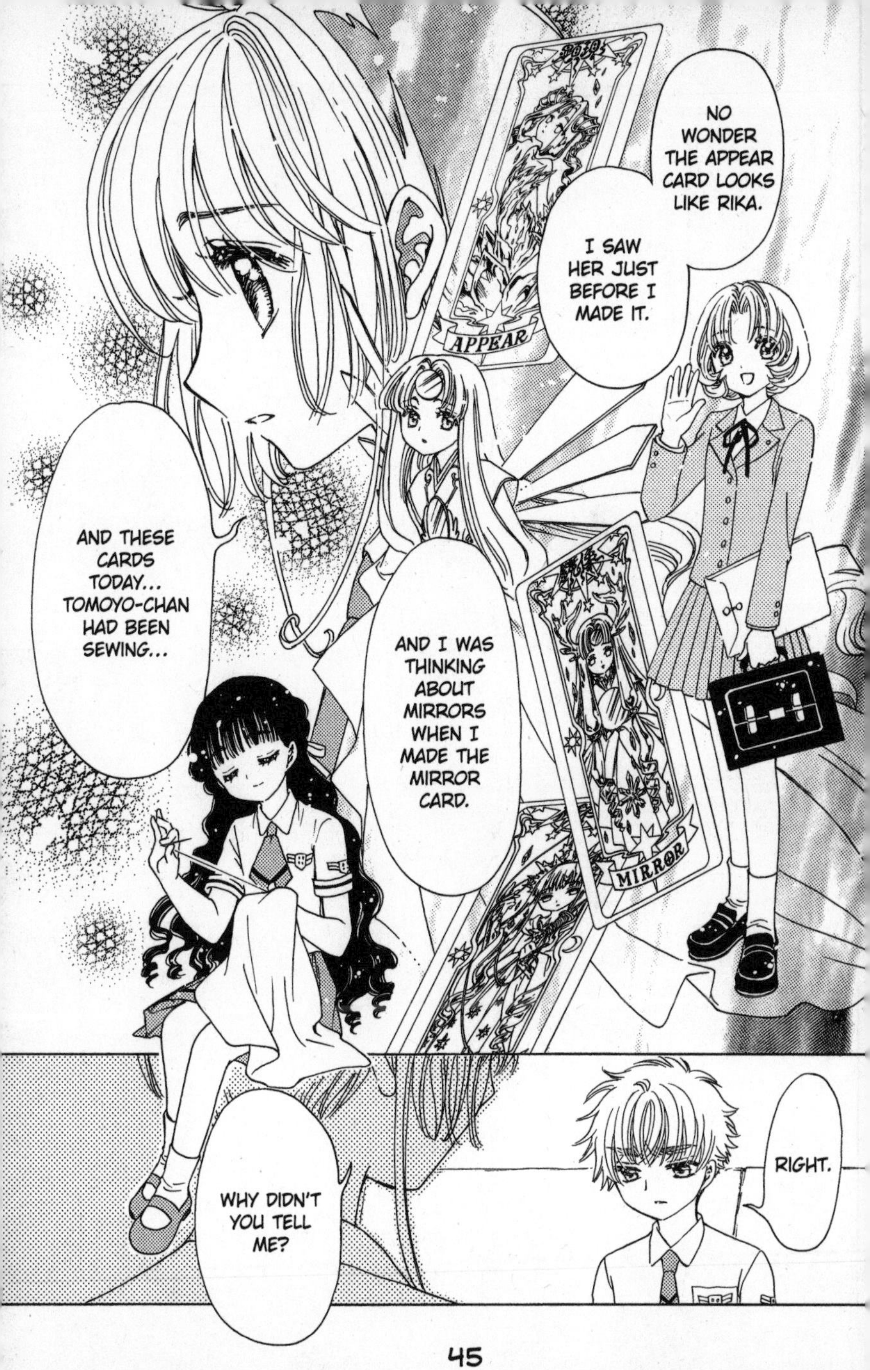
NO WONDER THE APPEAR CARD LOOKS LIKE RIKA.
I SAW HER JUST BEFORE I MADE IT.
APPEAR
AND I WAS THINKING ABOUT MIRRORS WHEN I MADE THE MIRROR CARD.
MIRROR
AND THESE CARDS TODAY... TOMOYO-CHAN HAD BEEN SEWING...
RIGHT.
WHY DIDN'T YOU TELL ME?

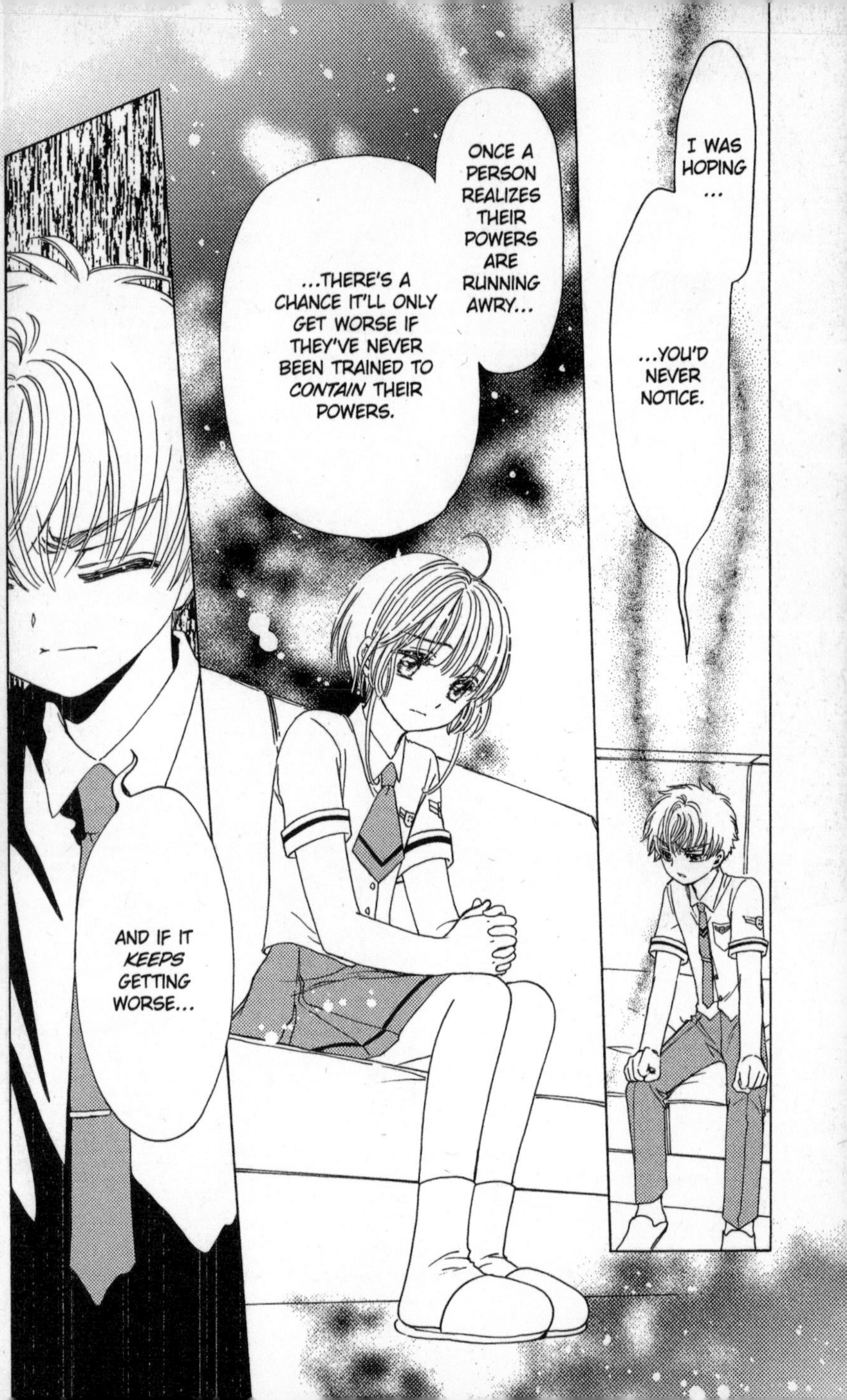
I WAS HOPING ...
...YOU'D NEVER NOTICE.
ONCE A PERSON REALIZES THEIR POWERS ARE RUNNING AWRY...
...THERE'S A CHANCE IT'LL ONLY GET WORSE IF THEY'VE NEVER BEEN TRAINED TO *CONTAIN* THEIR POWERS.
AND IF IT *KEEPS* GETTING WORSE...

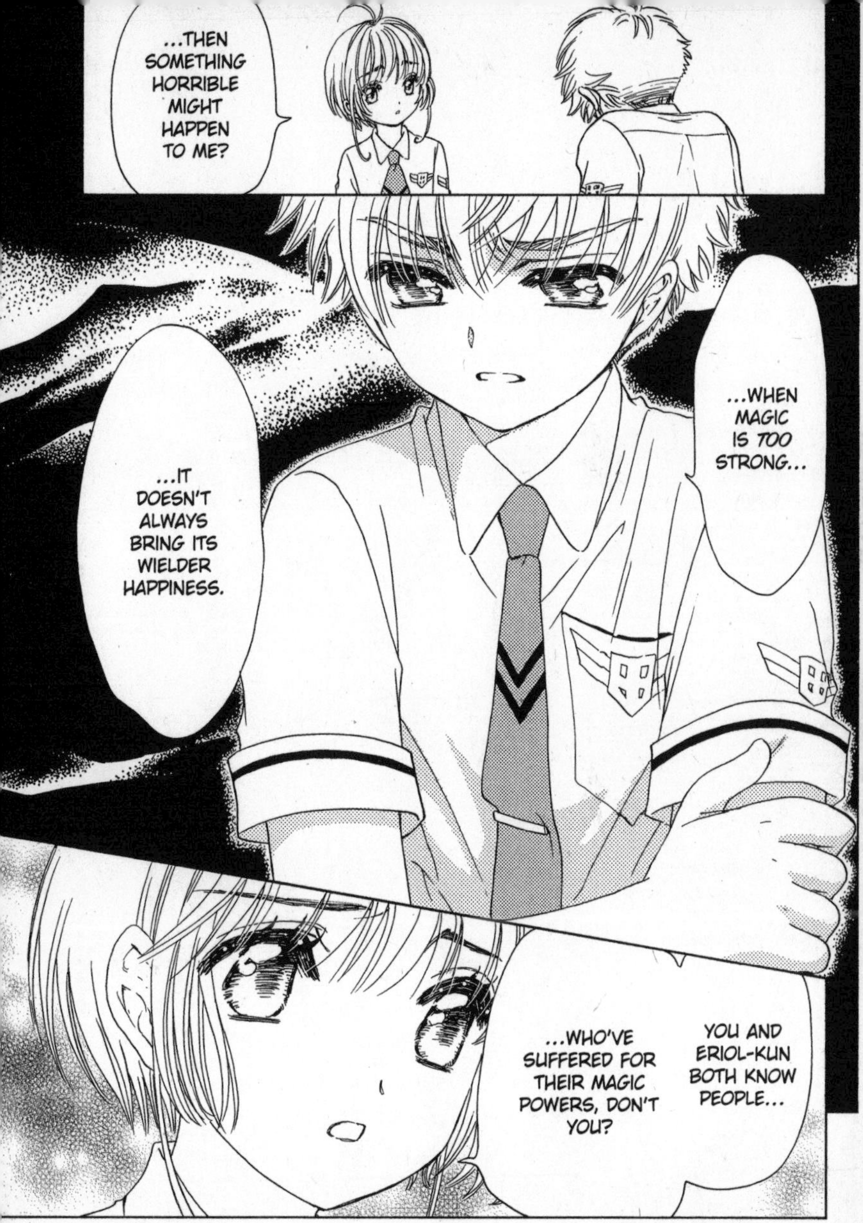
...THEN SOMETHING HORRIBLE MIGHT HAPPEN TO ME?
...WHEN MAGIC IS *TOO* STRONG...
...IT DOESN'T ALWAYS BRING ITS WIELDER HAPPINESS.
YOU AND ERIOL-KUN BOTH KNOW PEOPLE...
...WHO'VE SUFFERED FOR THEIR MAGIC POWERS, DON'T YOU?

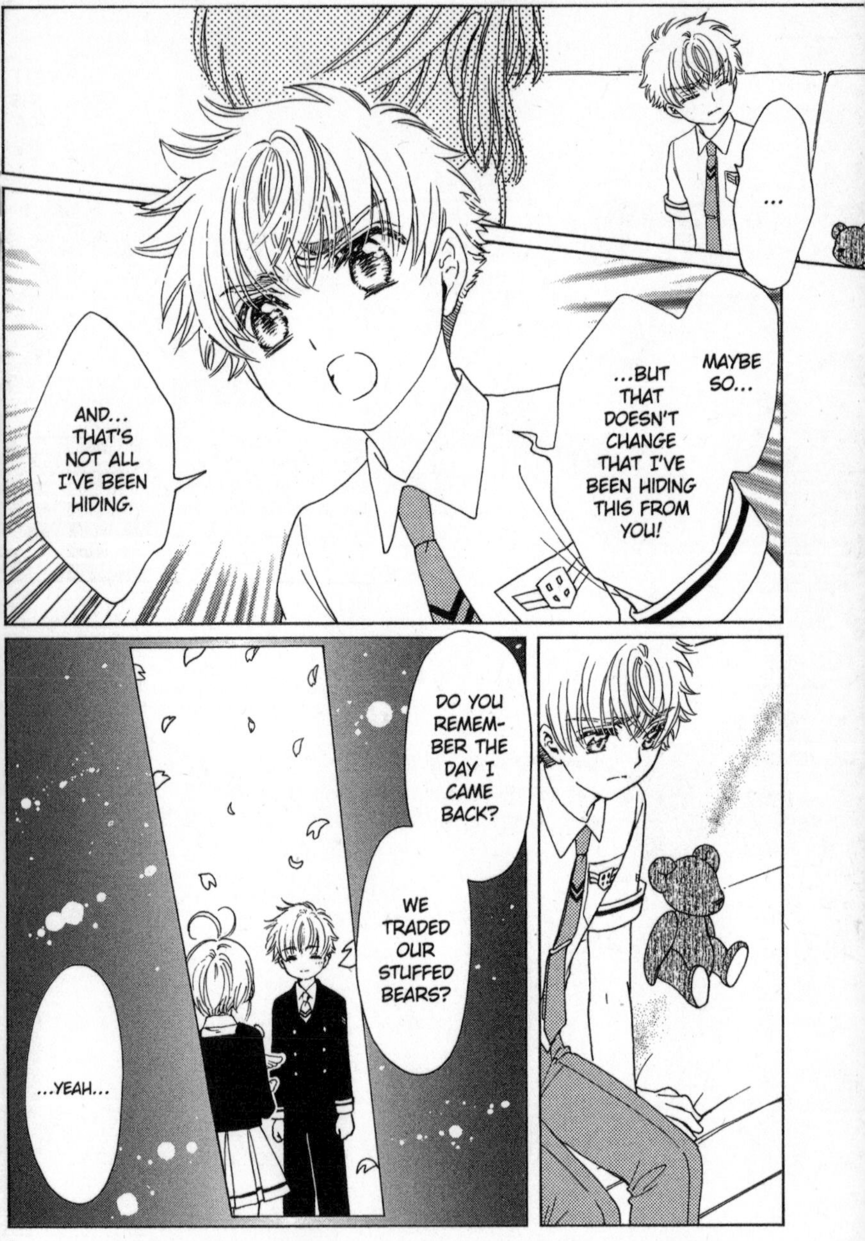
...
MAYBE SO...
...BUT THAT DOESN'T CHANGE THAT I'VE BEEN HIDING THIS FROM YOU!
AND... THAT'S NOT ALL I'VE BEEN HIDING.
DO YOU REMEMBER THE DAY I CAME BACK?
WE TRADED OUR STUFFED BEARS?
...YEAH...

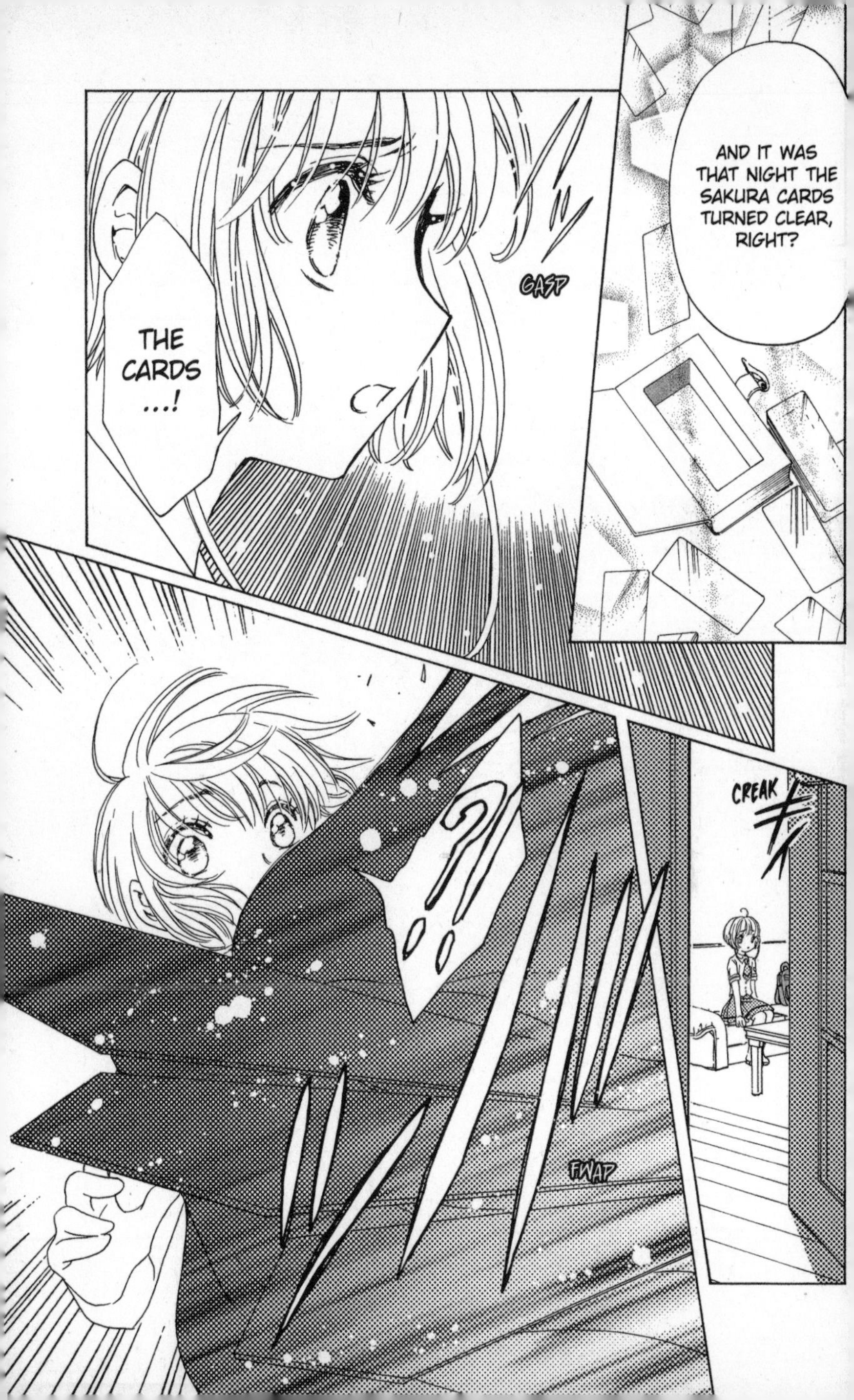
AND IT WAS THAT NIGHT THE SAKURA CARDS TURNED CLEAR, RIGHT?
GASP
THE CARDS ...!
CREAK
?!
FWAP

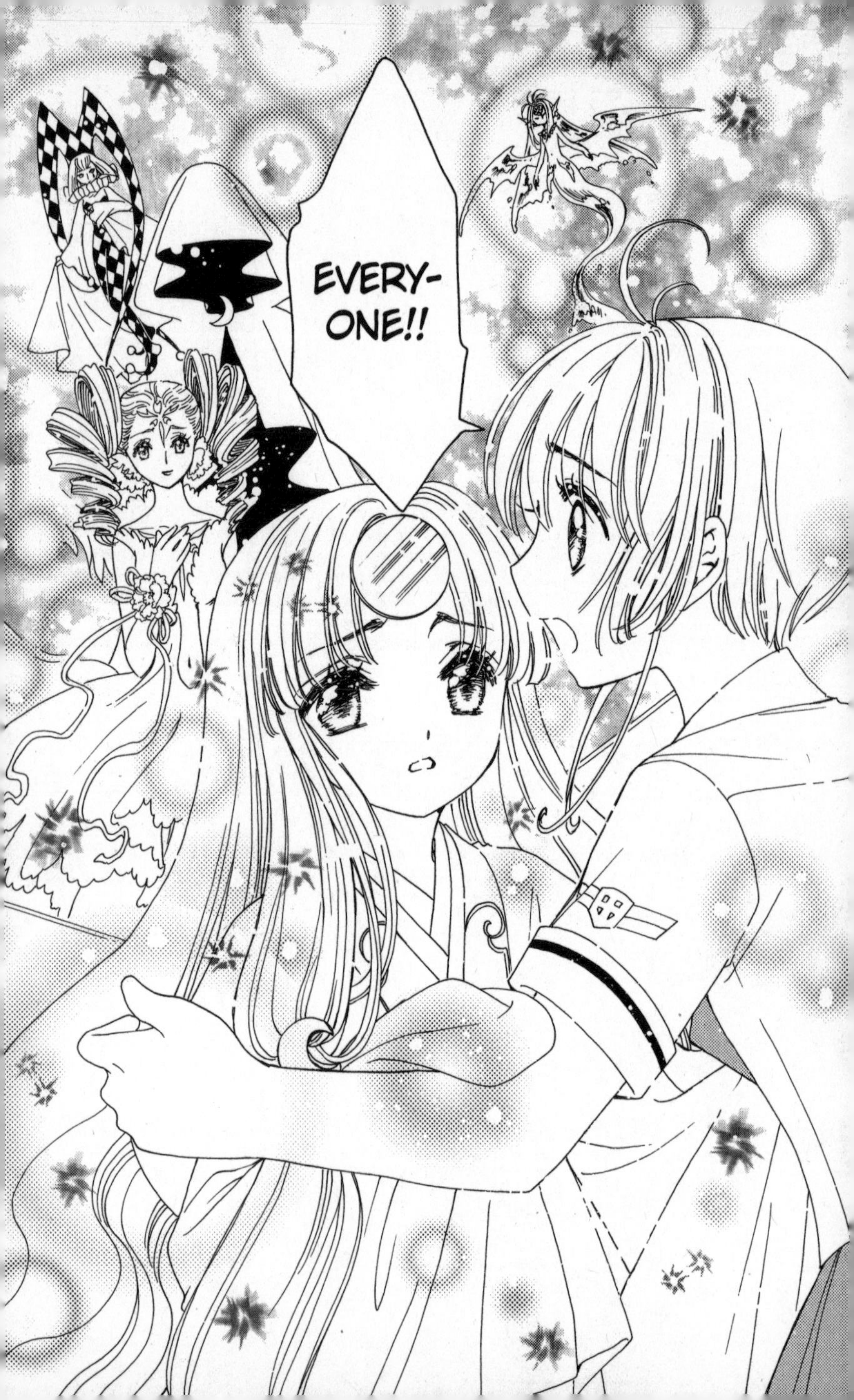
EVERY-
ONE!!

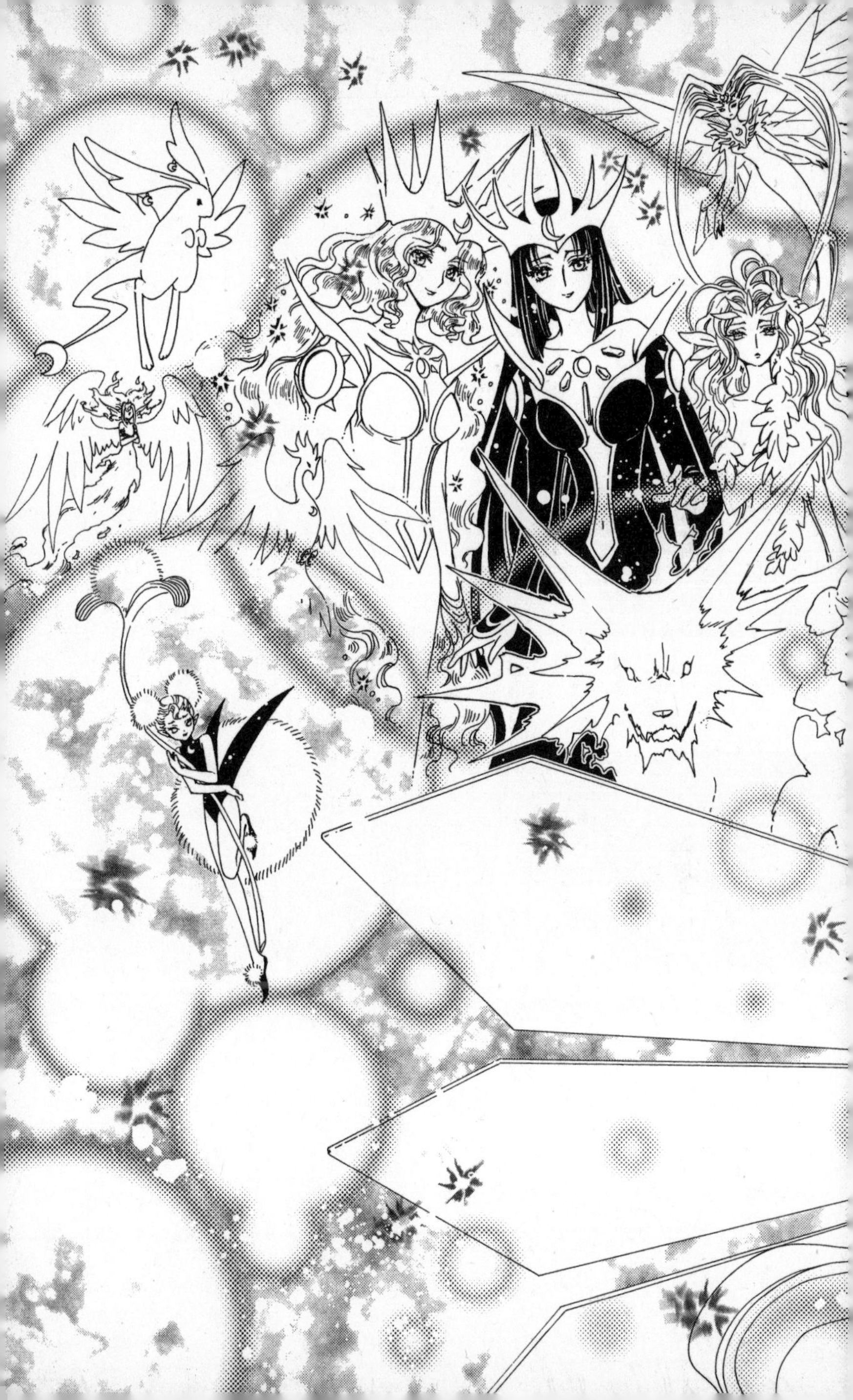

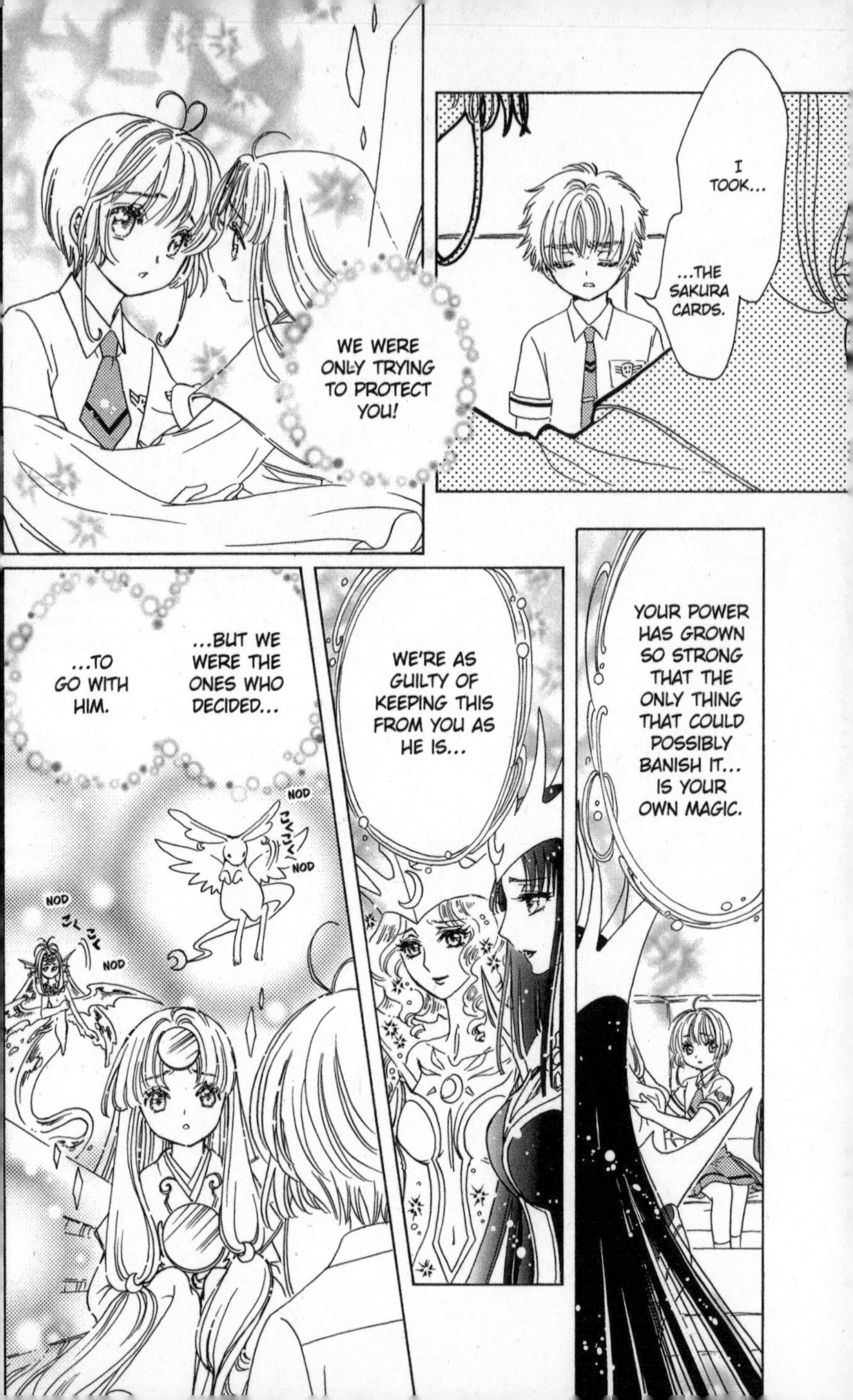
I TOOK...
...THE SAKURA CARDS.
WE WERE ONLY TRYING TO PROTECT YOU!
YOUR POWER HAS GROWN SO STRONG THAT THE ONLY THING THAT COULD POSSIBLY BANISH IT... IS YOUR OWN MAGIC.
WE'RE AS GUILTY OF KEEPING THIS FROM YOU AS HE IS...
...BUT WE WERE THE ONES WHO DECIDED...
...TO GO WITH HIM.
NOD
NOD
NOD
NOD

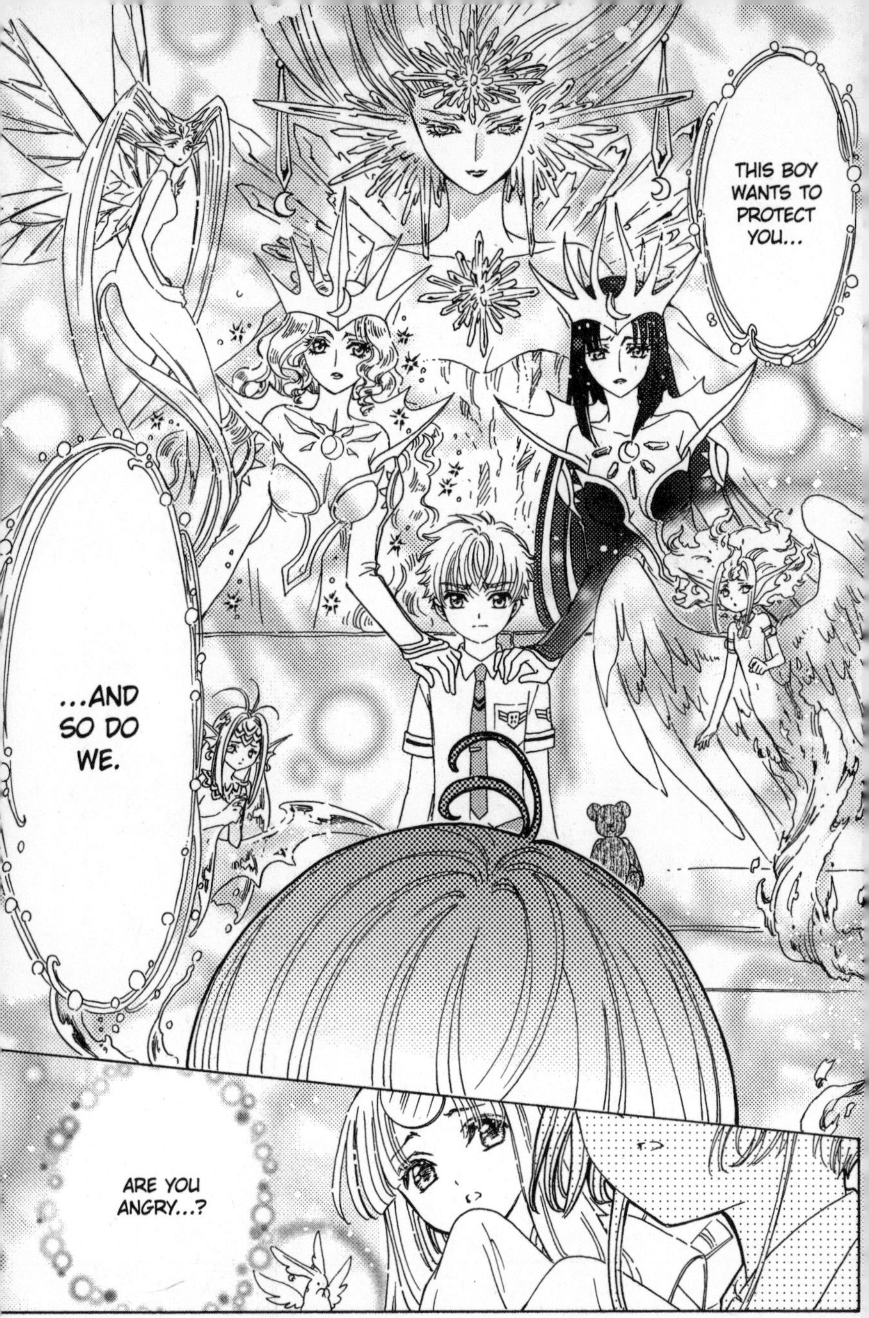
THIS BOY WANTS TO PROTECT YOU...
...AND SO DO WE.
ARE YOU ANGRY...?

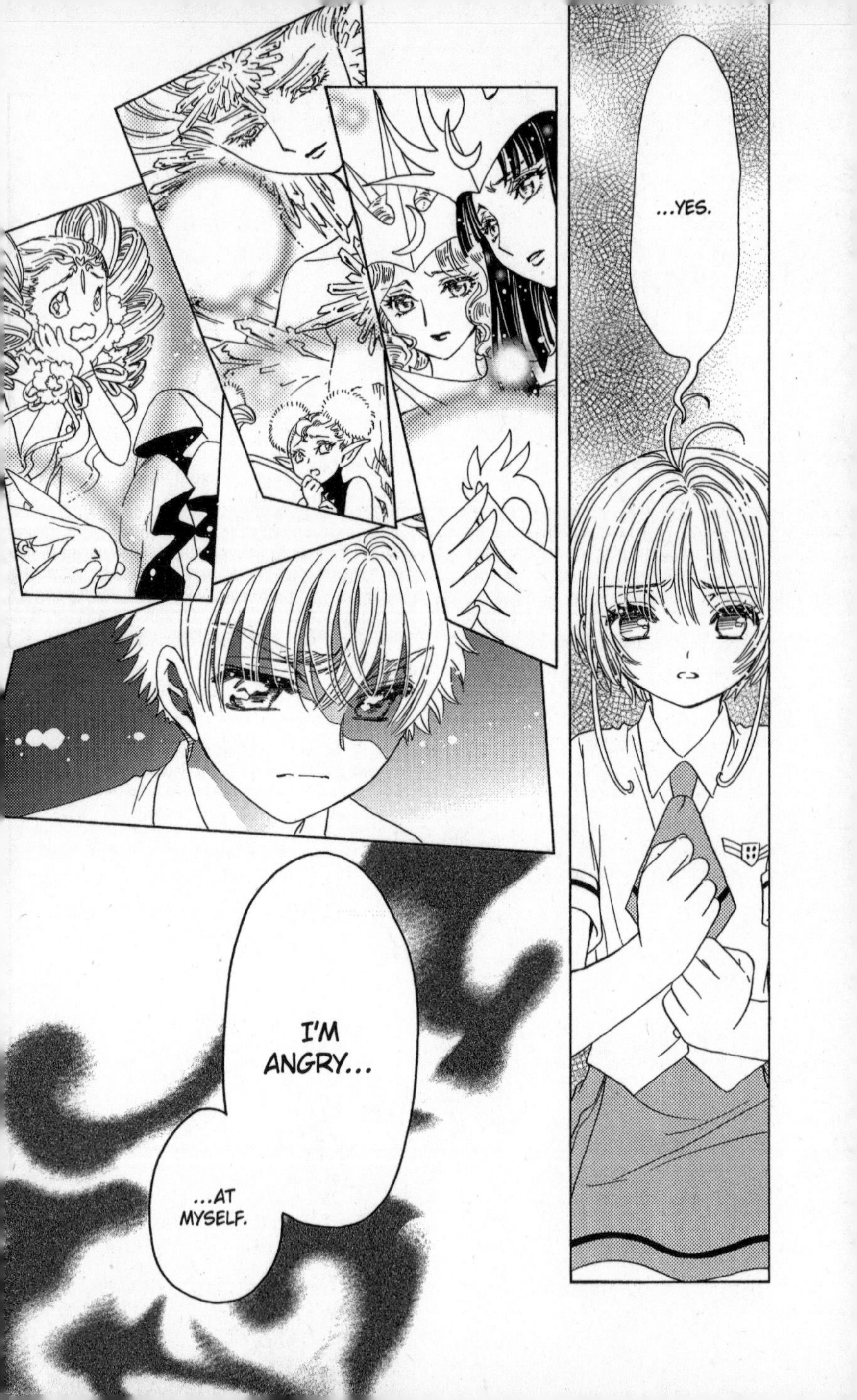
...YES.
I'M ANGRY...
...AT MYSELF.

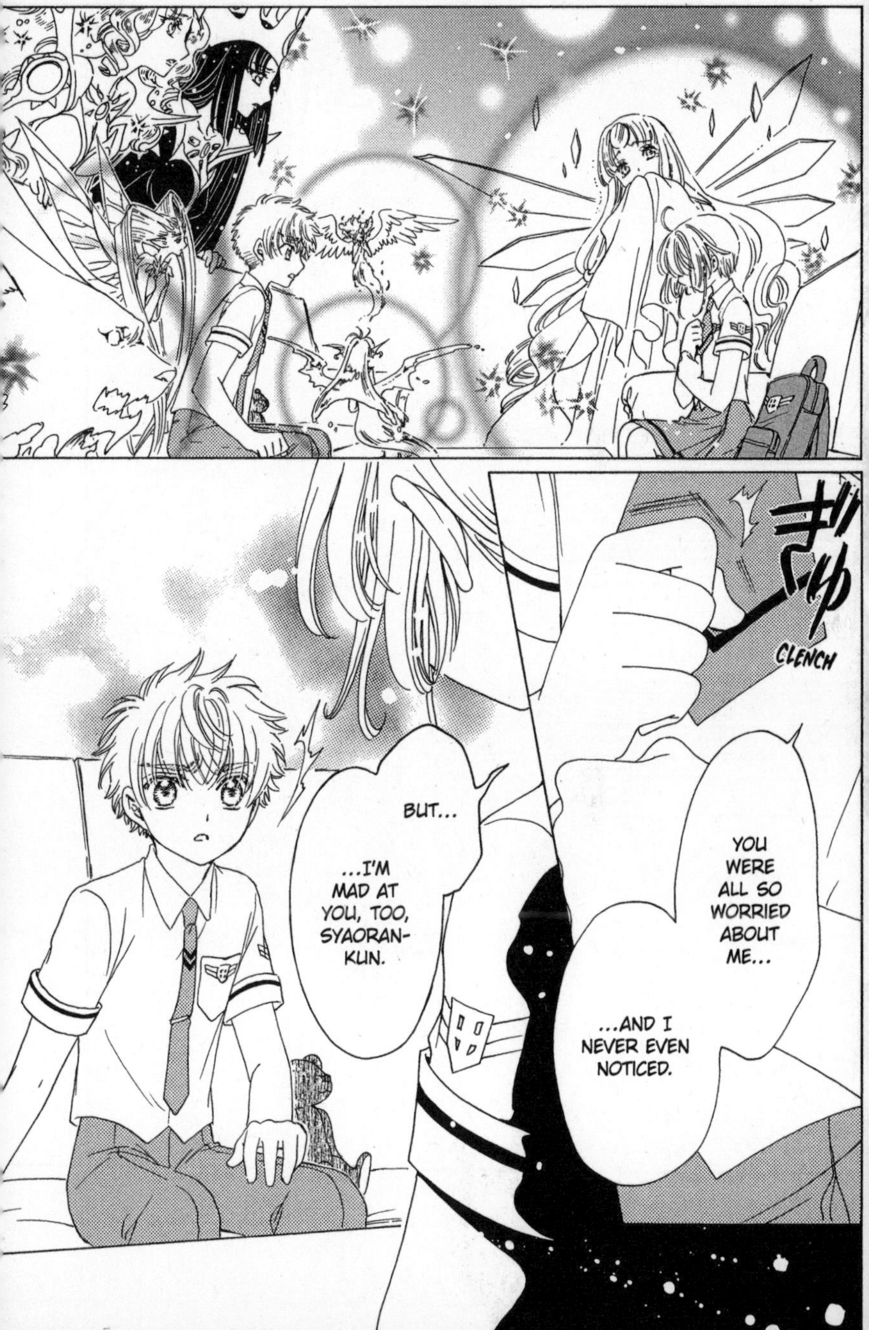
ぎゅ
CLENCH
YOU WERE ALL SO WORRIED ABOUT ME...
...AND I NEVER EVEN NOTICED.
BUT...
...I'M MAD AT YOU, TOO, SYAORAN-KUN.

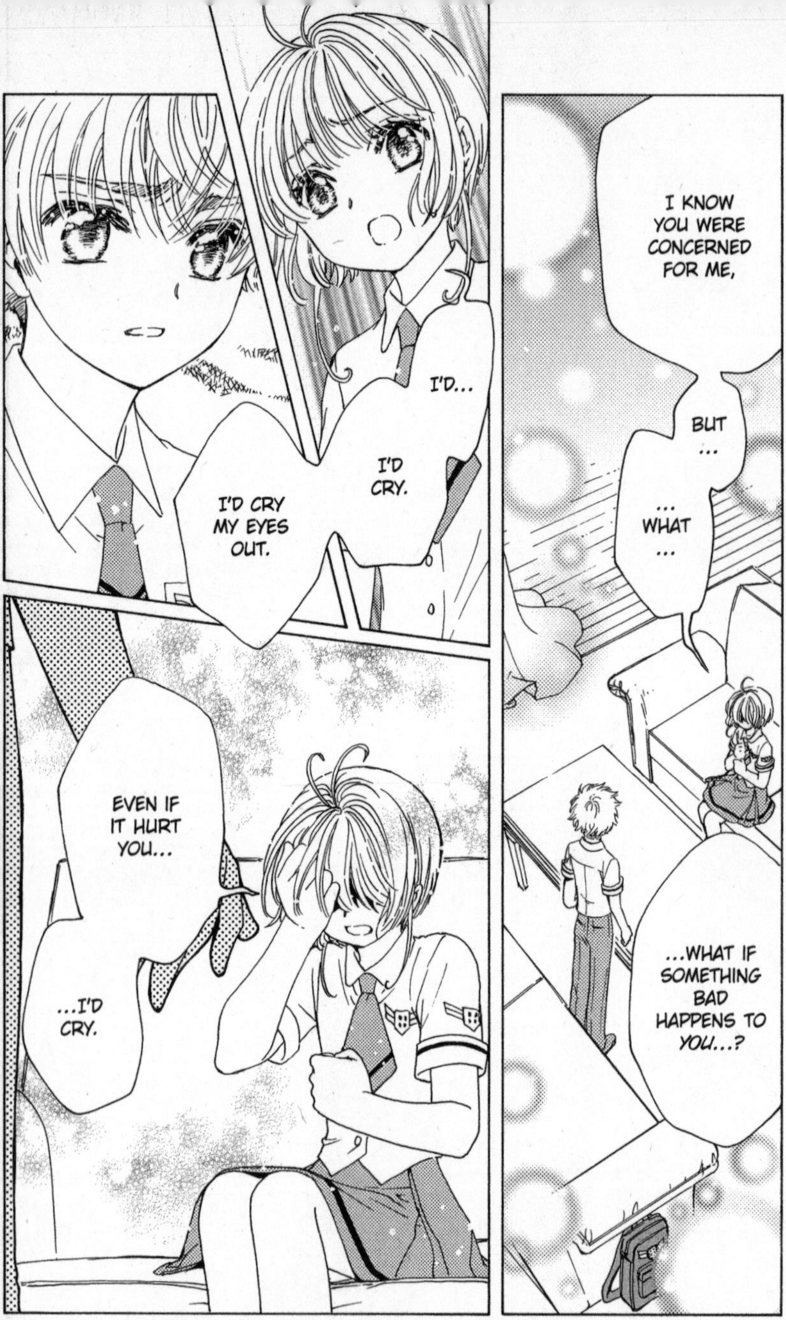
I KNOW YOU WERE CONCERNED FOR ME,
BUT ...
... WHAT ...
...WHAT IF SOMETHING BAD HAPPENS TO *YOU*...?
I'D...
I'D CRY.
I'D CRY MY EYES OUT.
EVEN IF IT HURT YOU...
...I'D CRY.

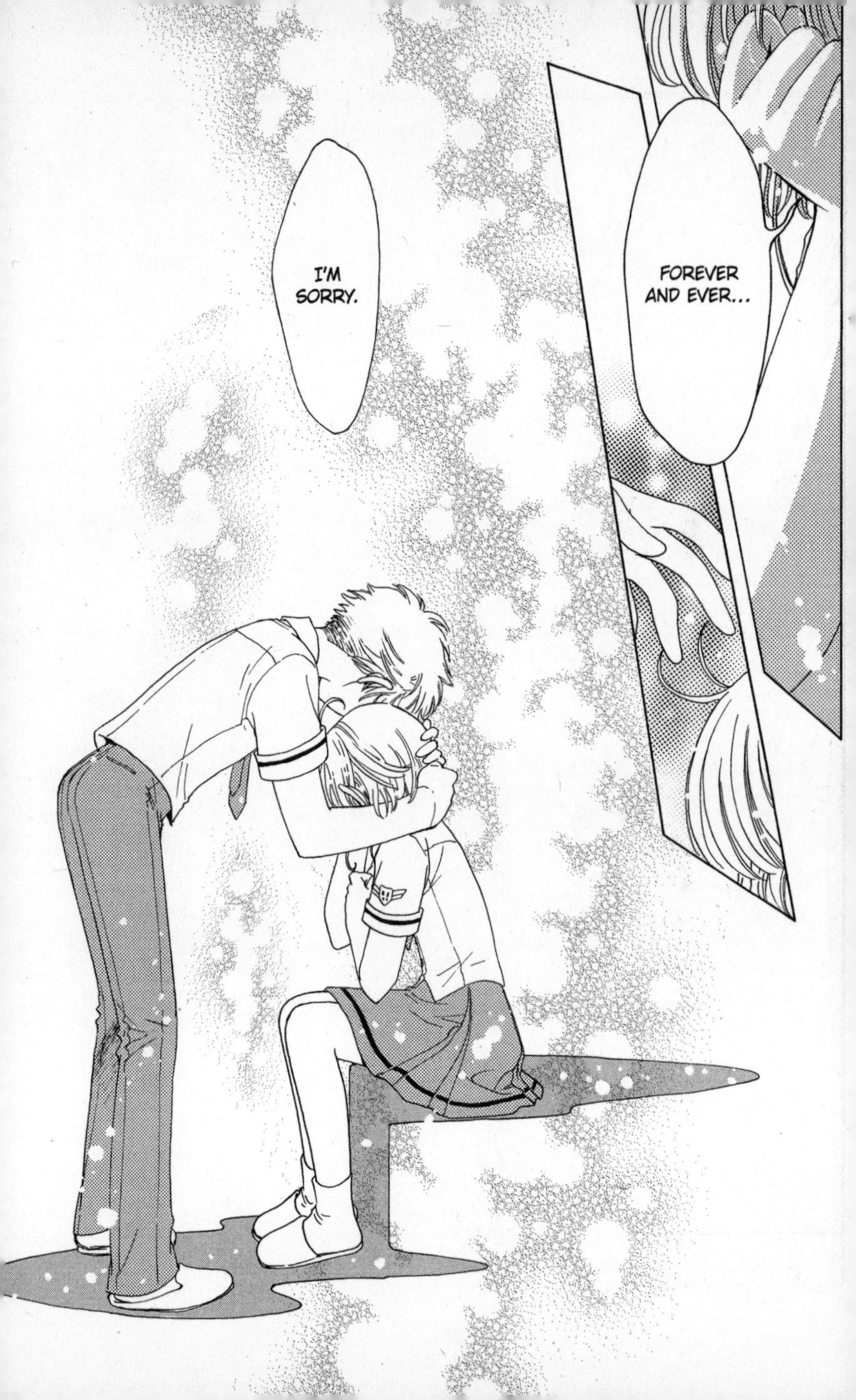
FOREVER AND EVER...
I'M SORRY.

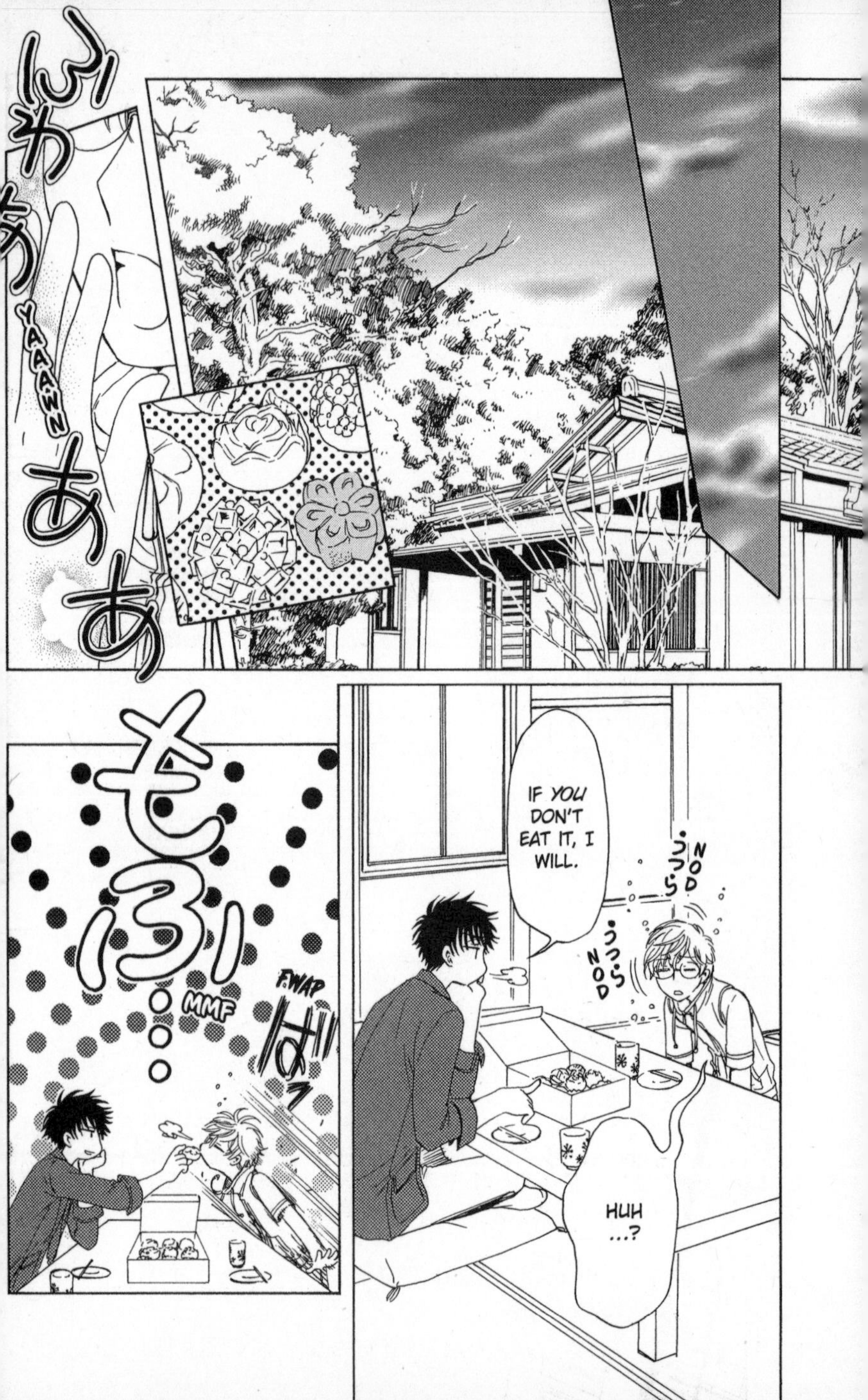
ふわぁああ
YAAAWN
IF YOU DON'T EAT IT, I WILL.
うつら NOD
うつら NOD
HUH ...?
もふ…
MMF
ばっ
F.WAP

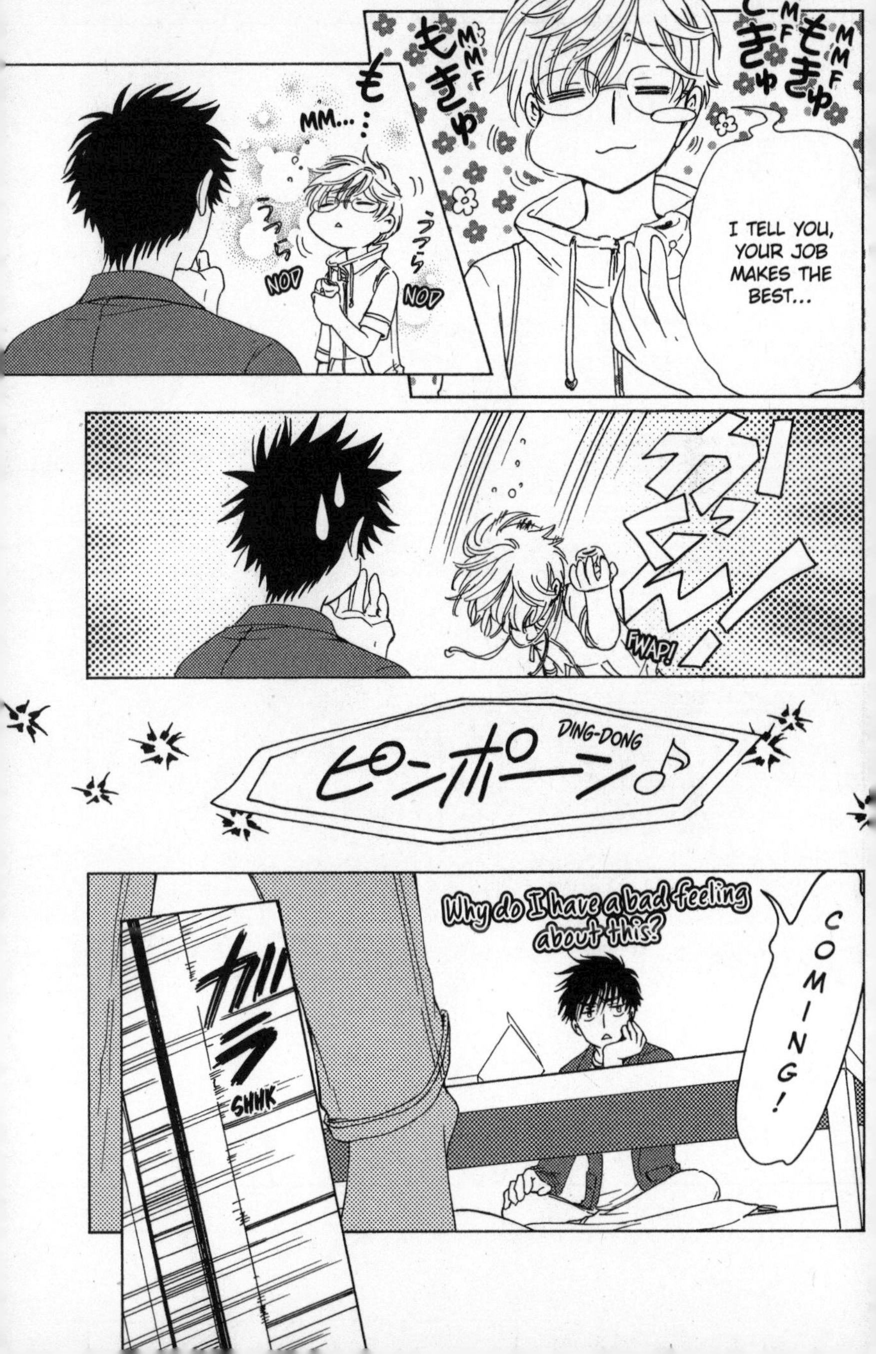

もきゅもきゅ
MMF MMF
I TELL YOU, YOUR JOB MAKES THE BEST...
もきゅ
MMF
も...
MM...
うつら
NOD
うつら
NOD
ガクン!
FWAP!
ピンポーン♪
DING-DONG
COMING!
Why do I have a bad feeling about this?
カラ
SHHK

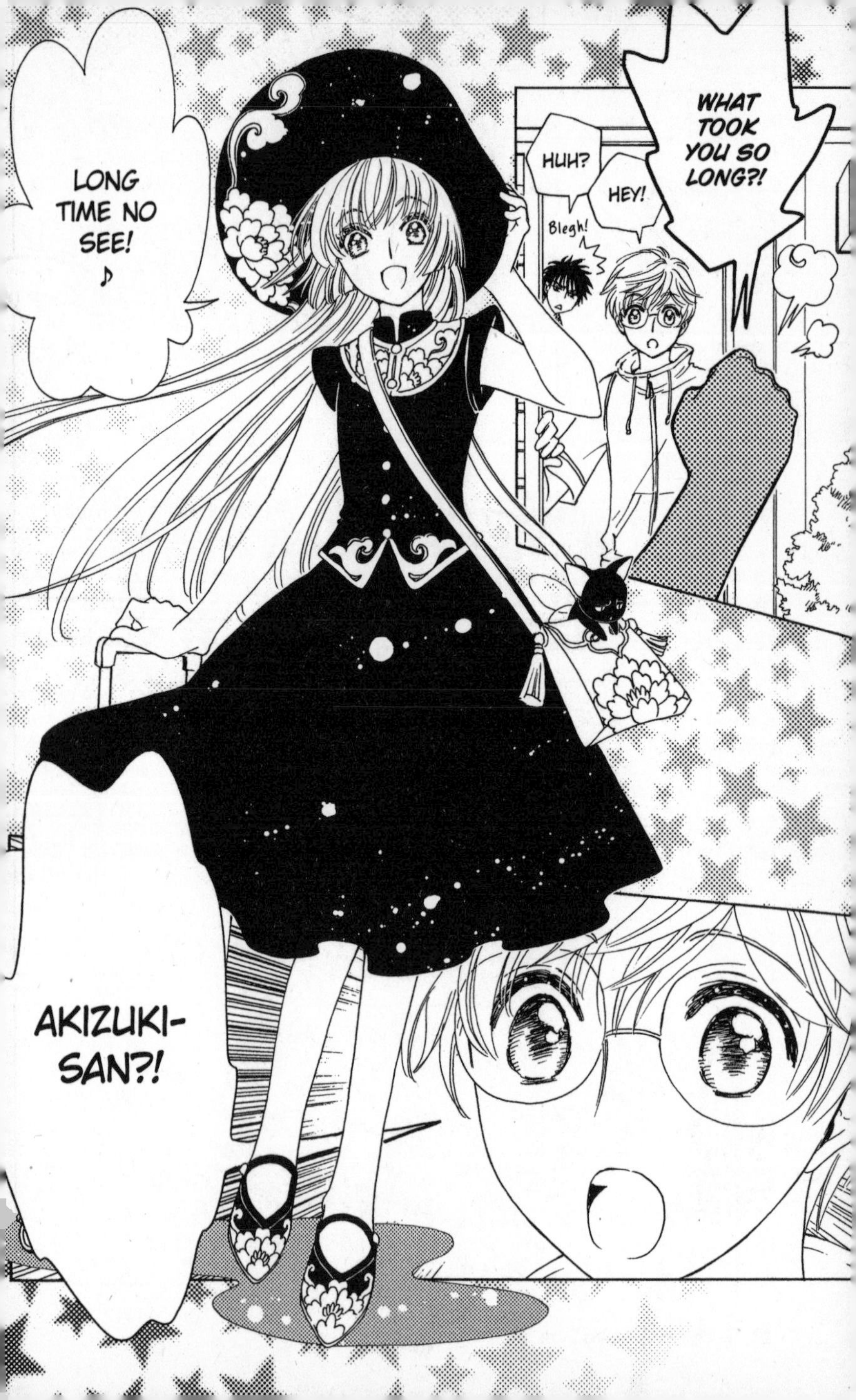
WHAT TOOK YOU SO LONG?!
HUH?
HEY!
Blegh!
LONG TIME NO SEE! ♪
AKIZUKI-SAN?!

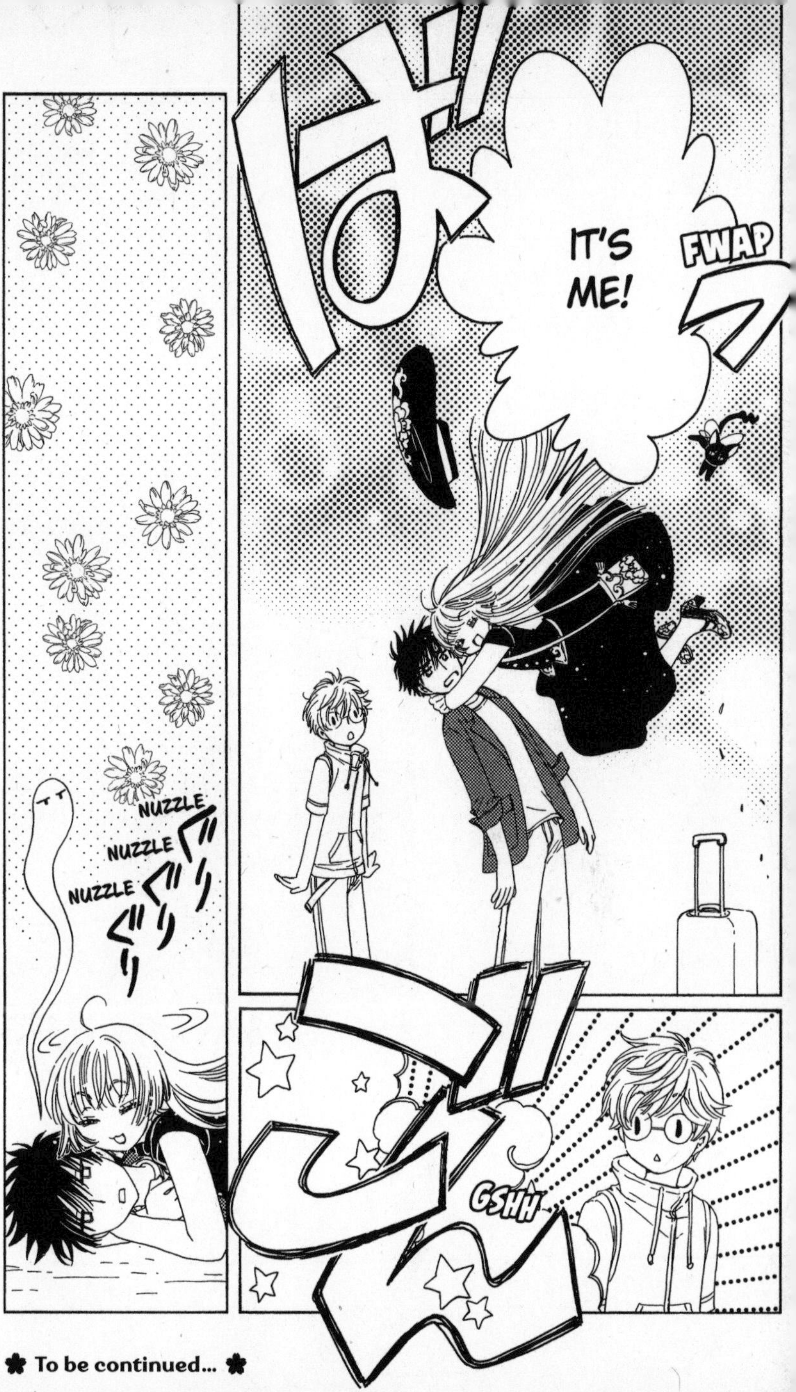
IT'S ME!
FWAP
GSHH
NUZZLE
NUZZLE
NUZZLE

✿ To be continued... ✿

Cardcaptor Sakura

CLEAR CARD

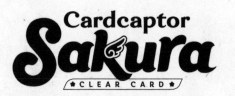

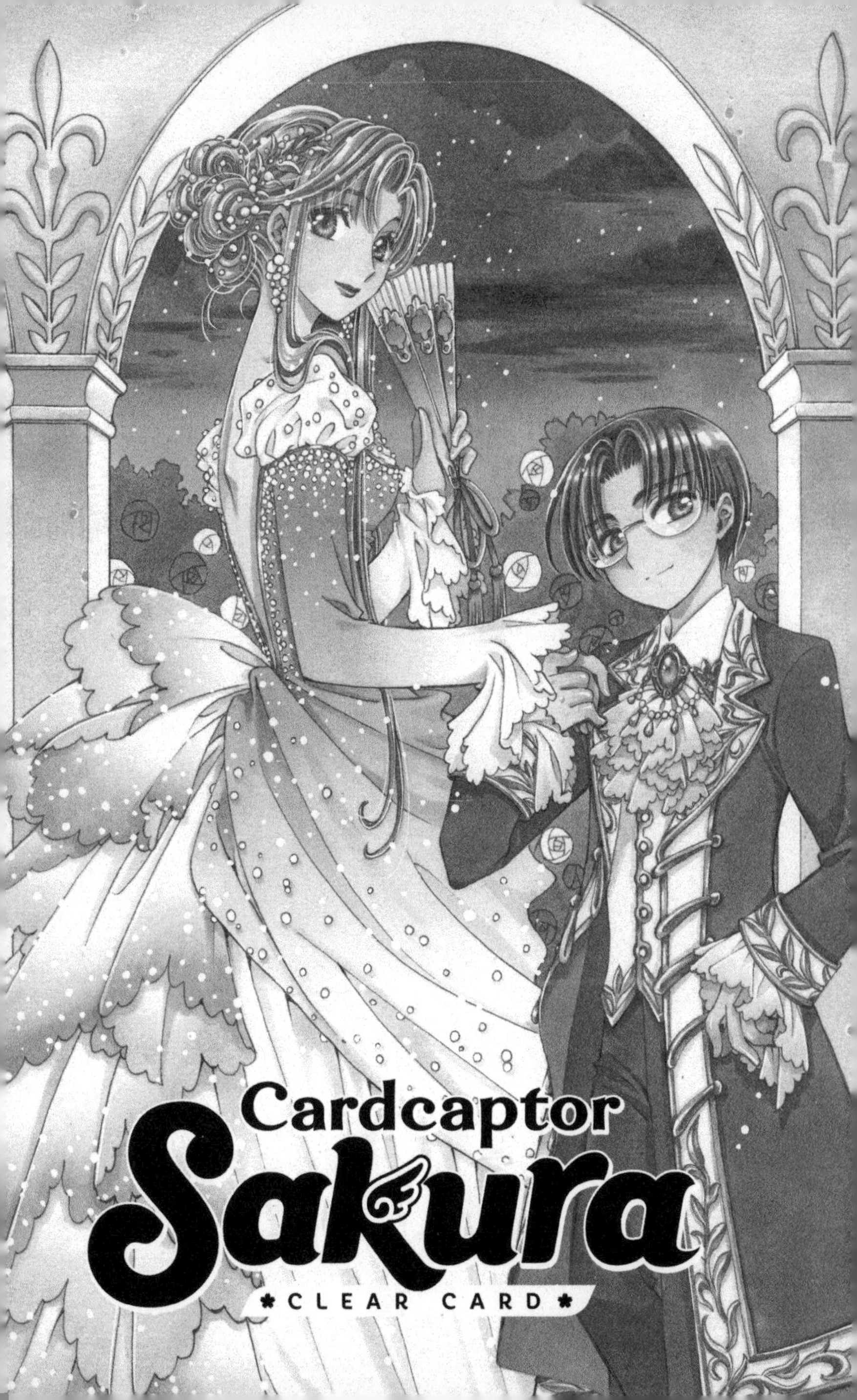
Cardcaptor
Sakura
CLEAR CARD

Cardcaptor Sakura

CLEAR CARD

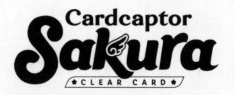

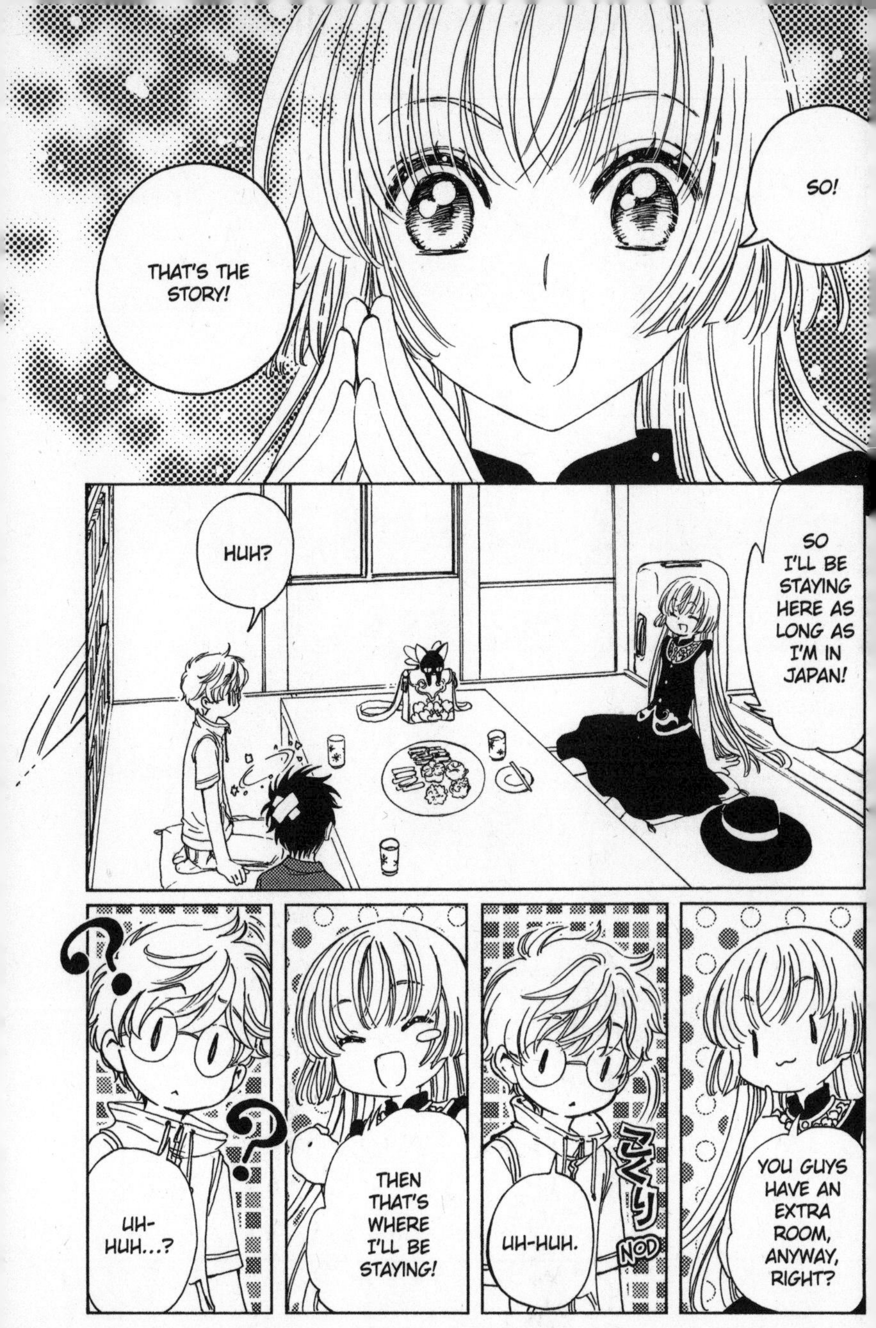
SO!
THAT'S THE STORY!
SO I'LL BE STAYING HERE AS LONG AS I'M IN JAPAN!
HUH?
YOU GUYS HAVE AN EXTRA ROOM, ANYWAY, RIGHT?
NOD
UH-HUH.
THEN THAT'S WHERE I'LL BE STAYING!
UH-HUH...?

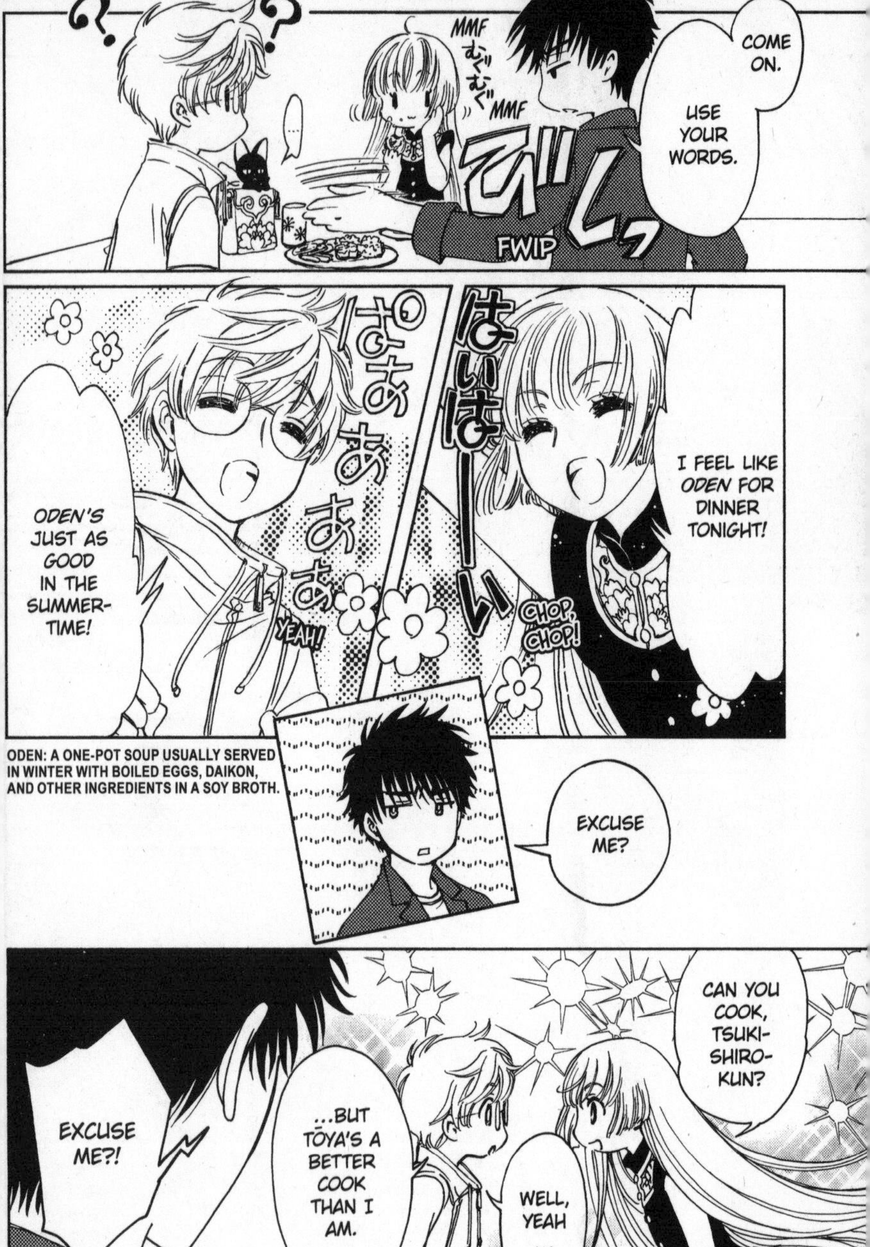
COME ON.
USE YOUR WORDS.
FWIP
MMF むぐむぐ MMF
...
I FEEL LIKE ODEN FOR DINNER TONIGHT!
はいはーい
CHOP, CHOP!
ぱあああああ
YEAH!
ODEN'S JUST AS GOOD IN THE SUMMER-TIME!
EXCUSE ME?
CAN YOU COOK, TSUKI-SHIRO-KUN?
WELL, YEAH ...
...BUT TOYA'S A BETTER COOK THAN I AM.
EXCUSE ME?!

ODEN: A ONE-POT SOUP USUALLY SERVED IN WINTER WITH BOILED EGGS, DAIKON, AND OTHER INGREDIENTS IN A SOY BROTH.

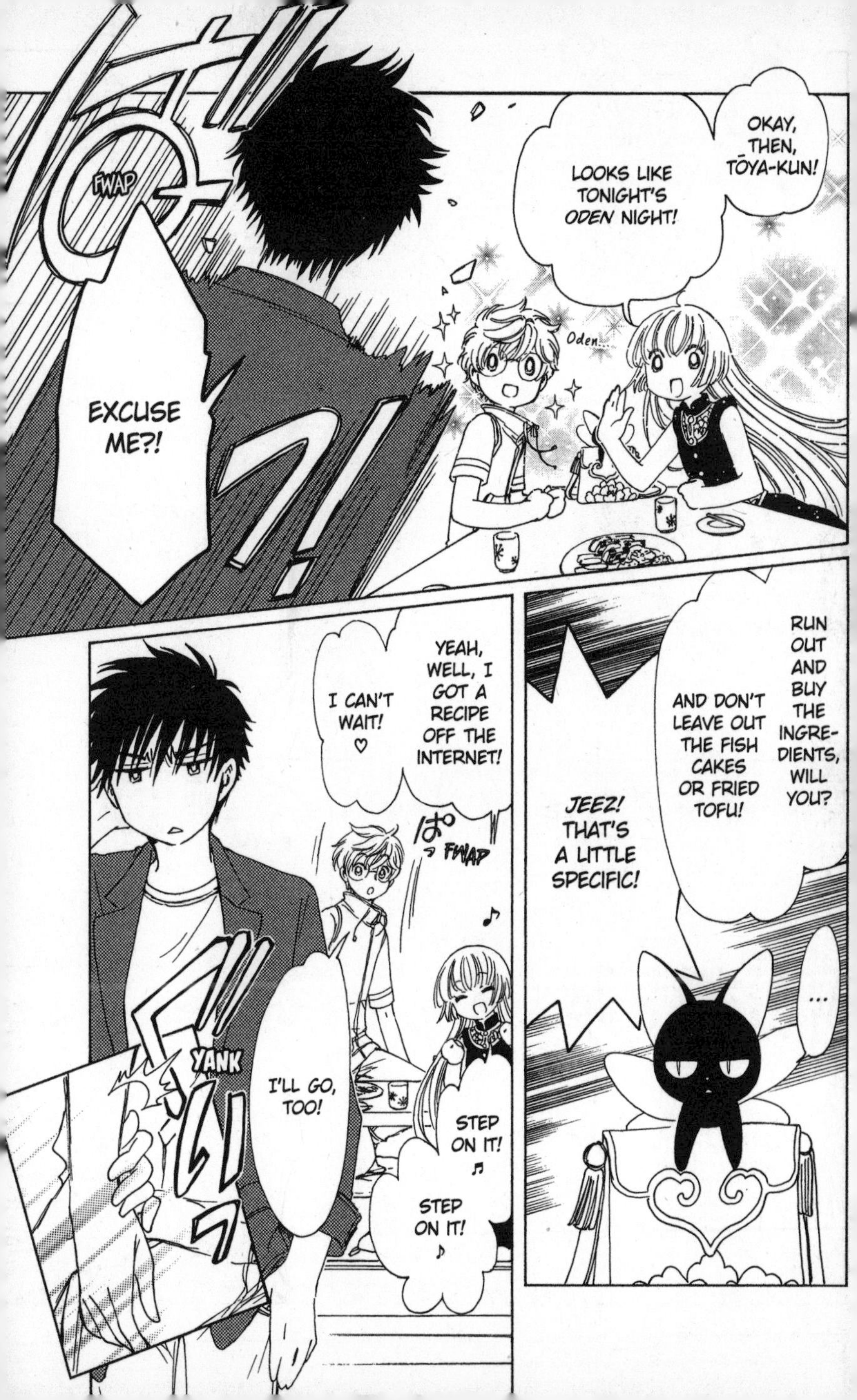
OKAY, THEN, TŌYA-KUN!
LOOKS LIKE TONIGHT'S ODEN NIGHT!
Oden...
FWAP
EXCUSE ME?!
RUN OUT AND BUY THE INGREDIENTS, WILL YOU?
AND DON'T LEAVE OUT THE FISH CAKES OR FRIED TOFU!
JEEZ! THAT'S A LITTLE SPECIFIC!
...
YEAH, WELL, I GOT A RECIPE OFF THE INTERNET!
I CAN'T WAIT! ♡
FWAP
STEP ON IT! ♪
STEP ON IT! ♪
I'LL GO, TOO!
YANK

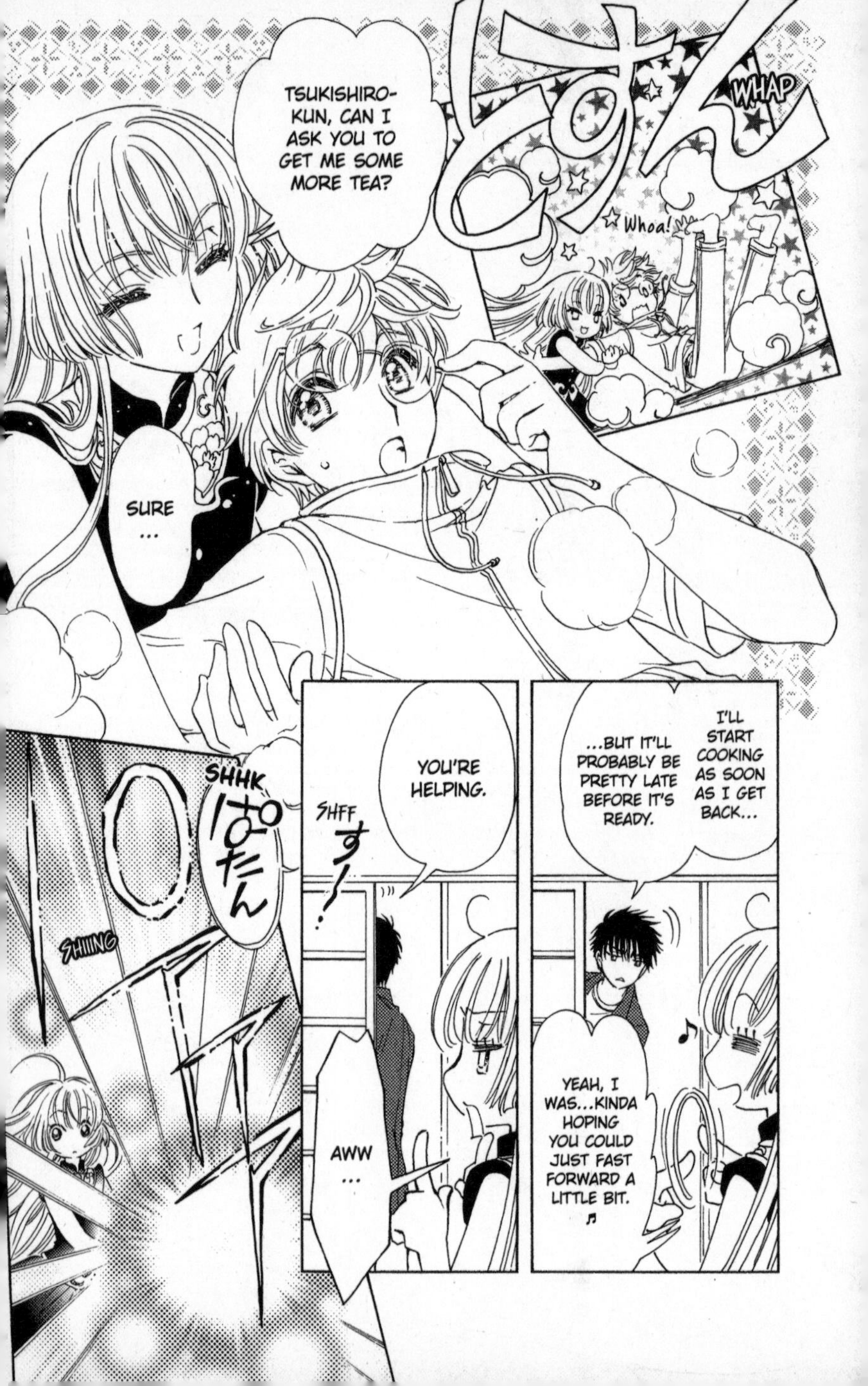
どすん
WHAP
Whoa!
TSUKISHIRO-KUN, CAN I ASK YOU TO GET ME SOME MORE TEA?
SURE ...
I'LL START COOKING AS SOON AS I GET BACK...
...BUT IT'LL PROBABLY BE PRETTY LATE BEFORE IT'S READY.
YEAH, I WAS...KINDA HOPING YOU COULD JUST FAST FORWARD A LITTLE BIT. ♪
YOU'RE HELPING.
SHFF
す!
AWW ...
SHHK
ぱたん
SHIING

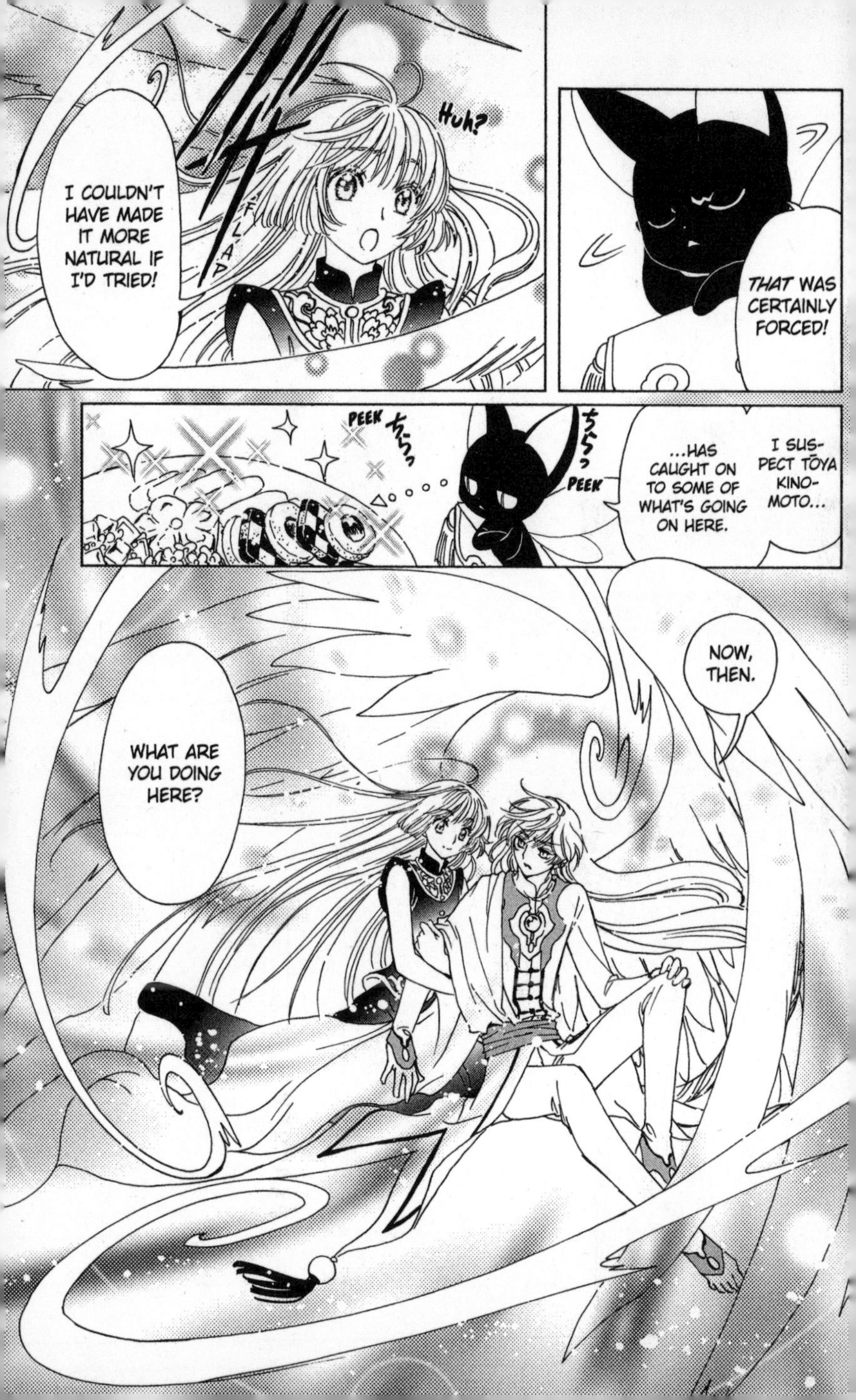
THAT WAS CERTAINLY FORCED!
Huh?
FLAP
I COULDN'T HAVE MADE IT MORE NATURAL IF I'D TRIED!
I SUS-PECT TŌYA KINO-MOTO...
...HAS CAUGHT ON TO SOME OF WHAT'S GOING ON HERE.
ちらっ
PEEK
ちらっ
PEEK
NOW, THEN.
WHAT ARE YOU DOING HERE?

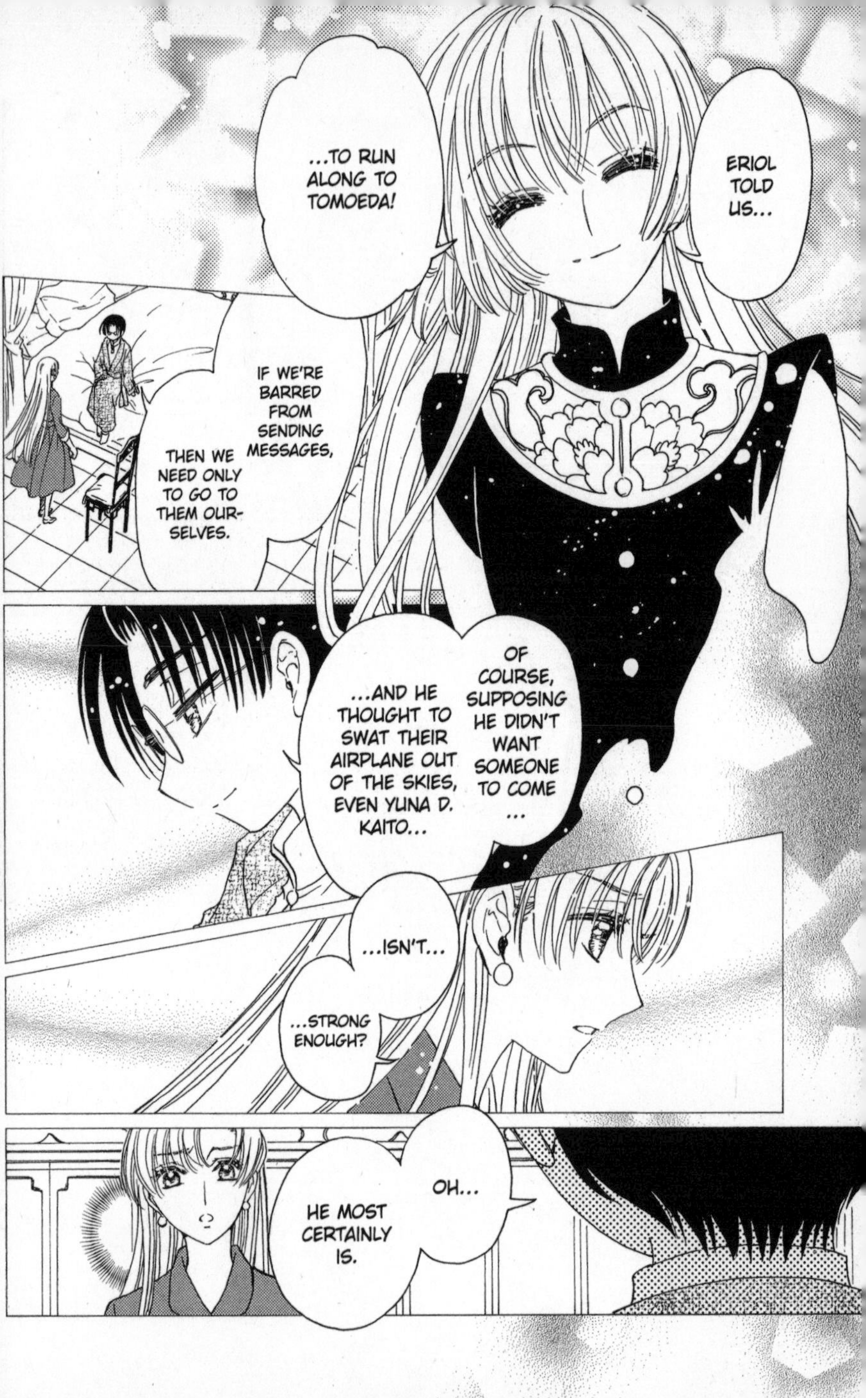
ERIOL TOLD US...
...TO RUN ALONG TO TOMOEDA!
IF WE'RE BARRED FROM SENDING MESSAGES,
THEN WE NEED ONLY TO GO TO THEM OURSELVES.
OF COURSE, SUPPOSING HE DIDN'T WANT SOMEONE TO COME...
...AND HE THOUGHT TO SWAT THEIR AIRPLANE OUT OF THE SKIES, EVEN YUNA D. KAITO...
...ISN'T...
...STRONG ENOUGH?
OH...
HE MOST CERTAINLY IS.

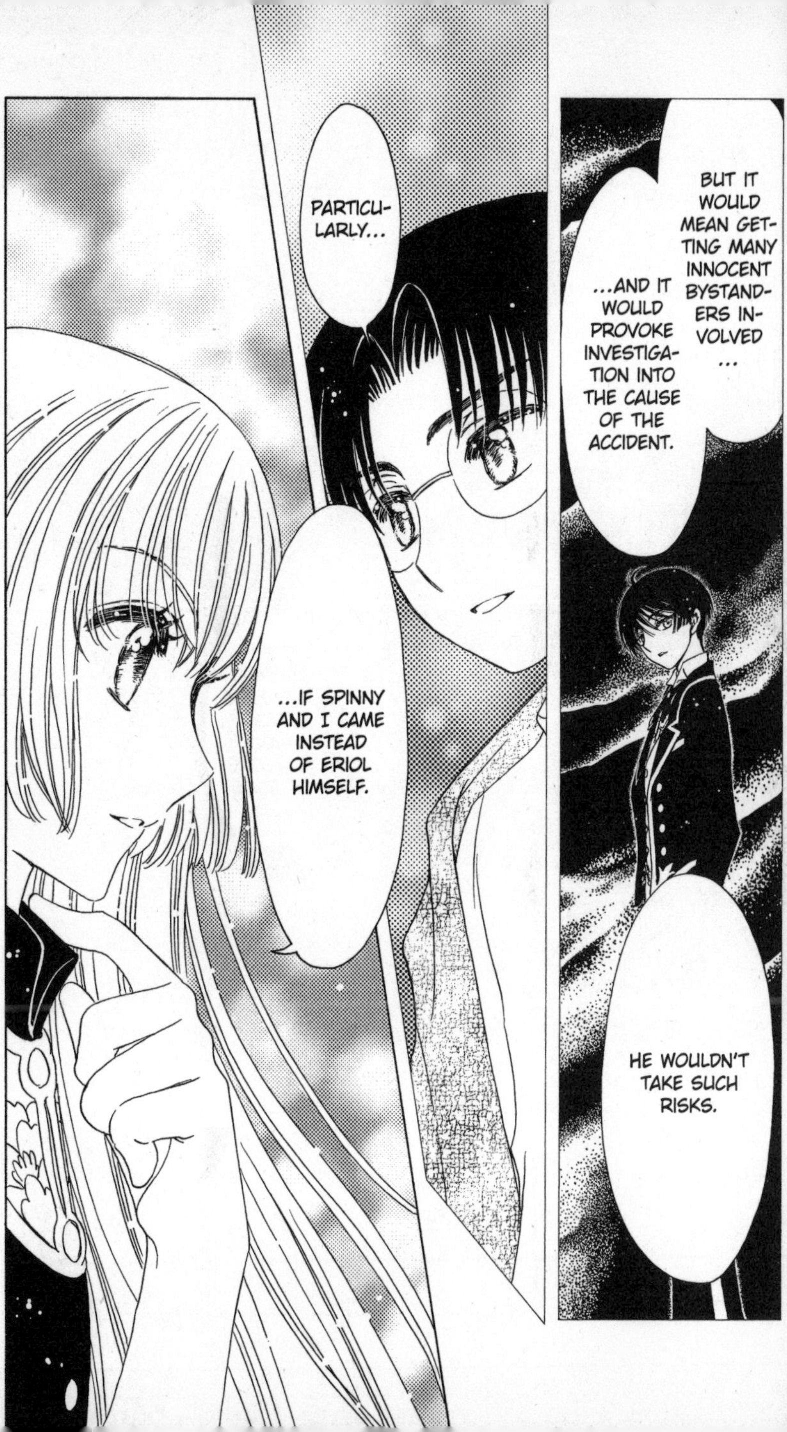
BUT IT WOULD MEAN GETTING MANY INNOCENT BYSTANDERS INVOLVED...
...AND IT WOULD PROVOKE INVESTIGATION INTO THE CAUSE OF THE ACCIDENT.
HE WOULDN'T TAKE SUCH RISKS.
PARTICULARLY...
...IF SPINNY AND I CAME INSTEAD OF ERIOL HIMSELF.

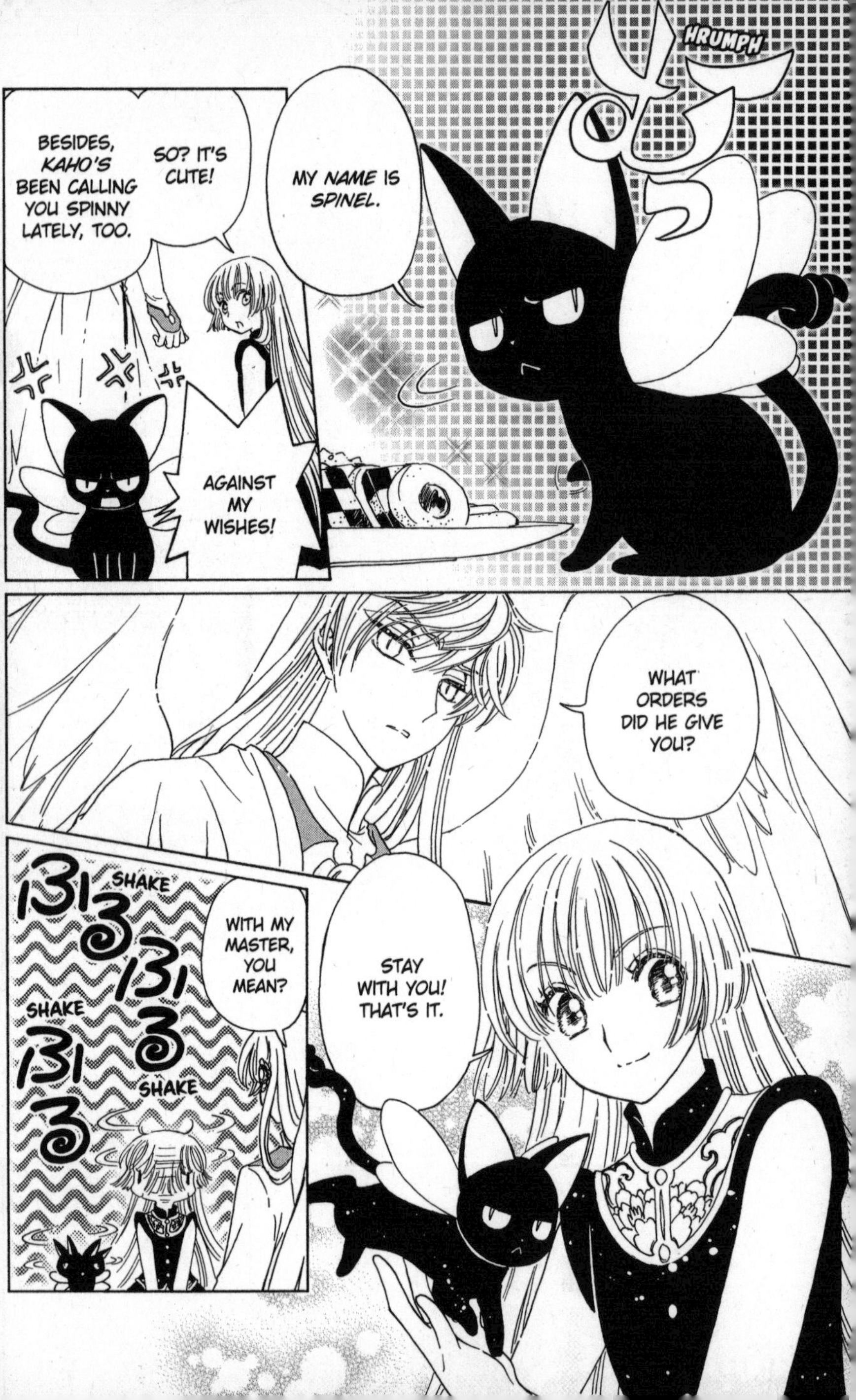
HRUMPH
MY NAME IS SPINEL.
SO? IT'S CUTE!
BESIDES, KAHO'S BEEN CALLING YOU SPINNY LATELY, TOO.
AGAINST MY WISHES!
WHAT ORDERS DID HE GIVE YOU?
STAY WITH YOU! THAT'S IT.
WITH MY MASTER, YOU MEAN?
SHAKE
SHAKE
SHAKE

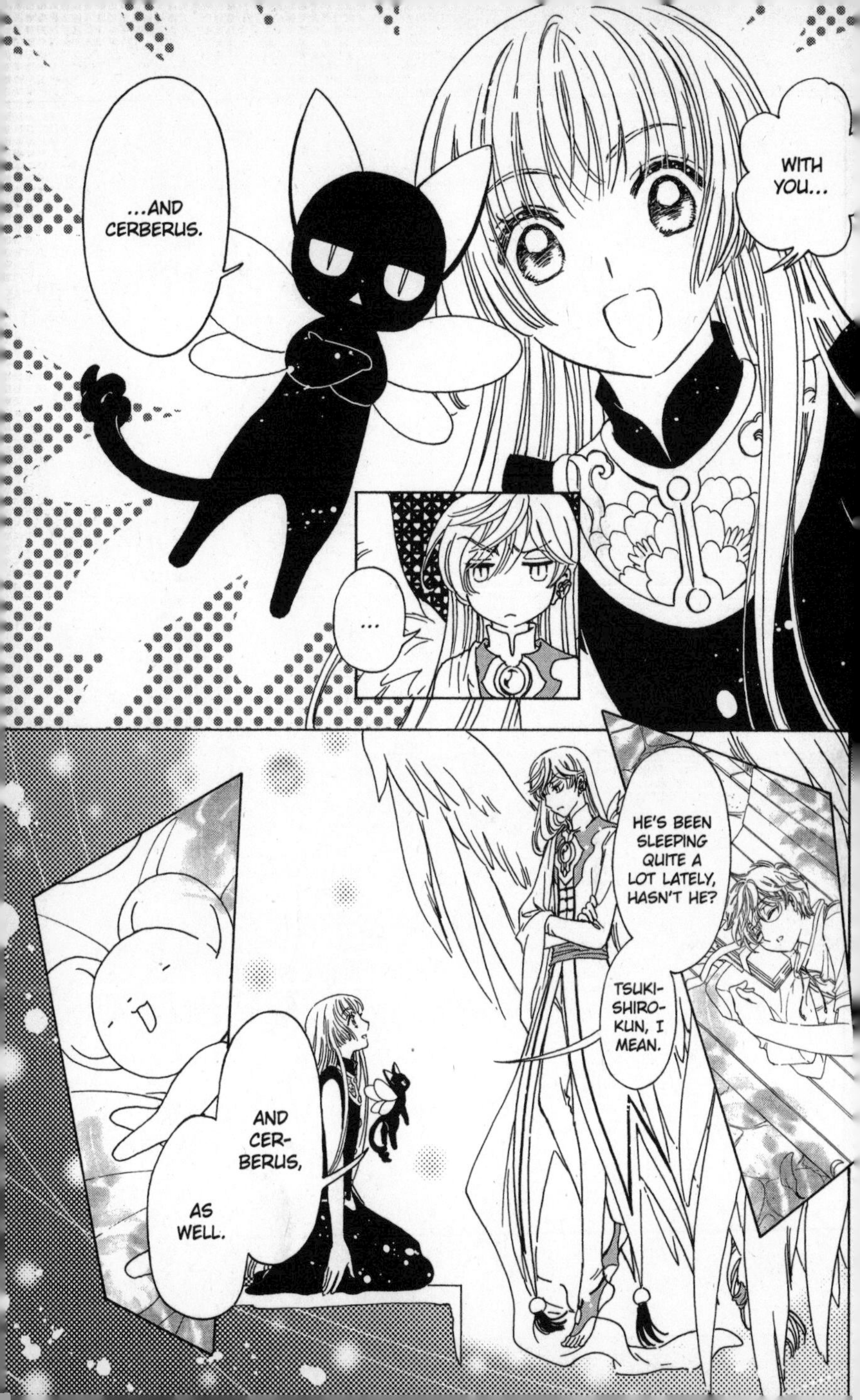
WITH YOU...
...AND CERBERUS.
...
HE'S BEEN SLEEPING QUITE A LOT LATELY, HASN'T HE?
TSUKISHIRO-KUN, I MEAN.
AND CERBERUS, AS WELL.

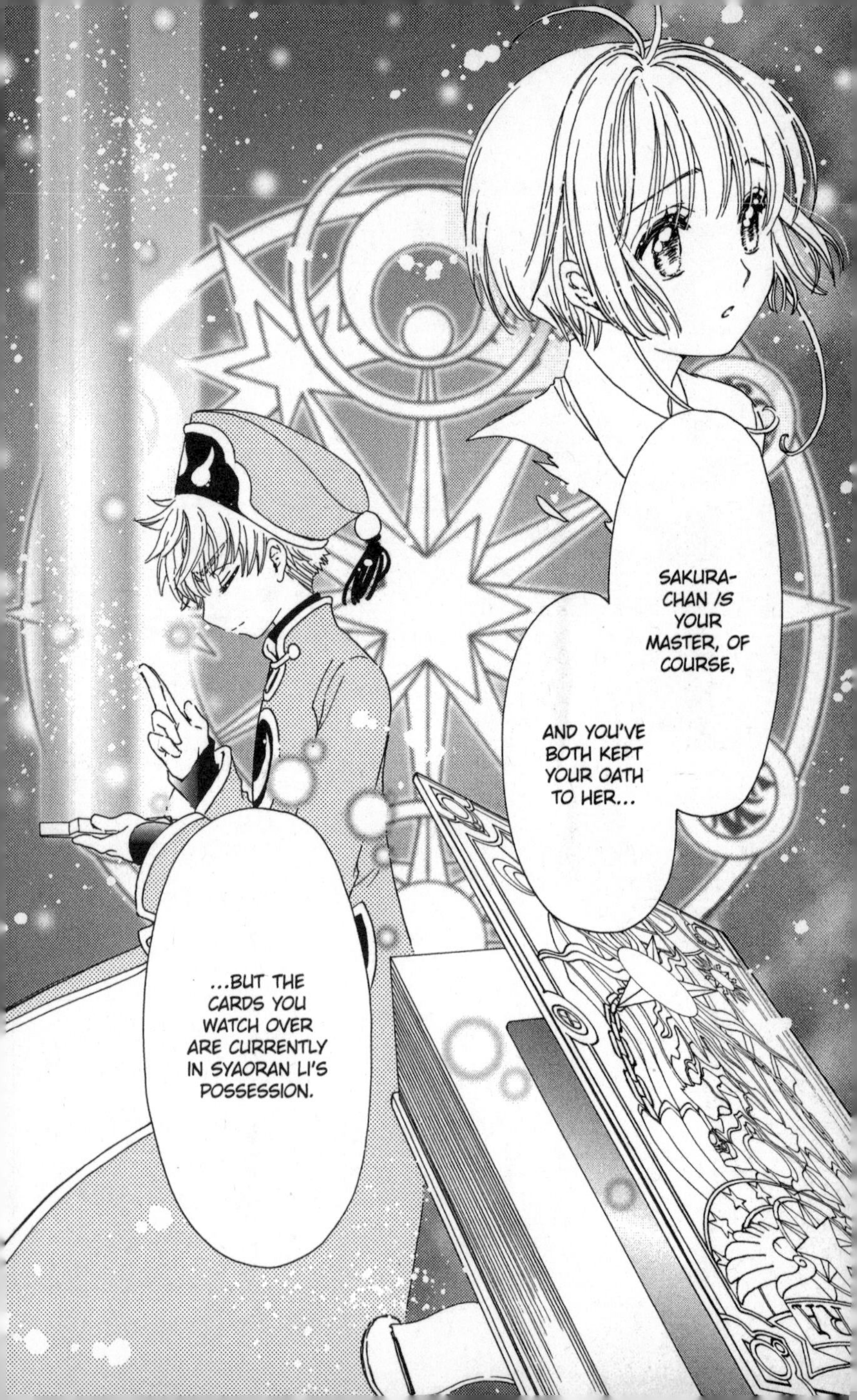
SAKURA-CHAN IS YOUR MASTER, OF COURSE,
AND YOU'VE BOTH KEPT YOUR OATH TO HER...
...BUT THE CARDS YOU WATCH OVER ARE CURRENTLY IN SYAORAN LI'S POSSESSION.

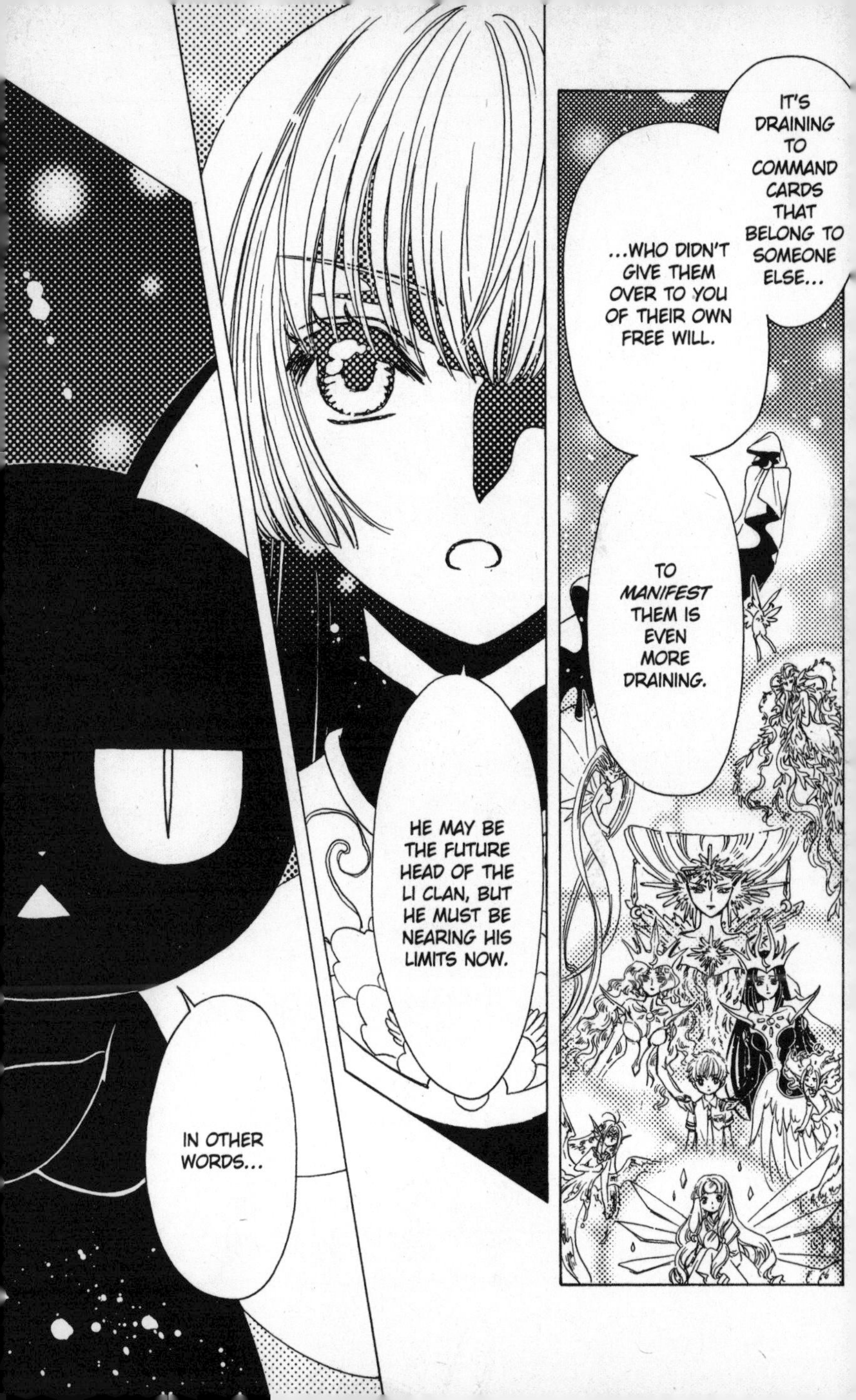
IT'S DRAINING TO COMMAND CARDS THAT BELONG TO SOMEONE ELSE...
...WHO DIDN'T GIVE THEM OVER TO YOU OF THEIR OWN FREE WILL.
TO *MANIFEST* THEM IS EVEN MORE DRAINING.
HE MAY BE THE FUTURE HEAD OF THE LI CLAN, BUT HE MUST BE NEARING HIS LIMITS NOW.
IN OTHER WORDS...

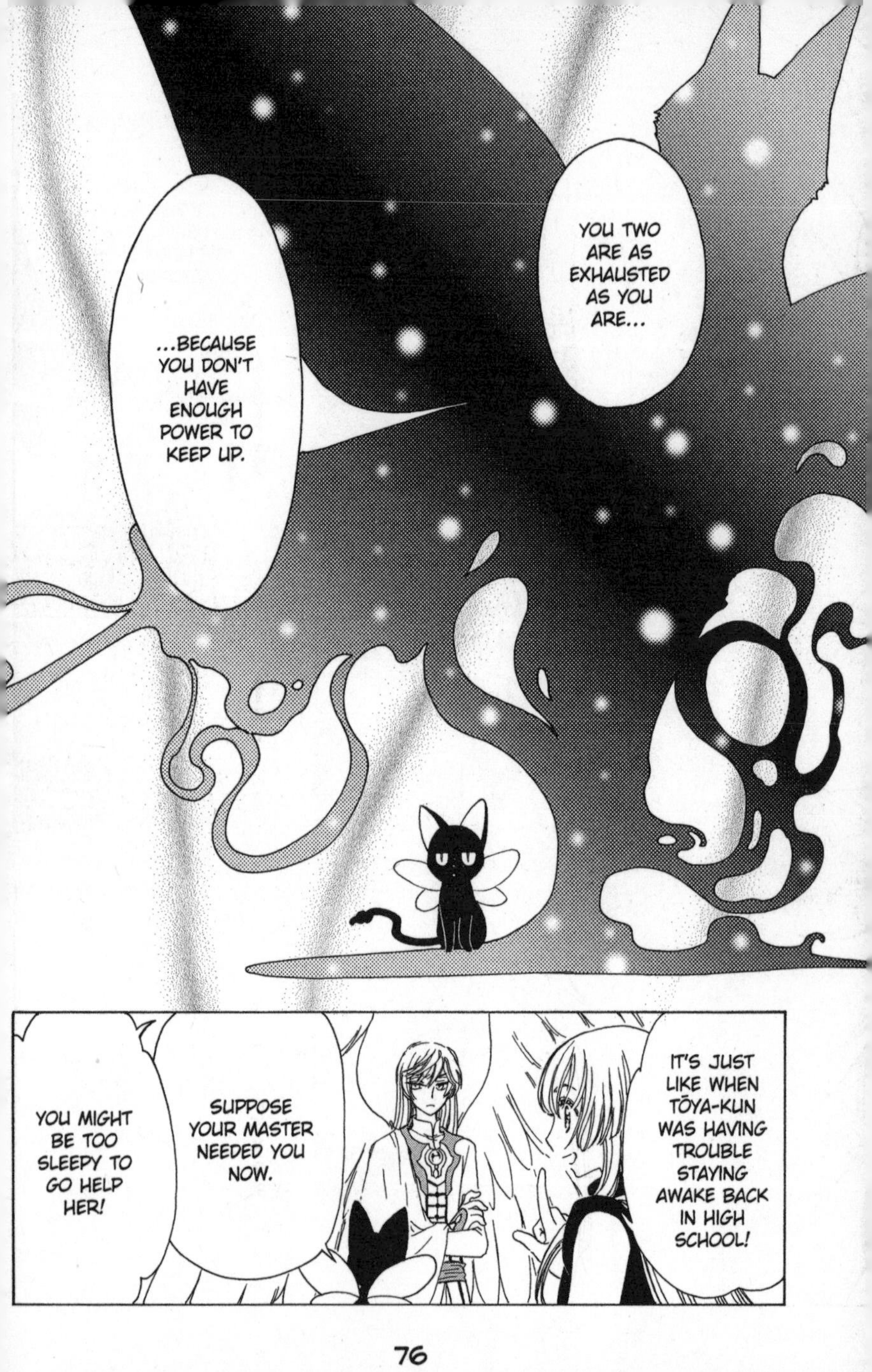
YOU TWO ARE AS EXHAUSTED AS YOU ARE...
...BECAUSE YOU DON'T HAVE ENOUGH POWER TO KEEP UP.
IT'S JUST LIKE WHEN TŌYA-KUN WAS HAVING TROUBLE STAYING AWAKE BACK IN HIGH SCHOOL!
SUPPOSE YOUR MASTER NEEDED YOU NOW.
YOU MIGHT BE TOO SLEEPY TO GO HELP HER!

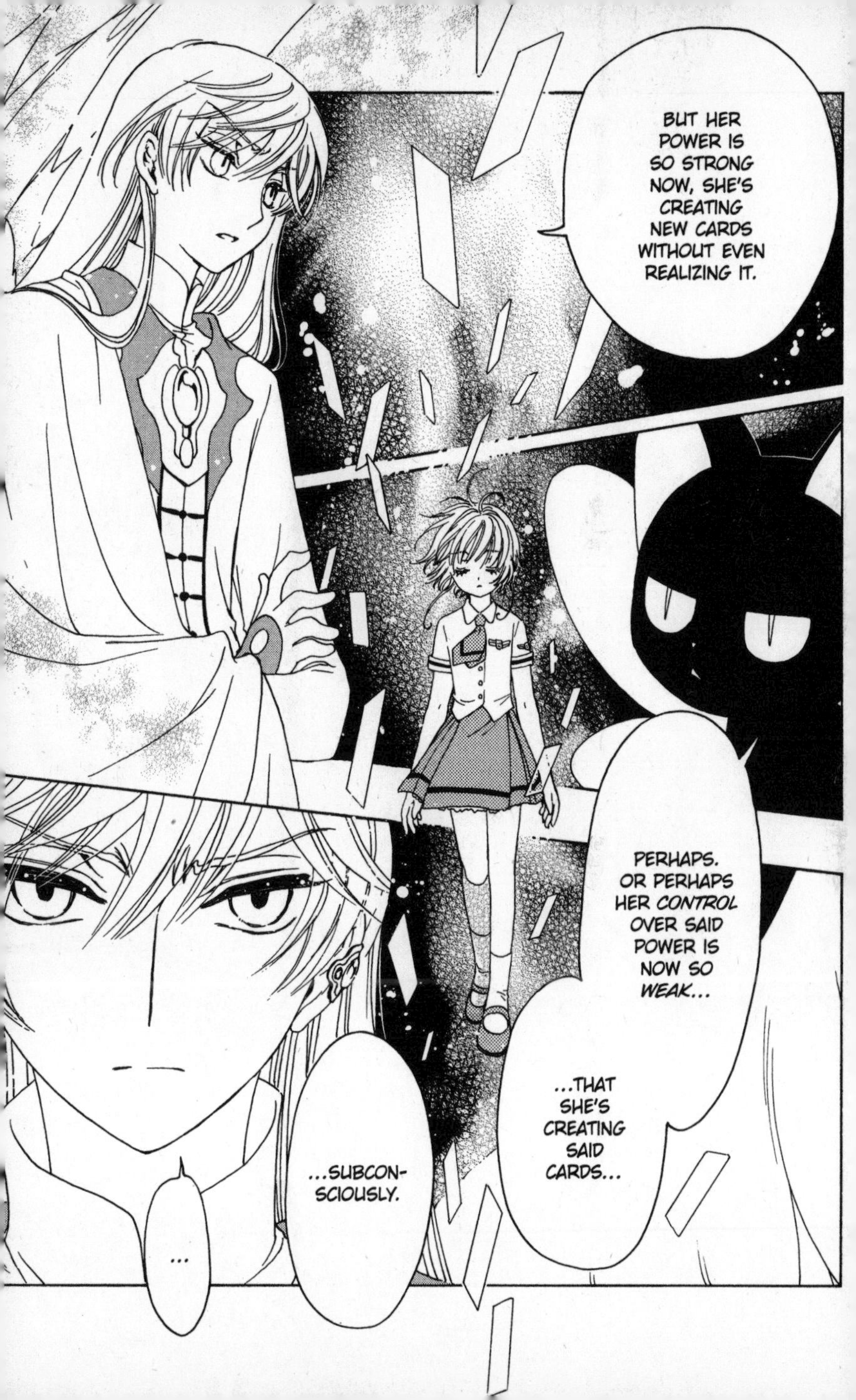
BUT HER POWER IS SO STRONG NOW, SHE'S CREATING NEW CARDS WITHOUT EVEN REALIZING IT.
PERHAPS. OR PERHAPS HER *CONTROL* OVER SAID POWER IS NOW SO *WEAK*...
...THAT SHE'S CREATING SAID CARDS...
...SUBCON-SCIOUSLY.
...

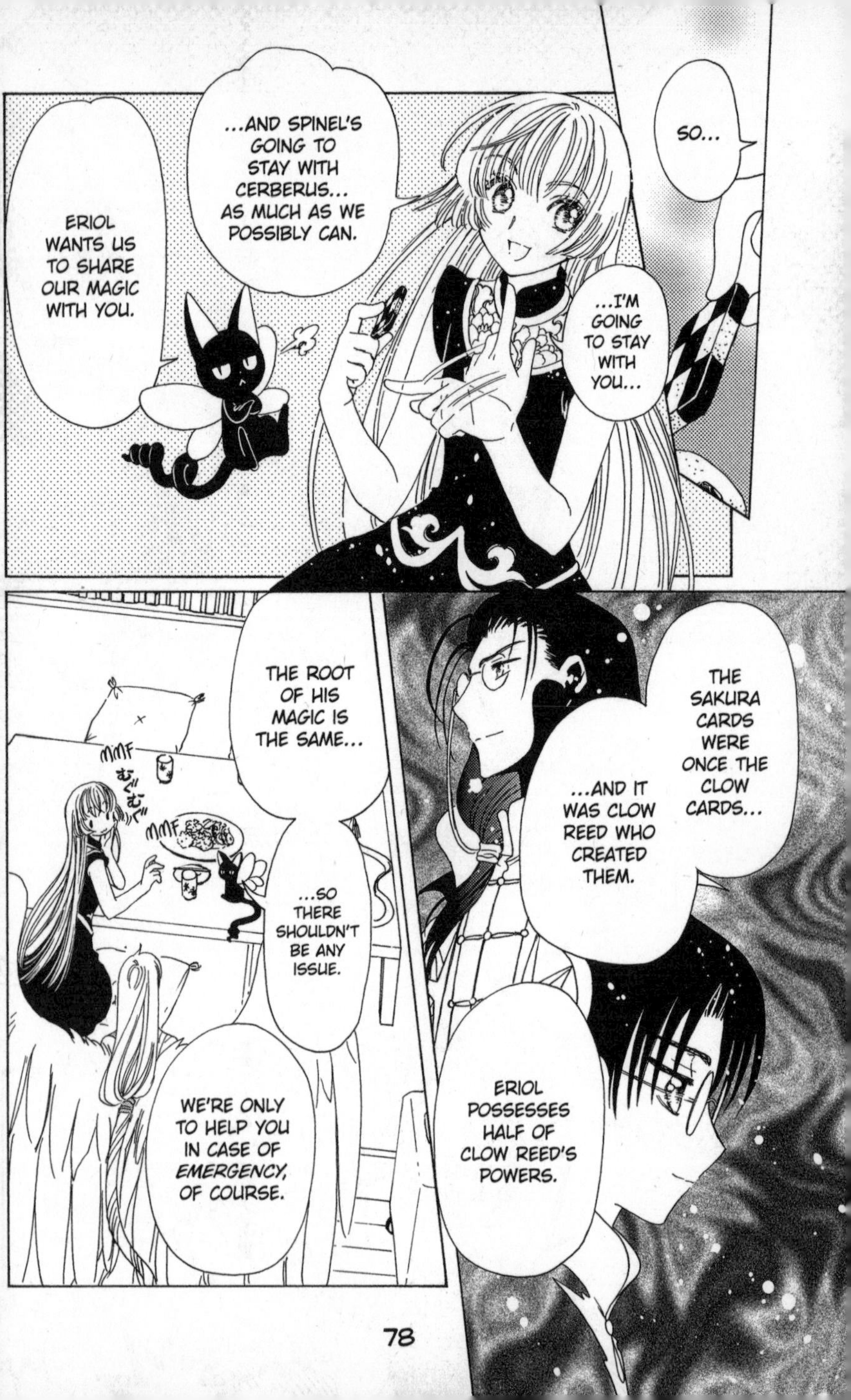
SO...
...I'M GOING TO STAY WITH YOU...
...AND SPINEL'S GOING TO STAY WITH CERBERUS... AS MUCH AS WE POSSIBLY CAN.
ERIOL WANTS US TO SHARE OUR MAGIC WITH YOU.
THE SAKURA CARDS WERE ONCE THE CLOW CARDS...
...AND IT WAS CLOW REED WHO CREATED THEM.
ERIOL POSSESSES HALF OF CLOW REED'S POWERS.
THE ROOT OF HIS MAGIC IS THE SAME...
...SO THERE SHOULDN'T BE ANY ISSUE.
MMF
むぐむぐ
MMF
WE'RE ONLY TO HELP YOU IN CASE OF *EMERGENCY*, OF COURSE.

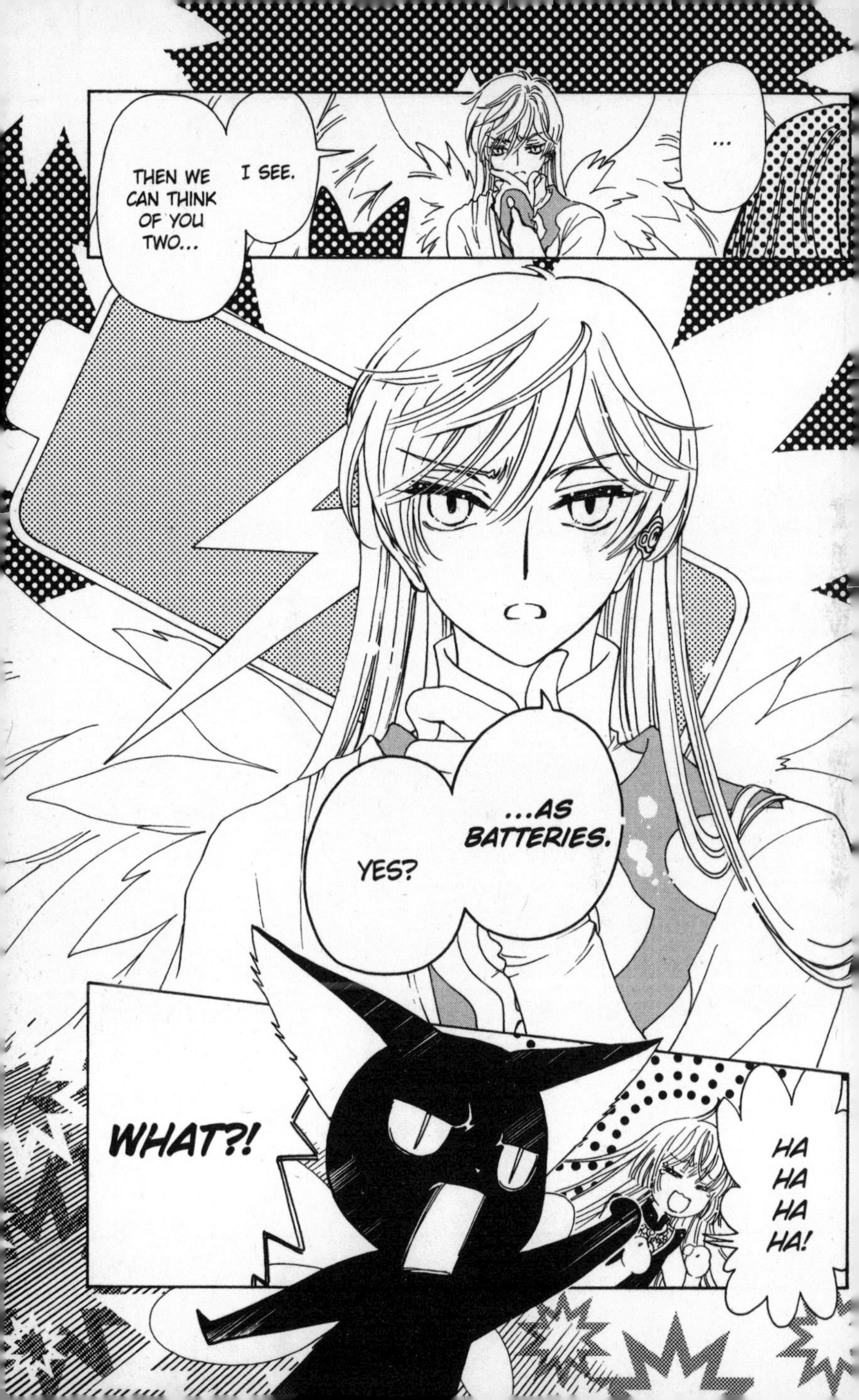
...
I SEE.
THEN WE CAN THINK OF YOU TWO...
...AS BATTERIES.
YES?
HA HA HA HA!
WHAT?!

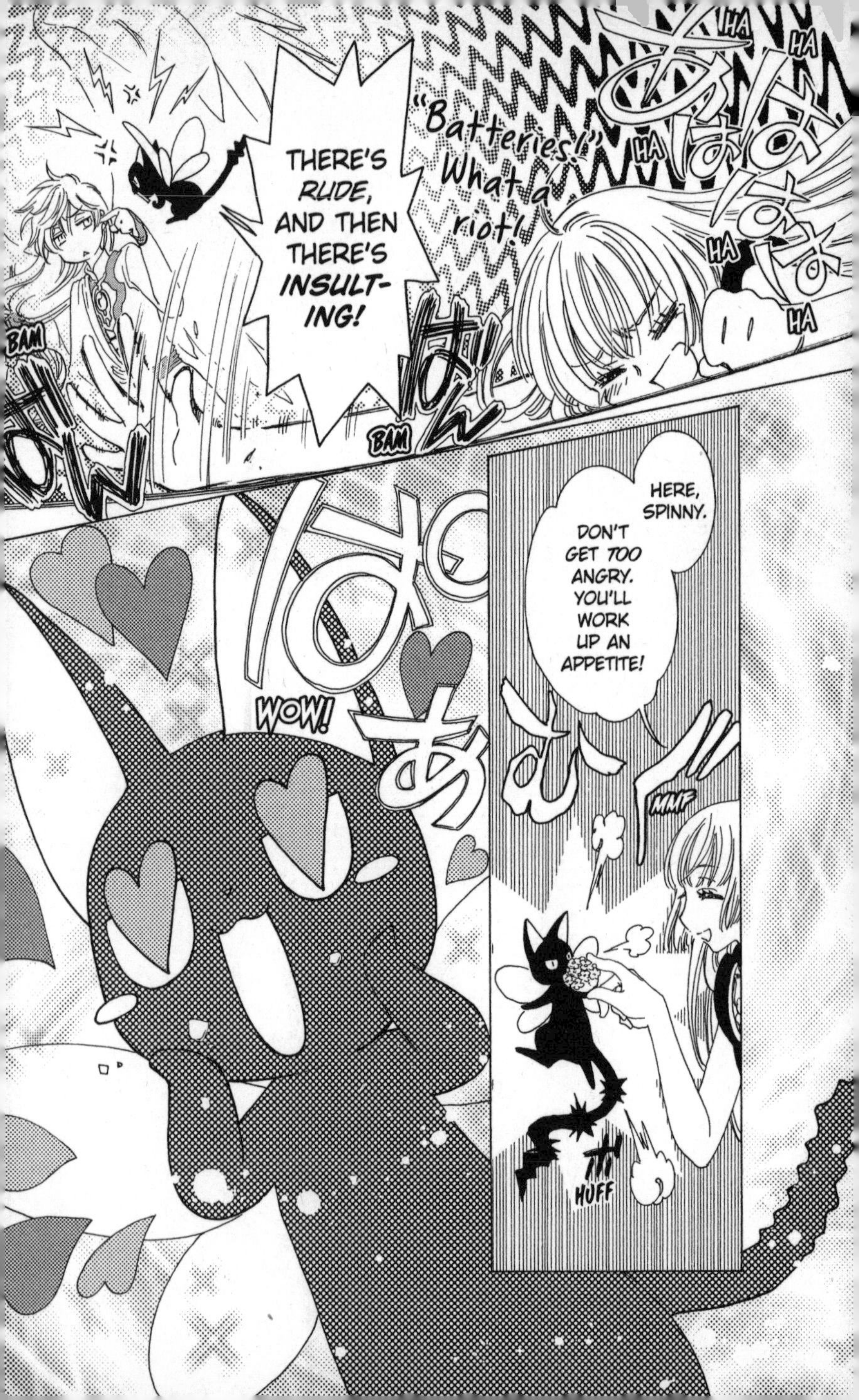
HA HA HA HA HA
"Batteries!" What a riot!
THERE'S RUDE, AND THEN THERE'S INSULTING!
BAM
BAM
HERE, SPINNY. DON'T GET TOO ANGRY. YOU'LL WORK UP AN APPETITE!
MMF
HUFF
WOW!

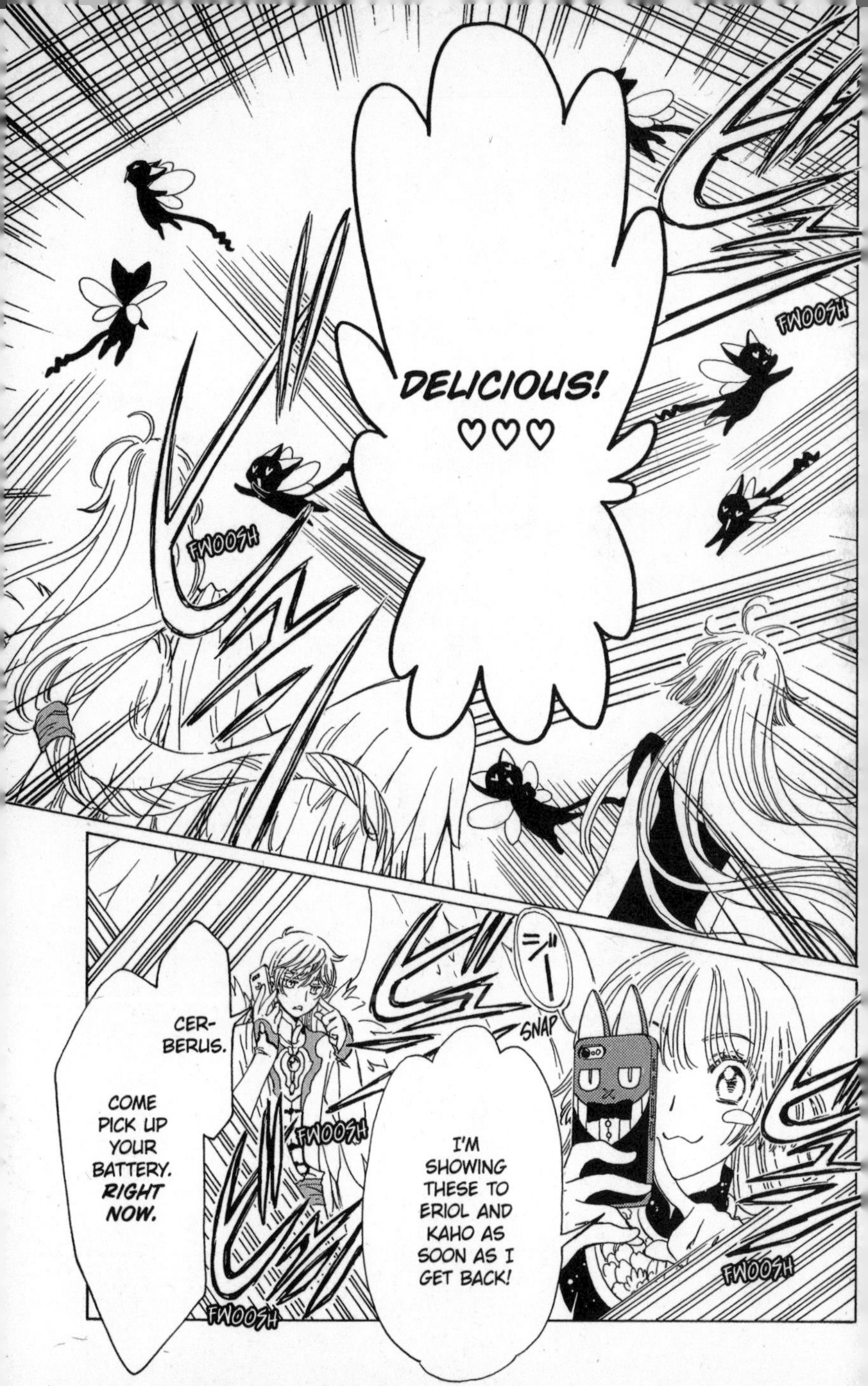

FWOOSH
DELICIOUS! ♡♡♡
FWOOSH
I'M SHOWING THESE TO ERIOL AND KAHO AS SOON AS I GET BACK!
FWOOSH
SNAP
CER-BERUS.
COME PICK UP YOUR BATTERY. ***RIGHT NOW.***
FWOOSH
FWOOSH

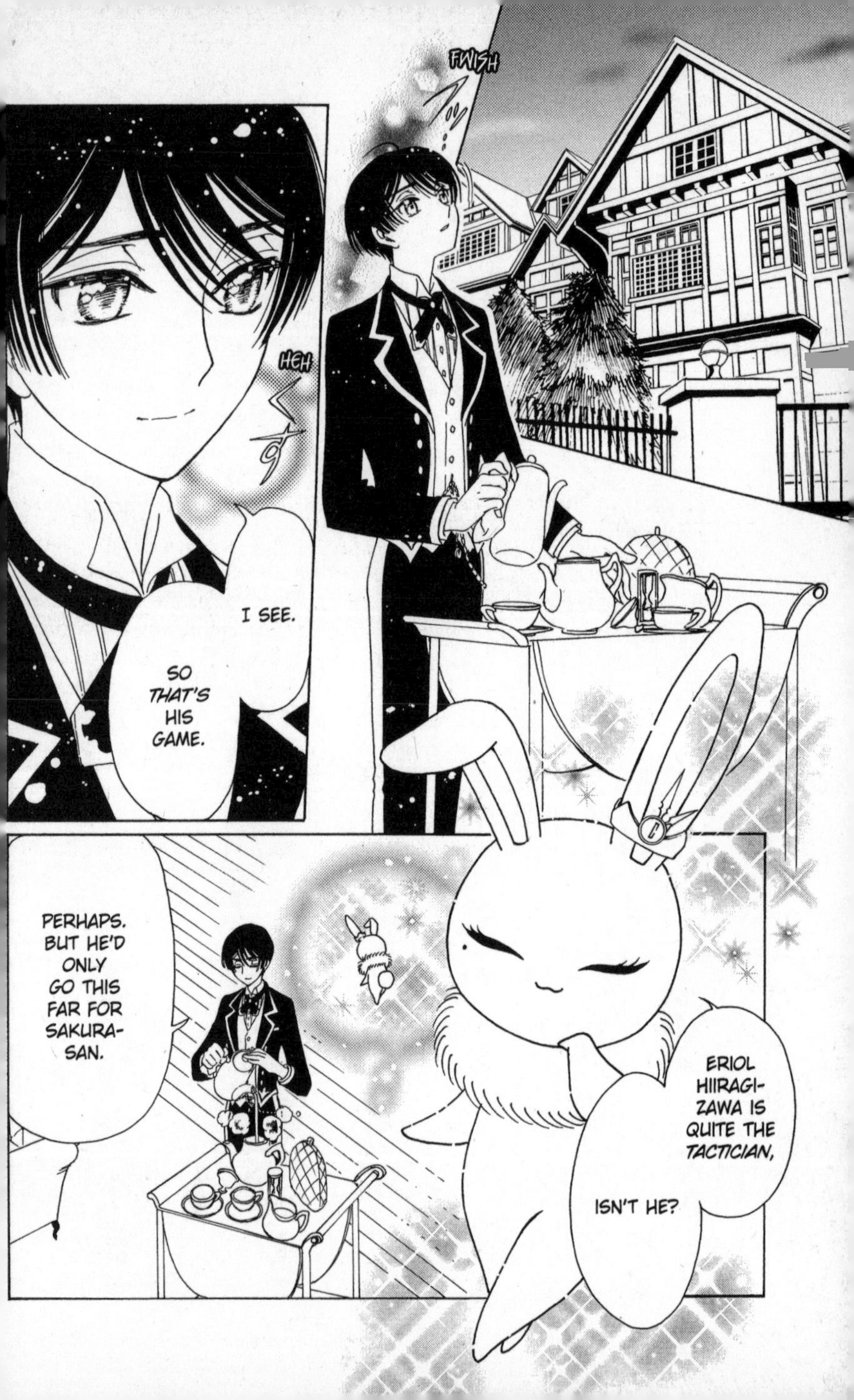
FWISH
HEH
I SEE.
SO THAT'S HIS GAME.
ERIOL HIIRAGI-ZAWA IS QUITE THE TACTICIAN,
ISN'T HE?
PERHAPS. BUT HE'D ONLY GO THIS FAR FOR SAKURA-SAN.

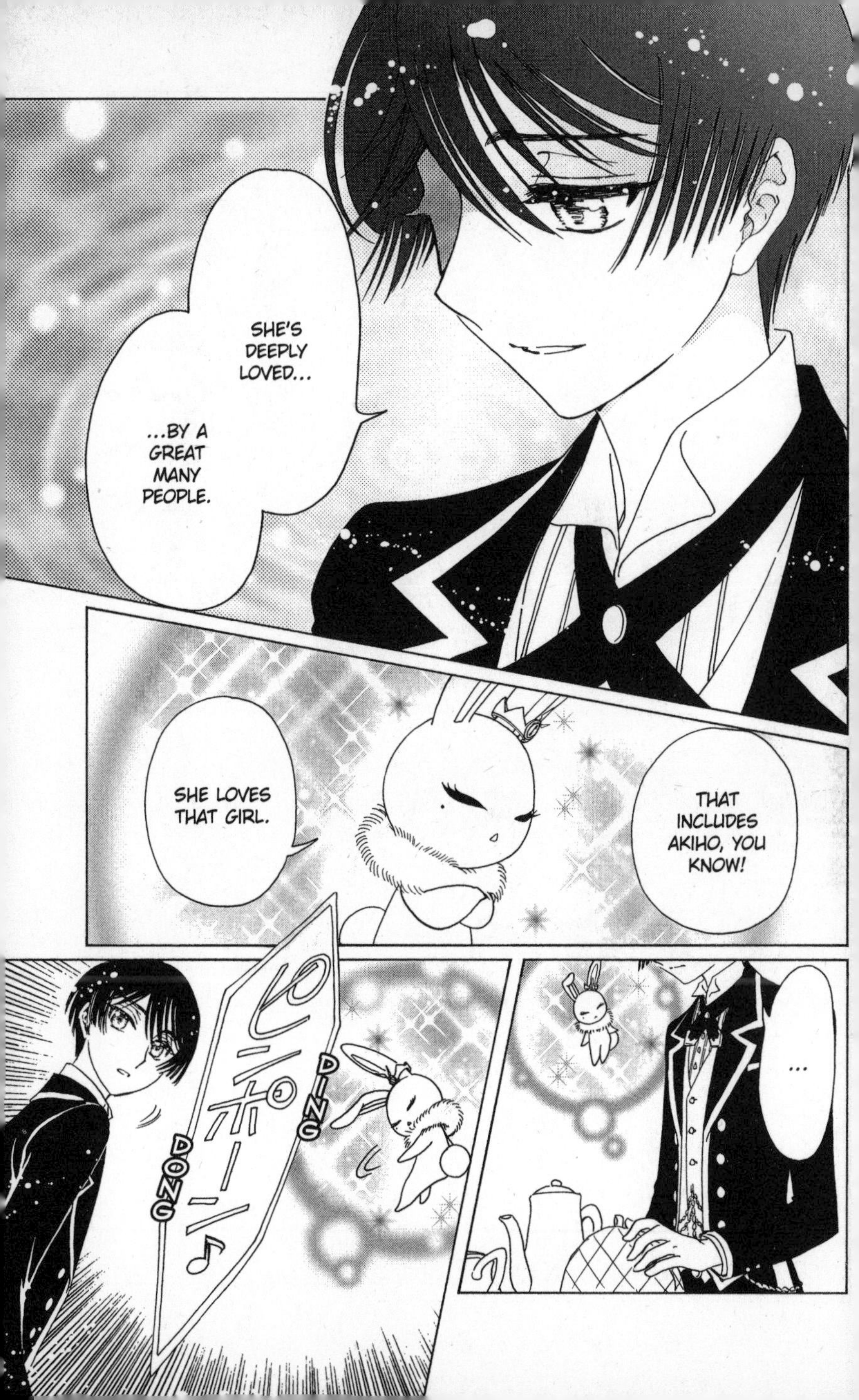
SHE'S DEEPLY LOVED...
...BY A GREAT MANY PEOPLE.
THAT INCLUDES AKIHO, YOU KNOW!
SHE LOVES THAT GIRL.
...
ピンポーン♪
DING
DONG

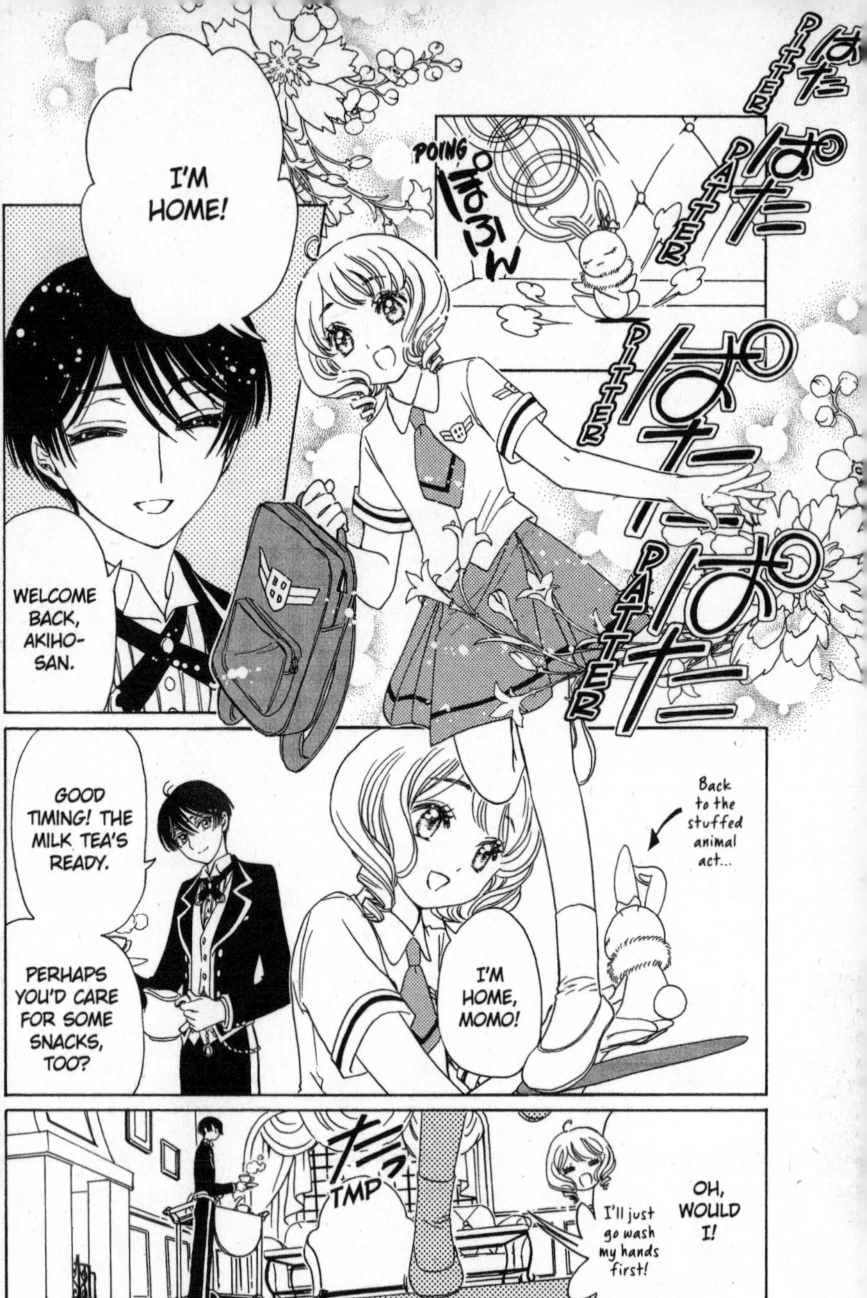
PITTER PATTER PITTER PATTER
POING
I'M HOME!
WELCOME BACK, AKIHO-SAN.
Back to the stuffed animal act...
I'M HOME, MOMO!
GOOD TIMING! THE MILK TEA'S READY.
PERHAPS YOU'D CARE FOR SOME SNACKS, TOO?
OH, WOULD I!
I'll just go wash my hands first!
TMP

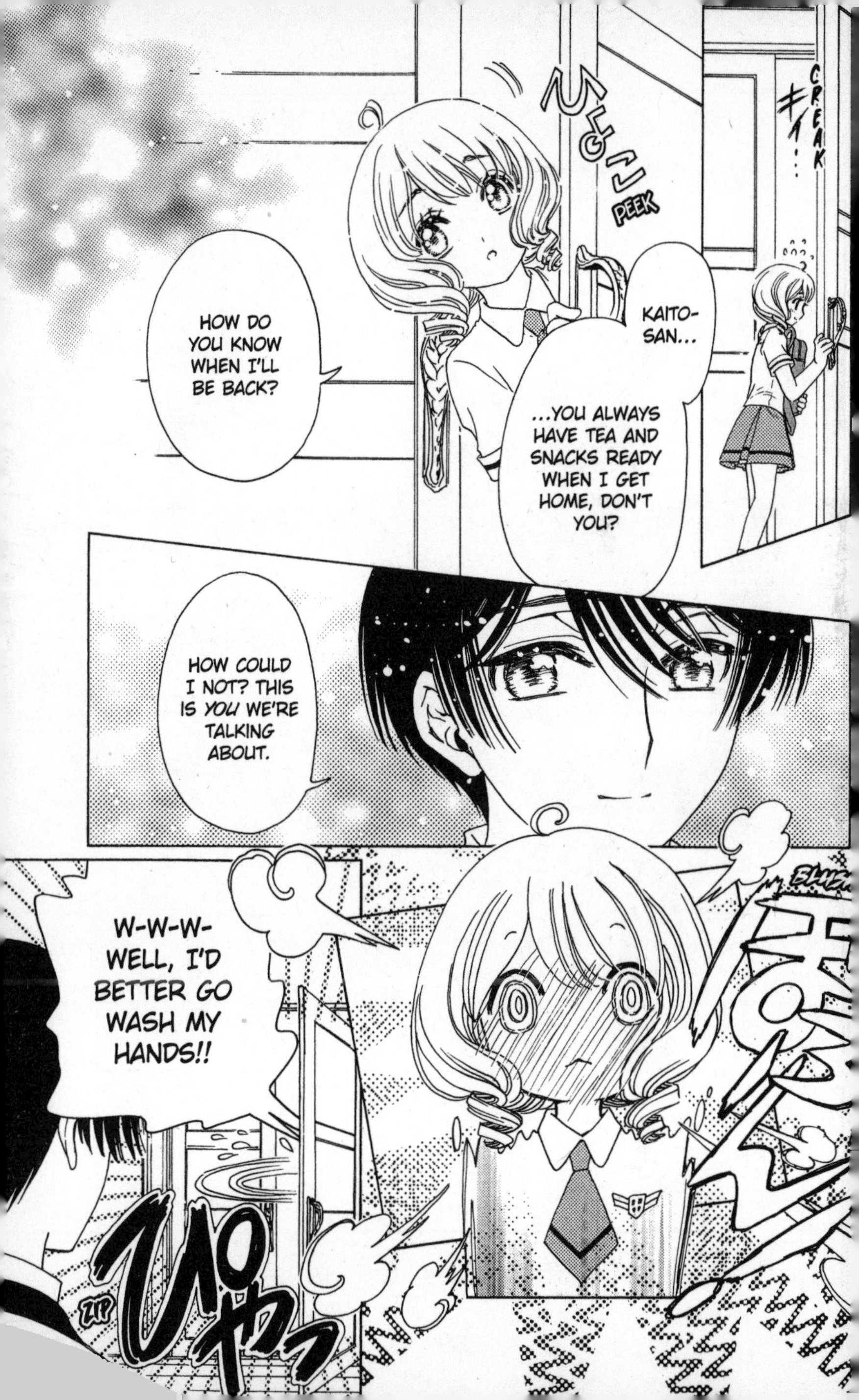
CREAK
PEEK
KAITO-SAN...
...YOU ALWAYS HAVE TEA AND SNACKS READY WHEN I GET HOME, DON'T YOU?
HOW DO YOU KNOW WHEN I'LL BE BACK?
HOW COULD I NOT? THIS IS *YOU* WE'RE TALKING ABOUT.
W-W-W-WELL, I'D BETTER GO WASH MY HANDS!!
ZIP

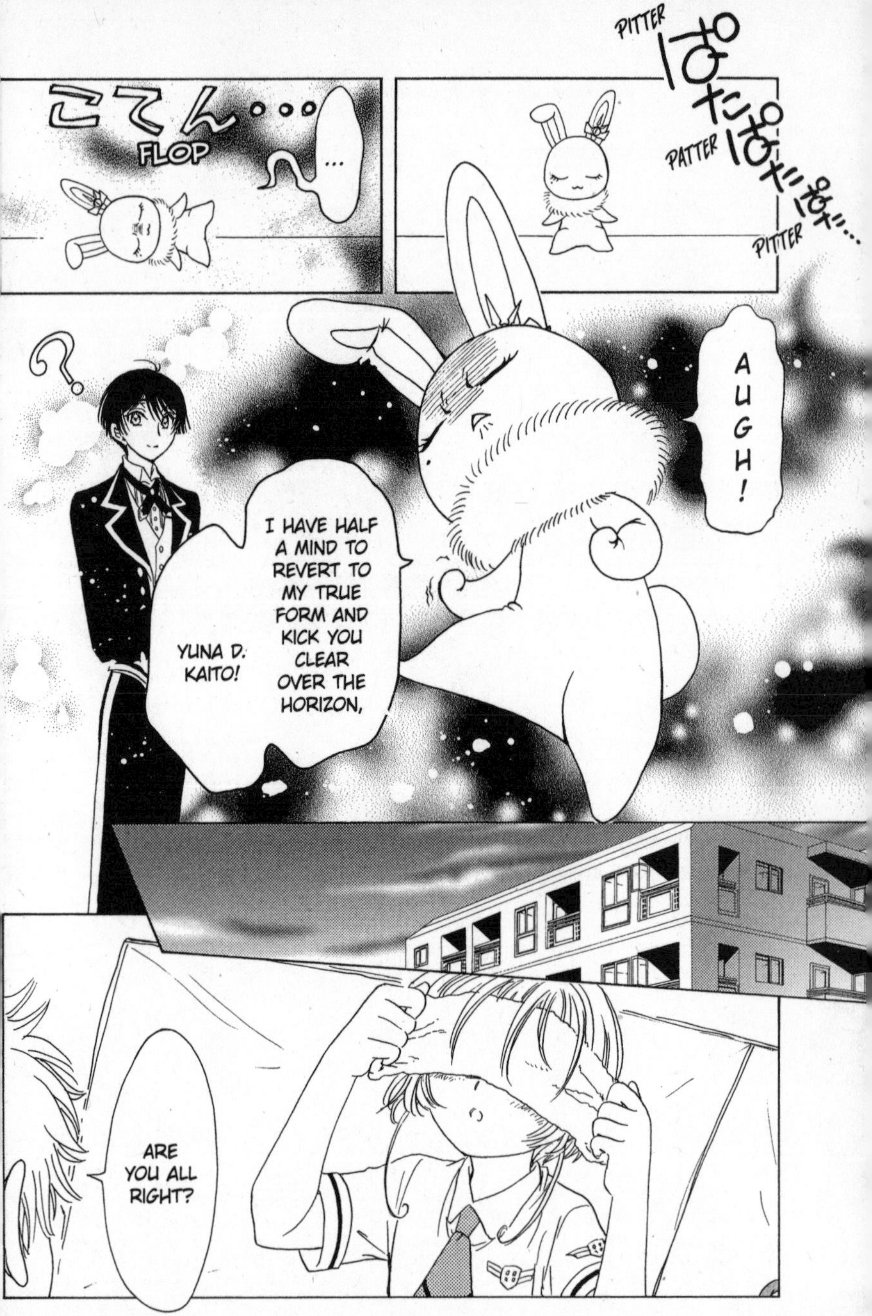
ぱたぱたぱた…
PITTER
PATTER
PITTER
こてん…
FLOP
...
AUGH!
I HAVE HALF A MIND TO REVERT TO MY TRUE FORM AND KICK YOU CLEAR OVER THE HORIZON,
YUNA D. KAITO!
ARE YOU ALL RIGHT?

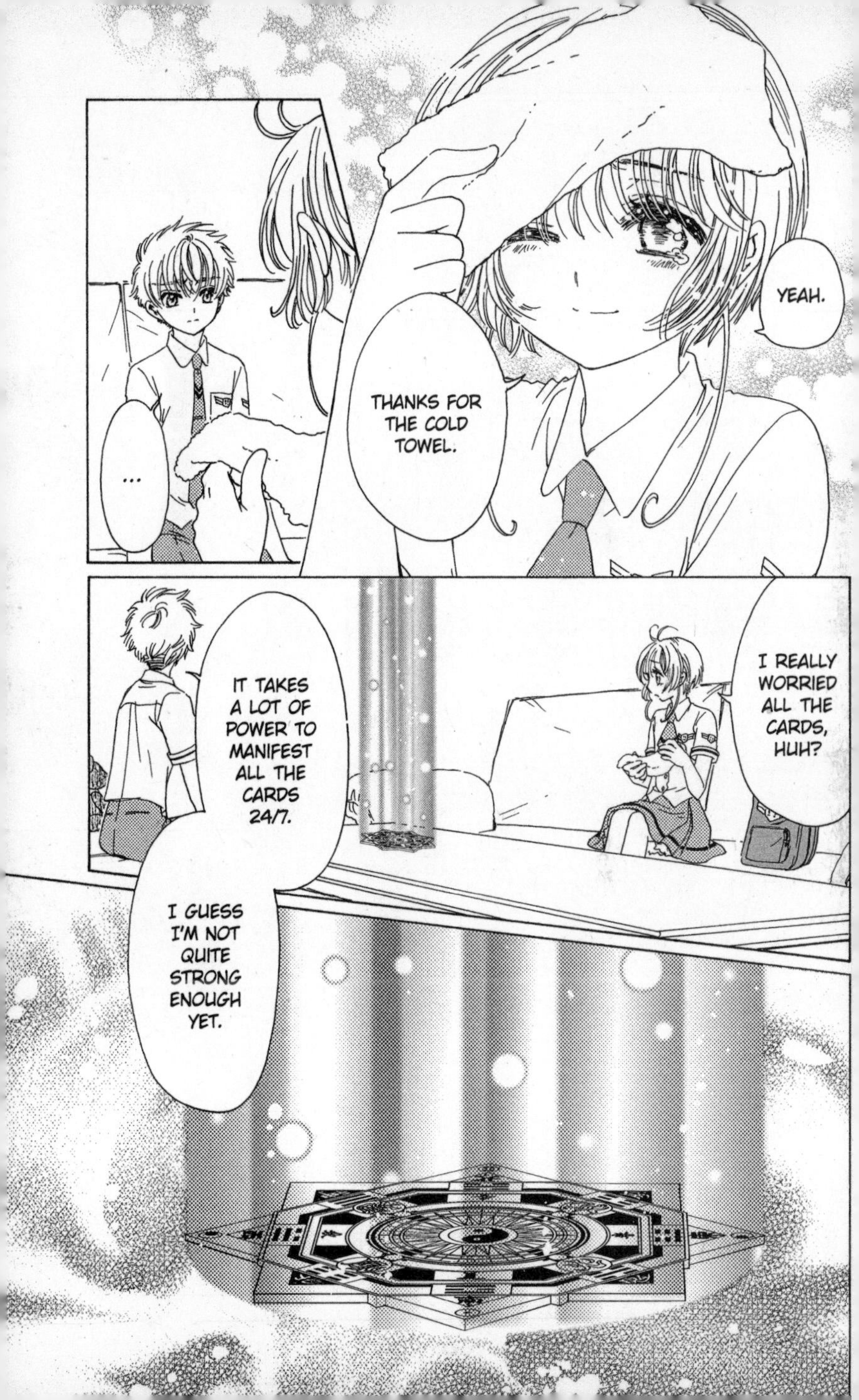
YEAH.
THANKS FOR THE COLD TOWEL.
...
I REALLY WORRIED ALL THE CARDS, HUH?
IT TAKES A LOT OF POWER TO MANIFEST ALL THE CARDS 24/7.
I GUESS I'M NOT QUITE STRONG ENOUGH YET.

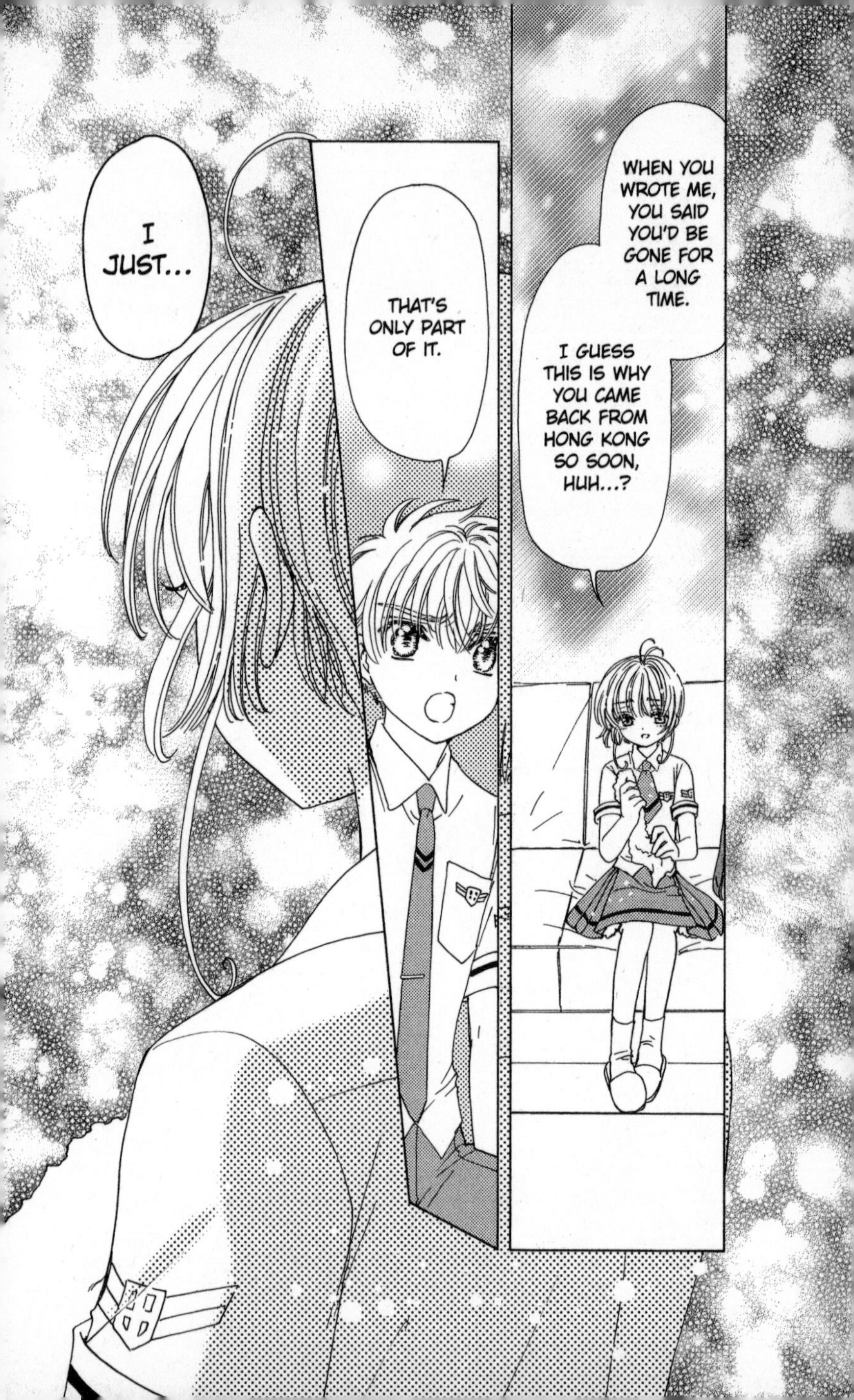
WHEN YOU WROTE ME, YOU SAID YOU'D BE GONE FOR A LONG TIME.
I GUESS THIS IS WHY YOU CAME BACK FROM HONG KONG SO SOON, HUH...?
THAT'S ONLY PART OF IT.
I JUST...

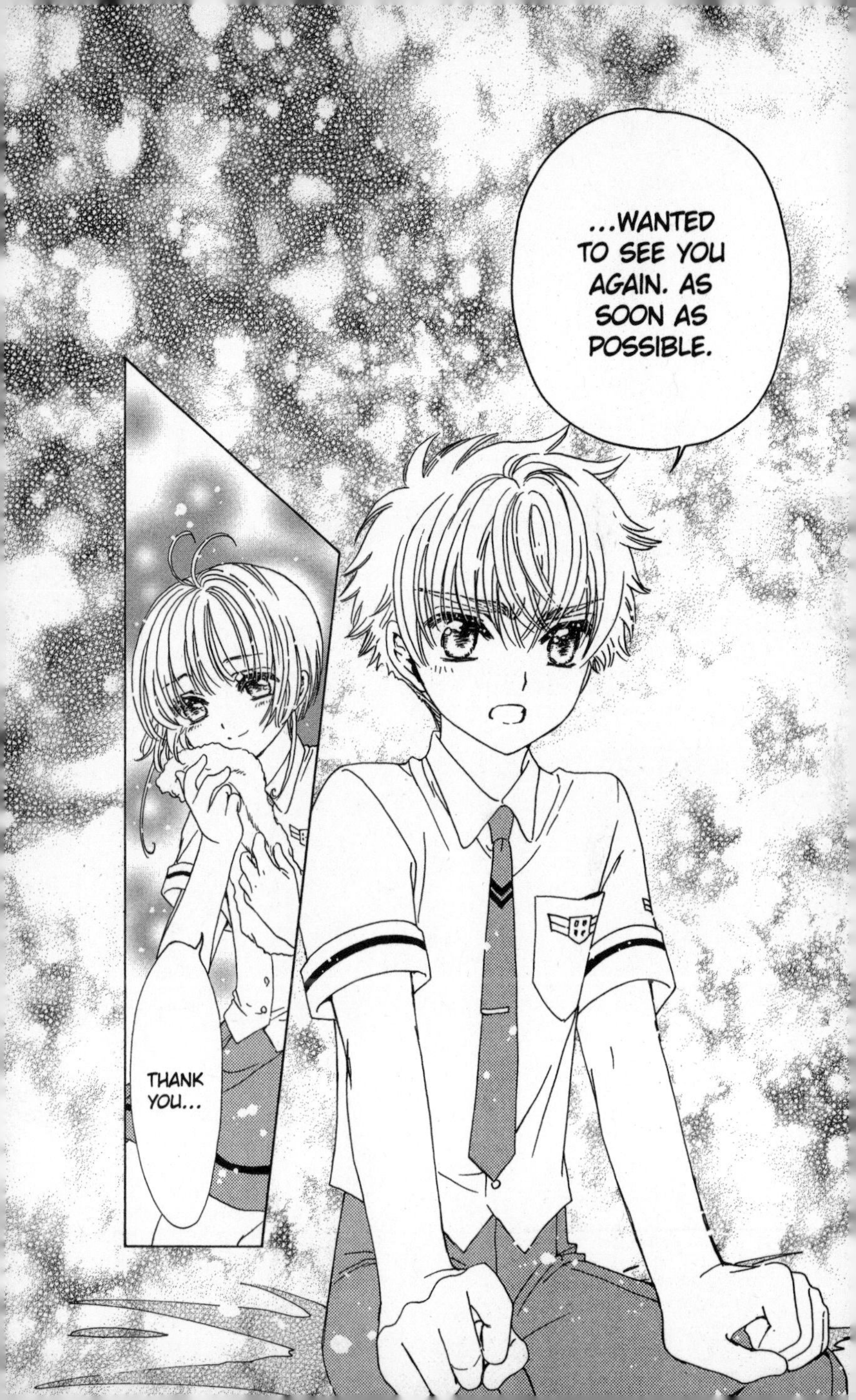
...WANTED TO SEE YOU AGAIN. AS SOON AS POSSIBLE.
THANK YOU...

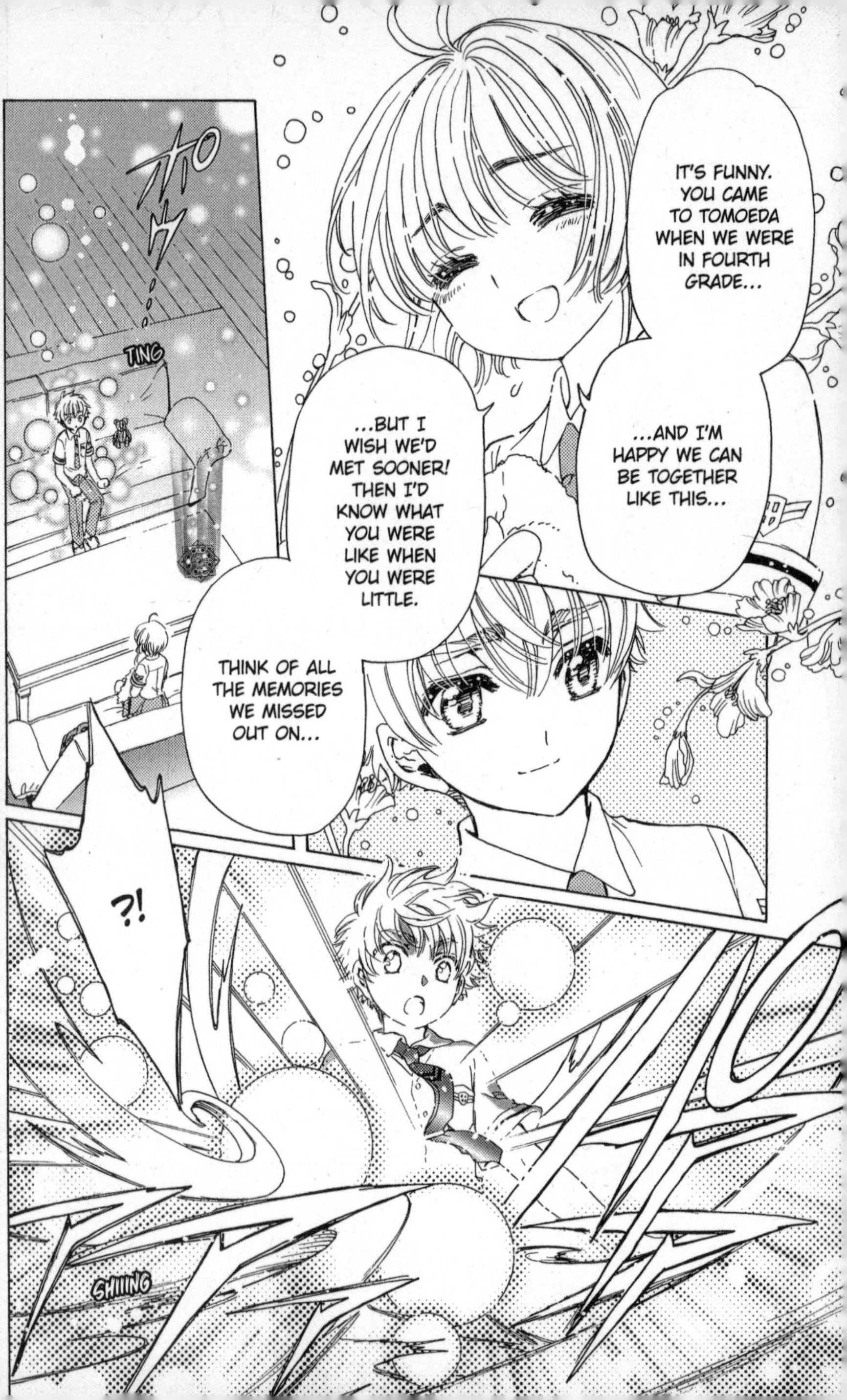
IT'S FUNNY. YOU CAME TO TOMOEDA WHEN WE WERE IN FOURTH GRADE...
...AND I'M HAPPY WE CAN BE TOGETHER LIKE THIS...
...BUT I WISH WE'D MET SOONER! THEN I'D KNOW WHAT YOU WERE LIKE WHEN YOU WERE LITTLE.
THINK OF ALL THE MEMORIES WE MISSED OUT ON...
TING
?!
SHIIING

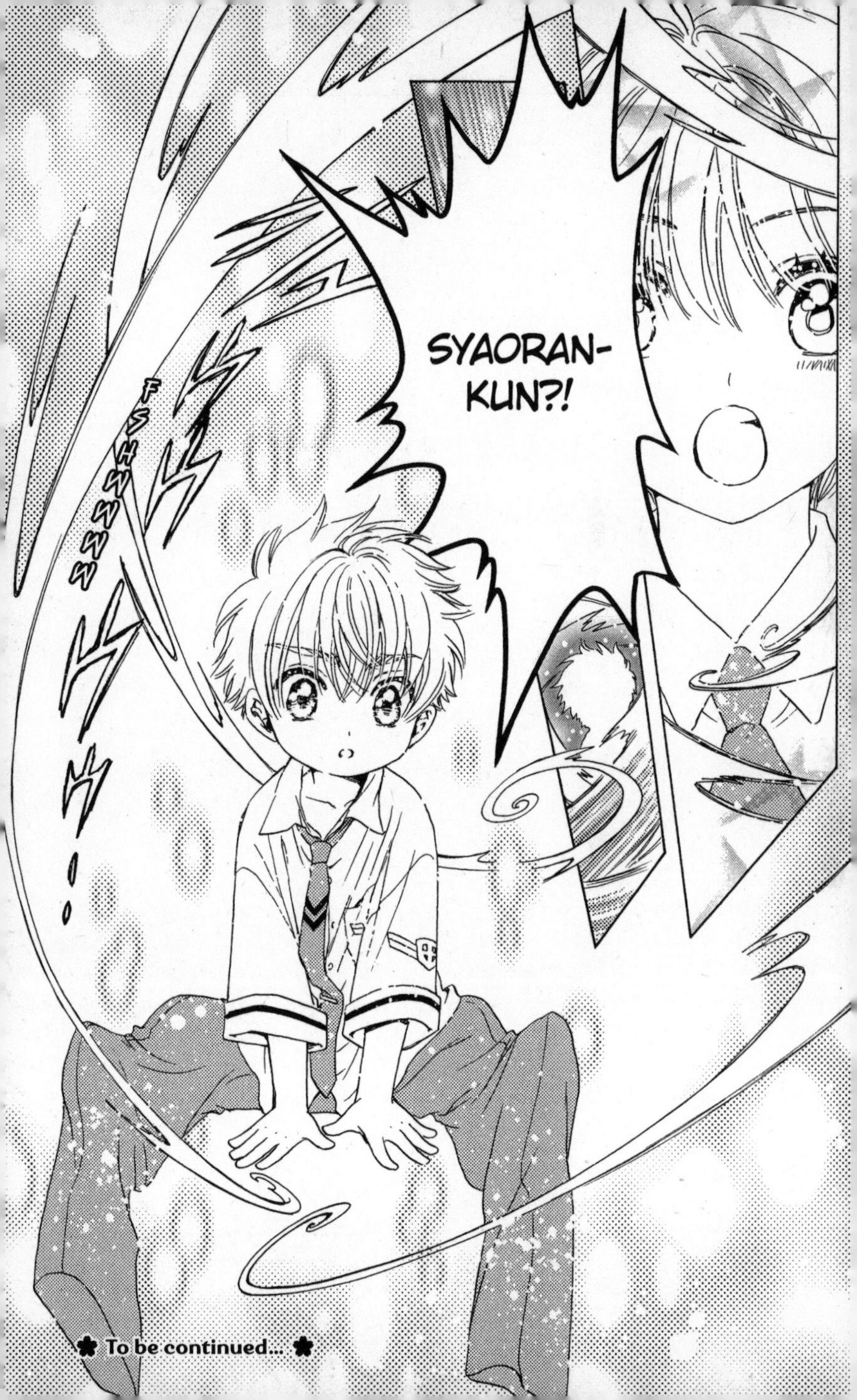
SYAORAN-KUN?!
FSHWWWWWW

✿ To be continued... ✿

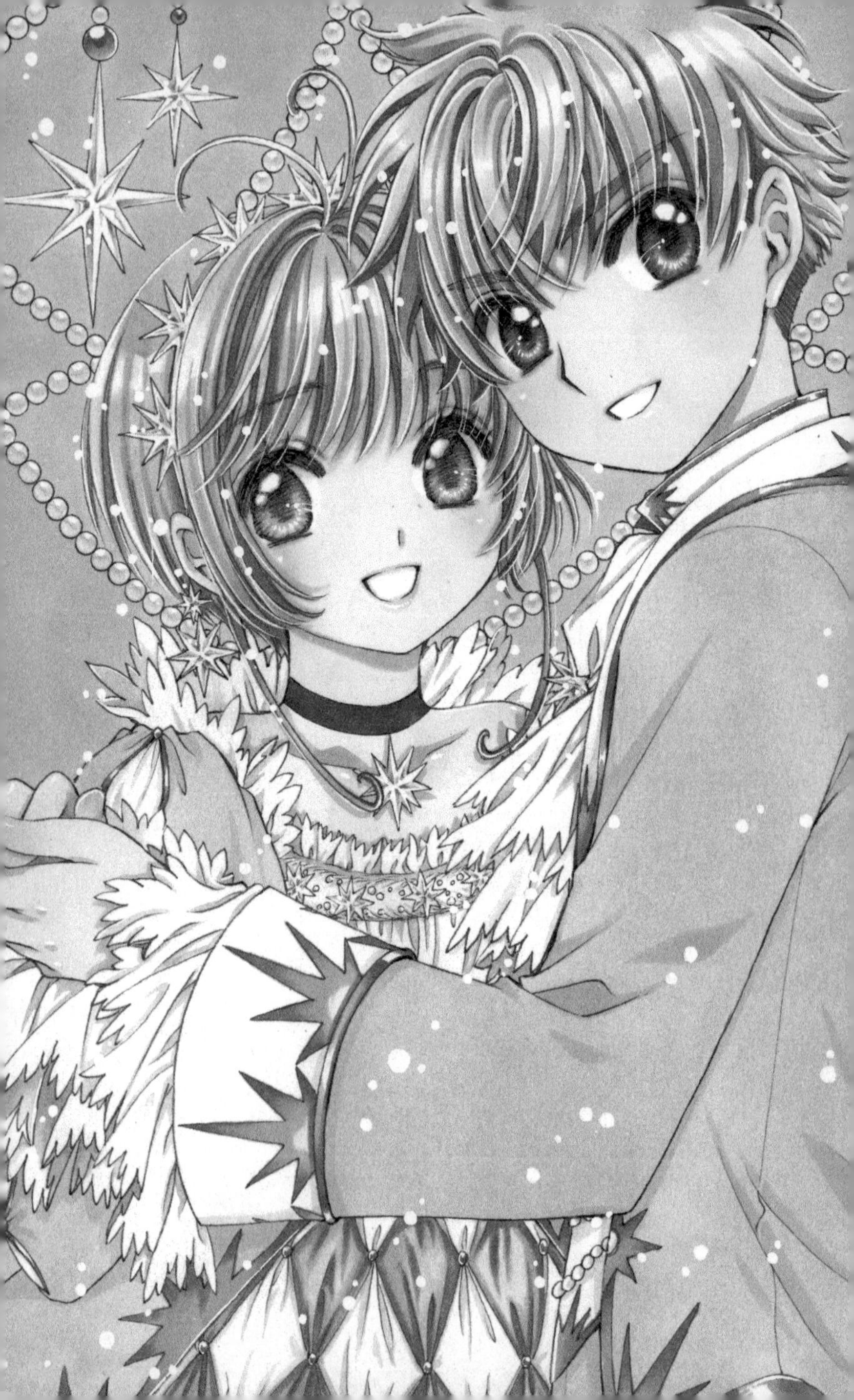

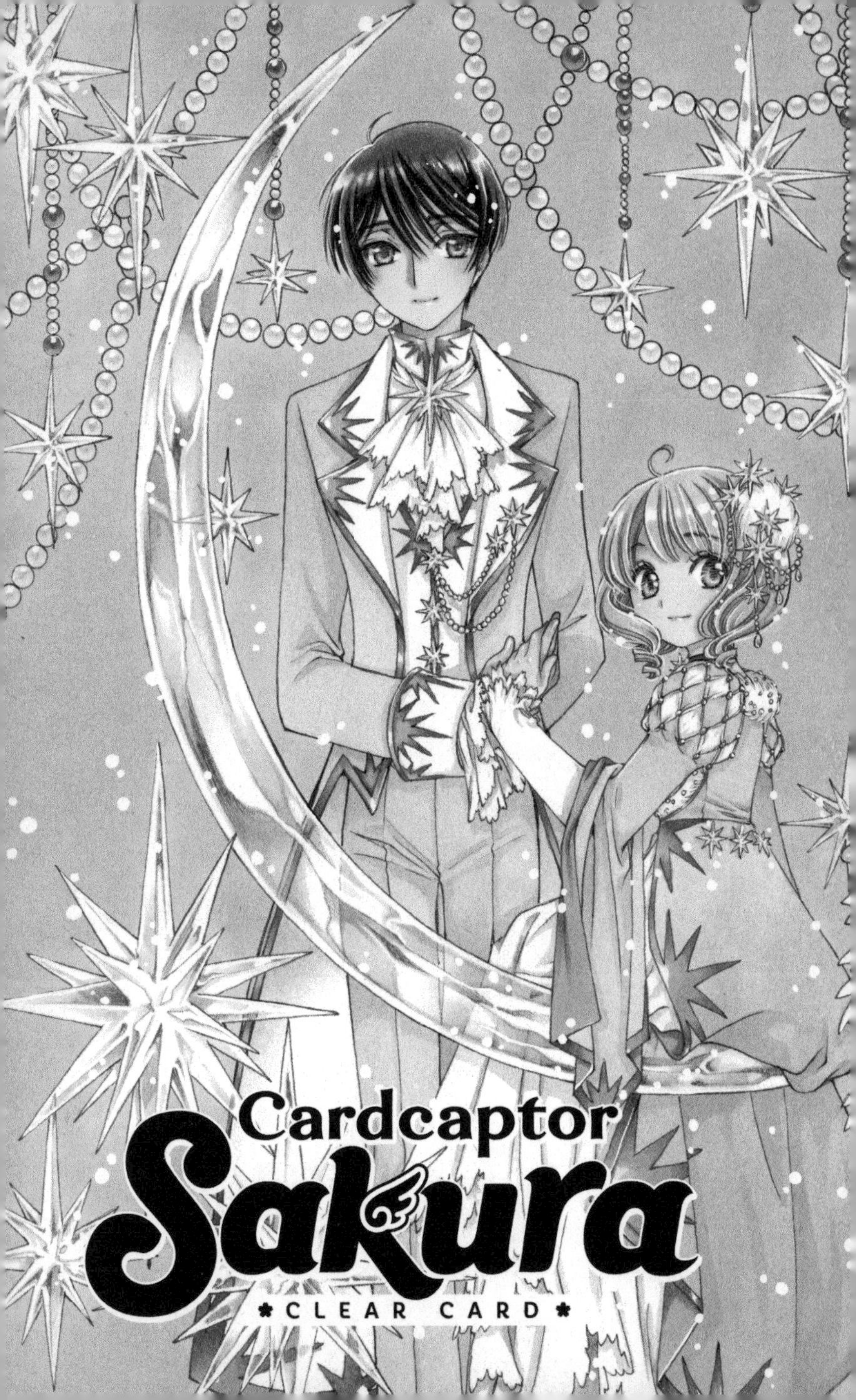
Cardcaptor
Sakura
CLEAR CARD

Cardcaptor Sakura

CLEAR CARD

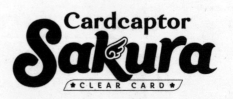

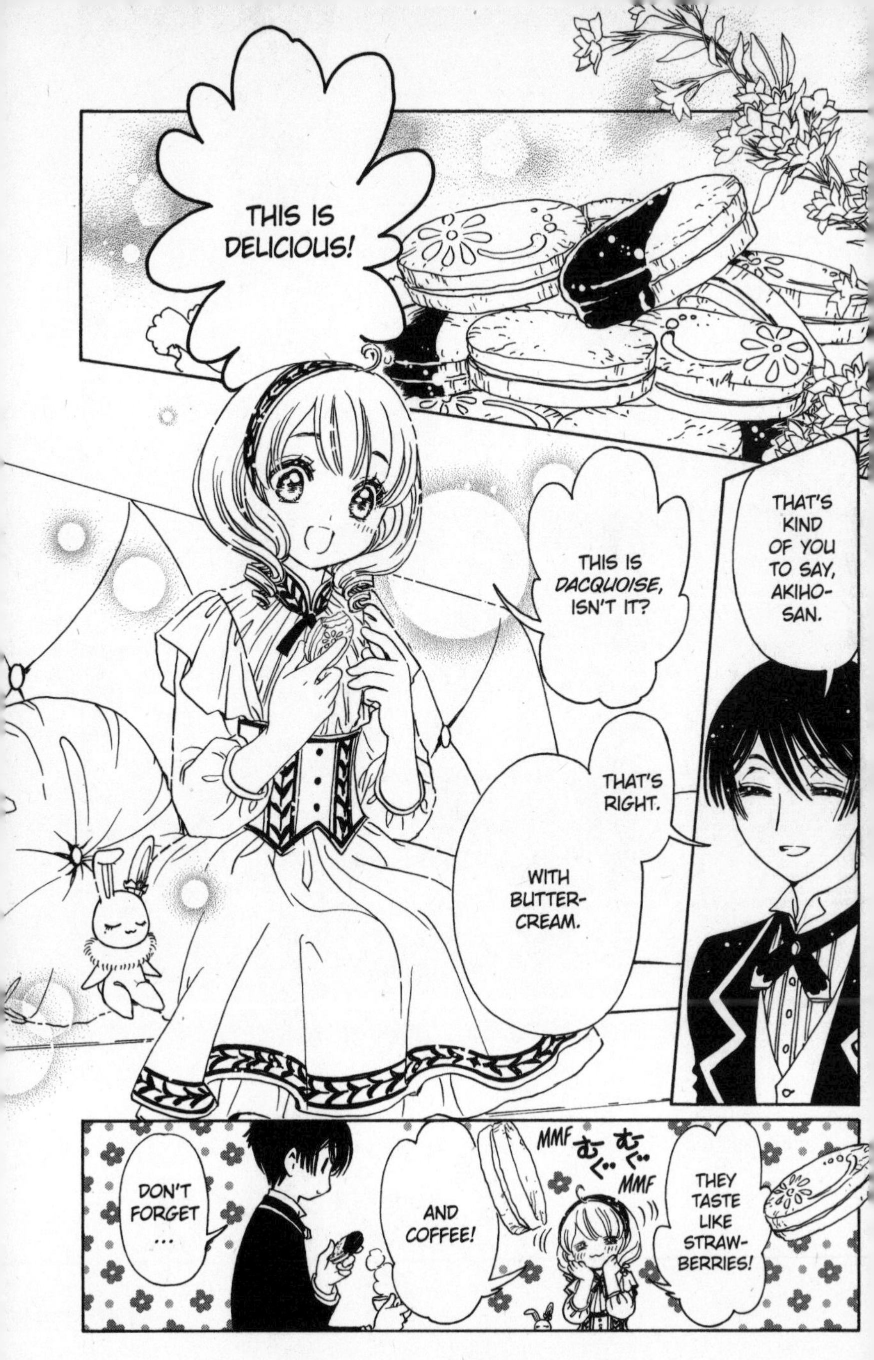
THIS IS DELICIOUS!
THAT'S KIND OF YOU TO SAY, AKIHO-SAN.
THIS IS *DACQUOISE*, ISN'T IT?
THAT'S RIGHT.
WITH BUTTER-CREAM.
THEY TASTE LIKE STRAW-BERRIES!
MMF むぐ むぐ MMF
AND COFFEE!
DON'T FORGET ...

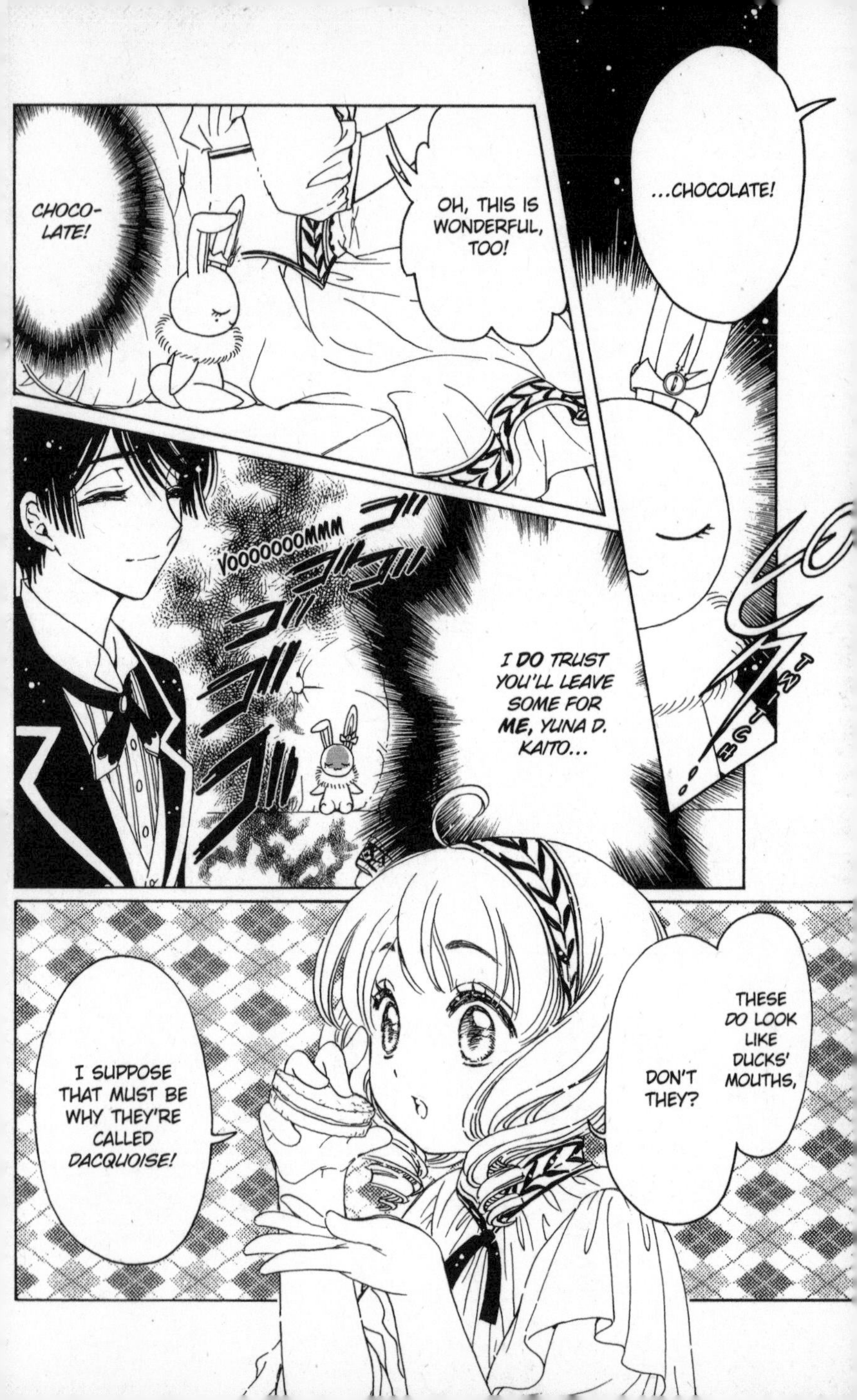
...CHOCOLATE!
OH, THIS IS WONDERFUL, TOO!
CHOCO-LATE!
TWITCH...
I DO TRUST YOU'LL LEAVE SOME FOR ME, YUNA D. KAITO...
VOOOOOOOMMM
THESE DO LOOK LIKE DUCKS' MOUTHS,
DON'T THEY?
I SUPPOSE THAT MUST BE WHY THEY'RE CALLED DACQUOISE!

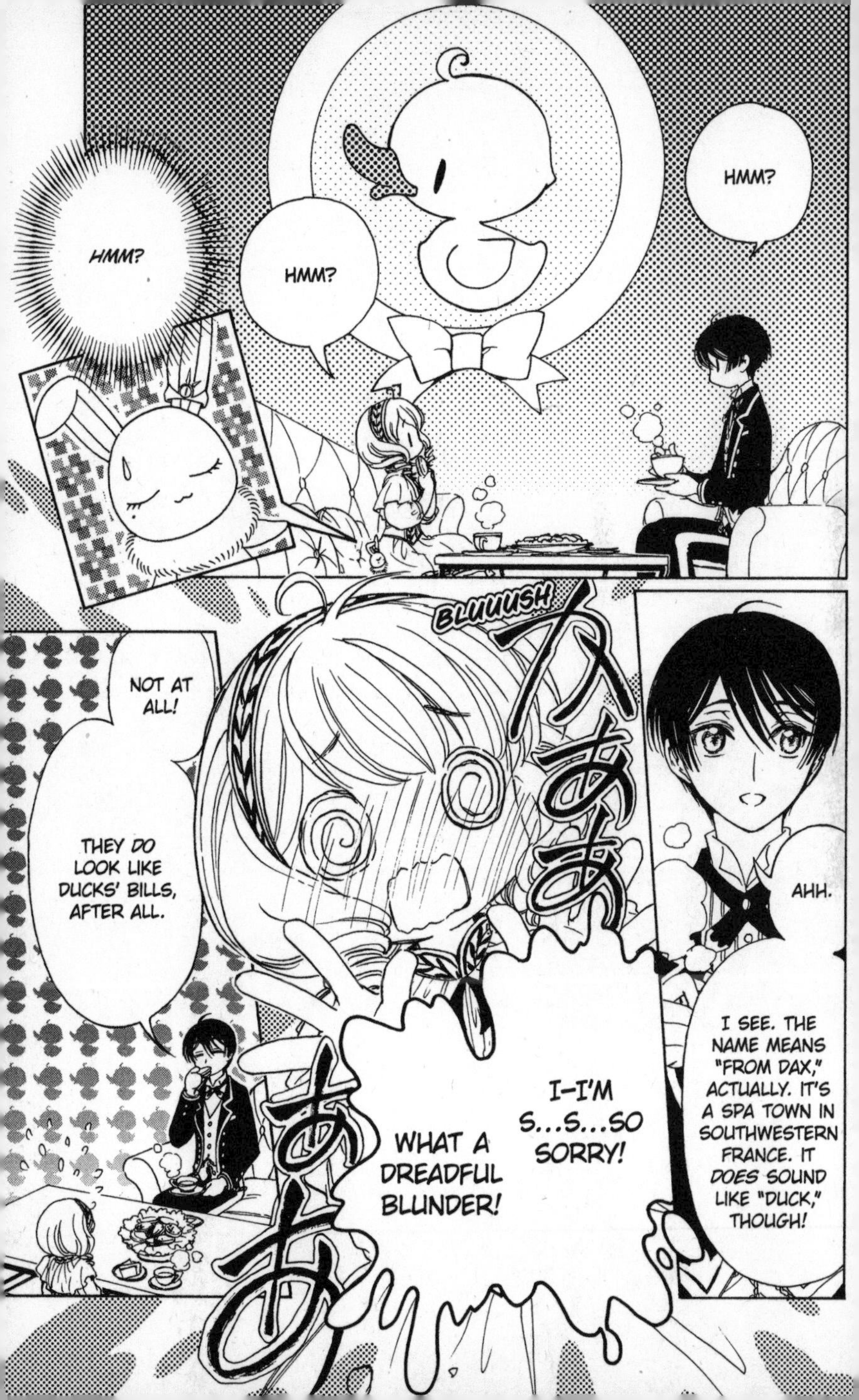
HMM?
HMM?
HMM?
AHH.
I SEE. THE NAME MEANS "FROM DAX," ACTUALLY. IT'S A SPA TOWN IN SOUTHWESTERN FRANCE. IT *DOES* SOUND LIKE "DUCK," THOUGH!
BLUUUSH
I-I'M S...S...SO SORRY!
WHAT A DREADFUL BLUNDER!
NOT AT ALL!
THEY *DO* LOOK LIKE DUCKS' BILLS, AFTER ALL.

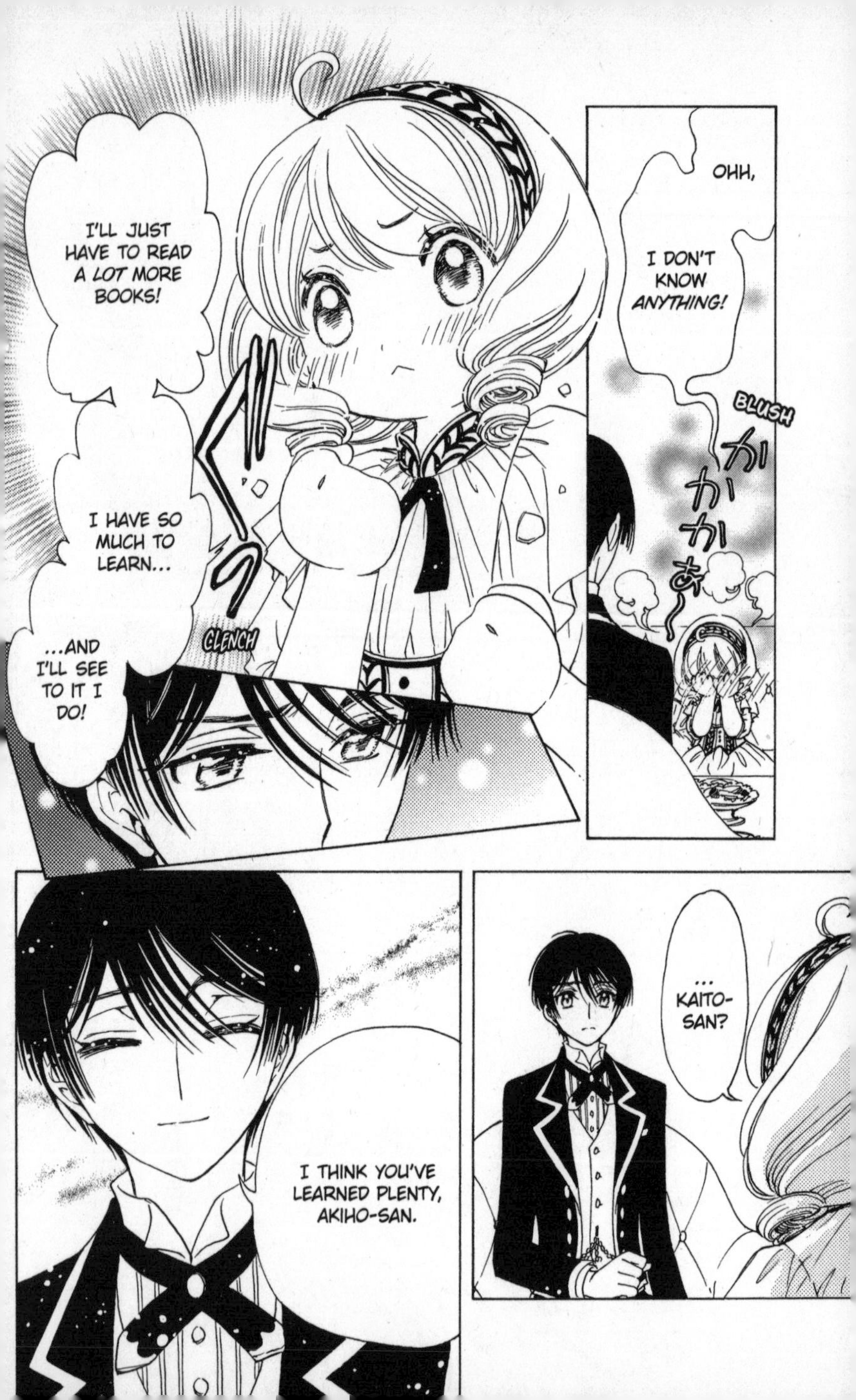
OHH,
I DON'T KNOW *ANYTHING!*
BLUSH
かかかあ~
I'LL JUST HAVE TO READ A *LOT* MORE BOOKS!
CLENCH
I HAVE SO MUCH TO LEARN...
...AND I'LL SEE TO IT I DO!
... KAITO-SAN?
I THINK YOU'VE LEARNED PLENTY, AKIHO-SAN.

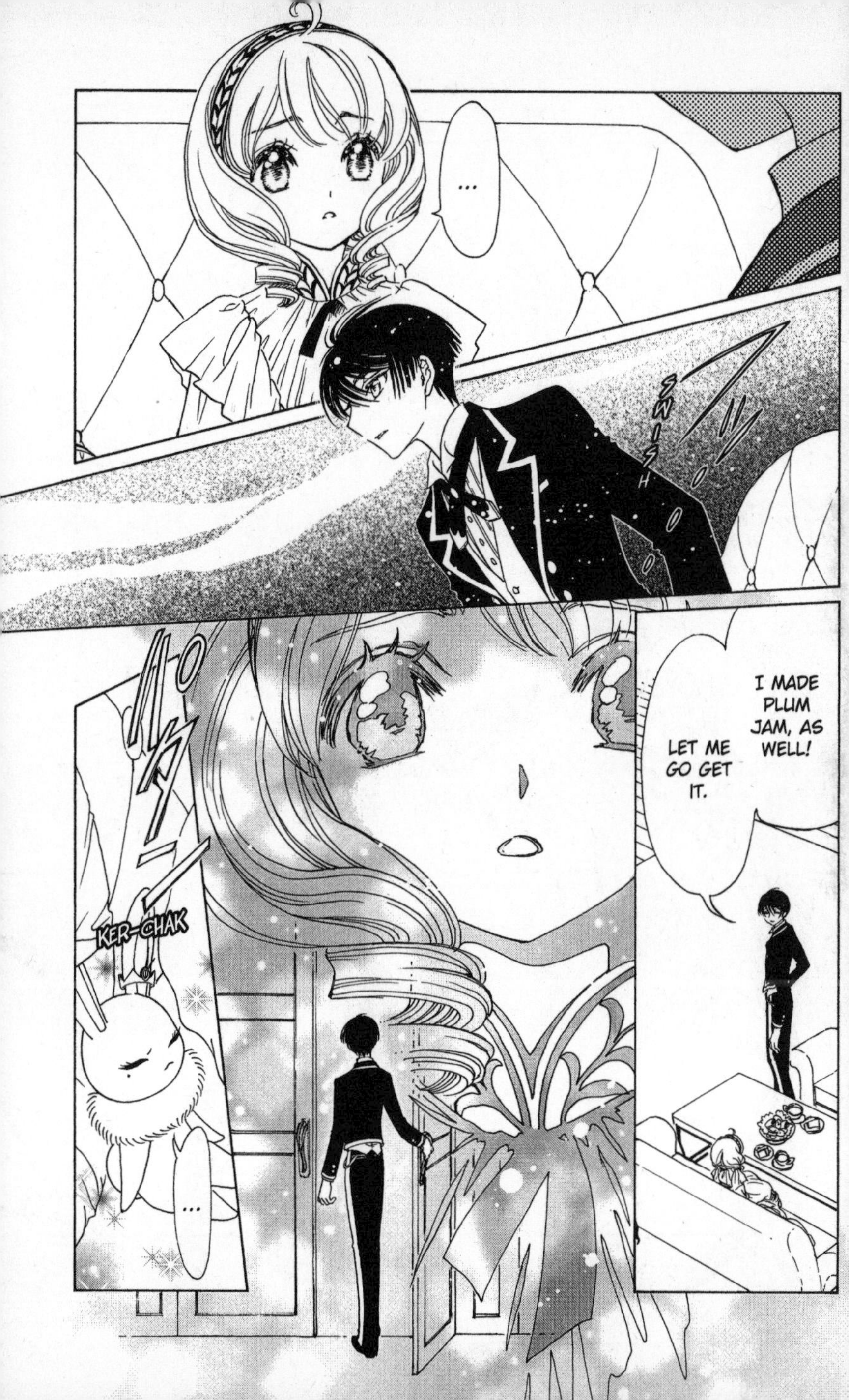
...
SWISHOO
I MADE PLUM JAM, AS WELL!
LET ME GO GET IT.
KER-CHAK
...

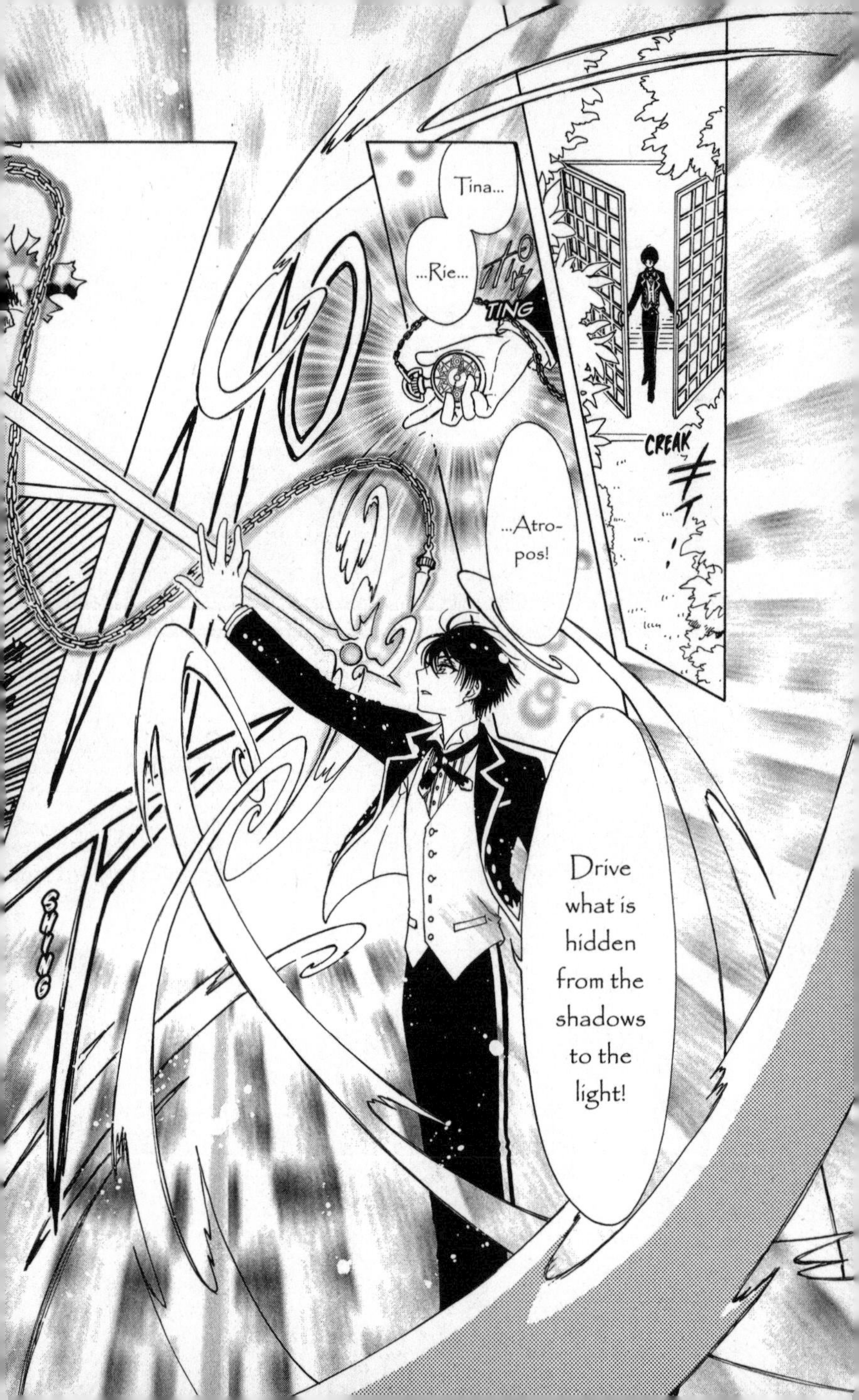
CREAK
Tina...
...Rie...
TING
...Atro-pos!
Drive what is hidden from the shadows to the light!
SHING

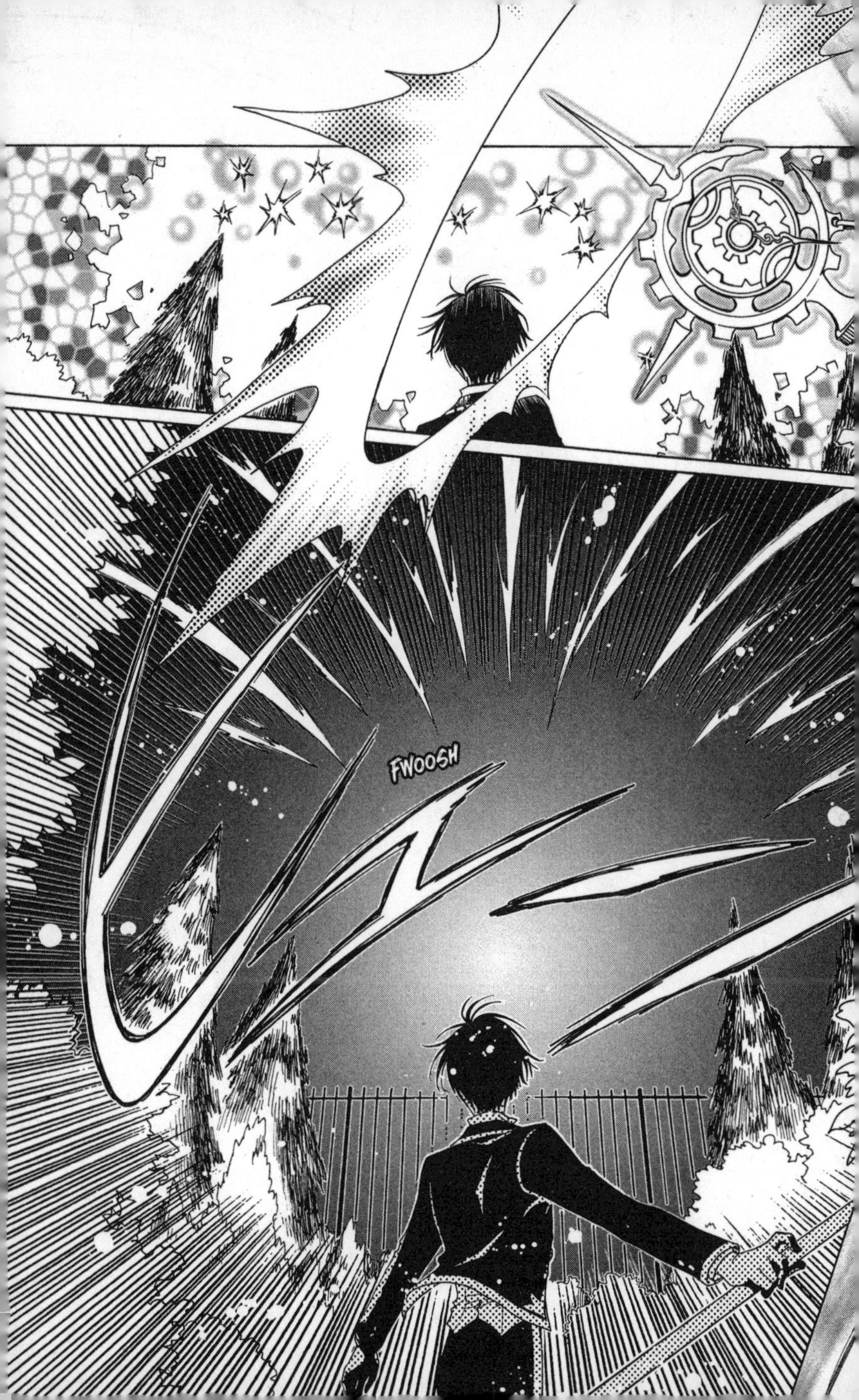
FWOOSH

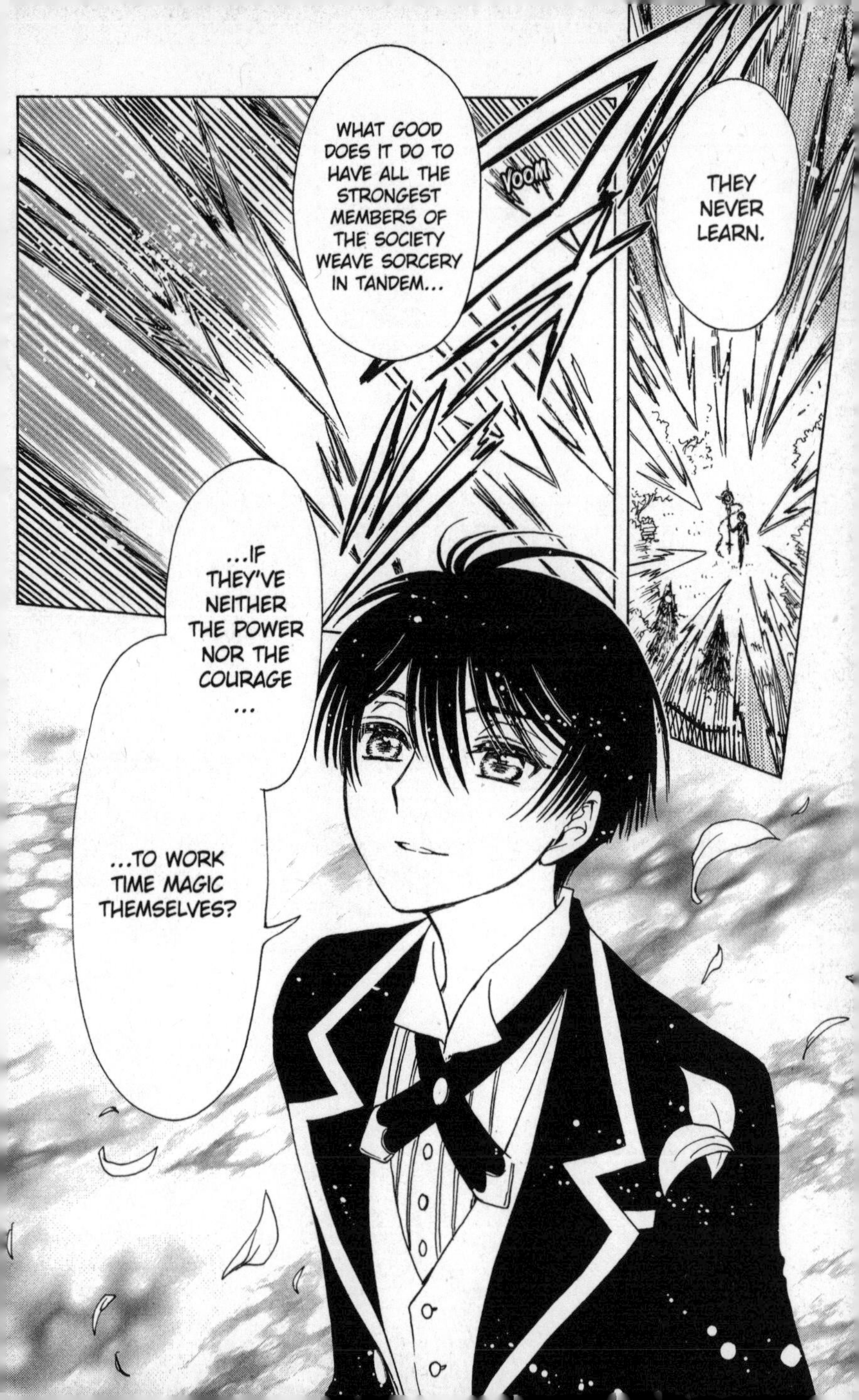
THEY NEVER LEARN.
VOOM
WHAT GOOD DOES IT DO TO HAVE ALL THE STRONGEST MEMBERS OF THE SOCIETY WEAVE SORCERY IN TANDEM...
...IF THEY'VE NEITHER THE POWER NOR THE COURAGE ...
...TO WORK TIME MAGIC THEMSELVES?

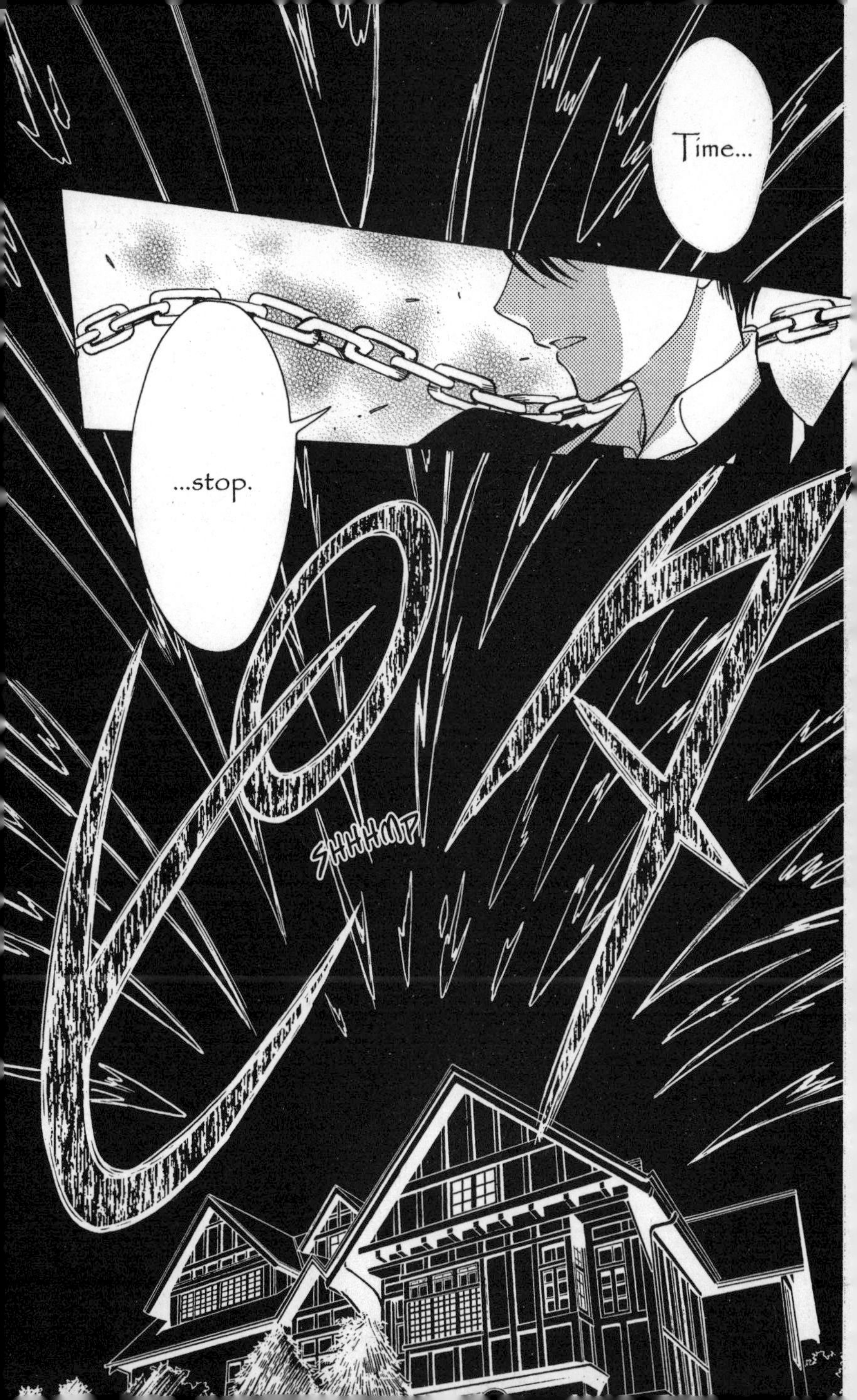
Time...
...stop.
SHHHMP

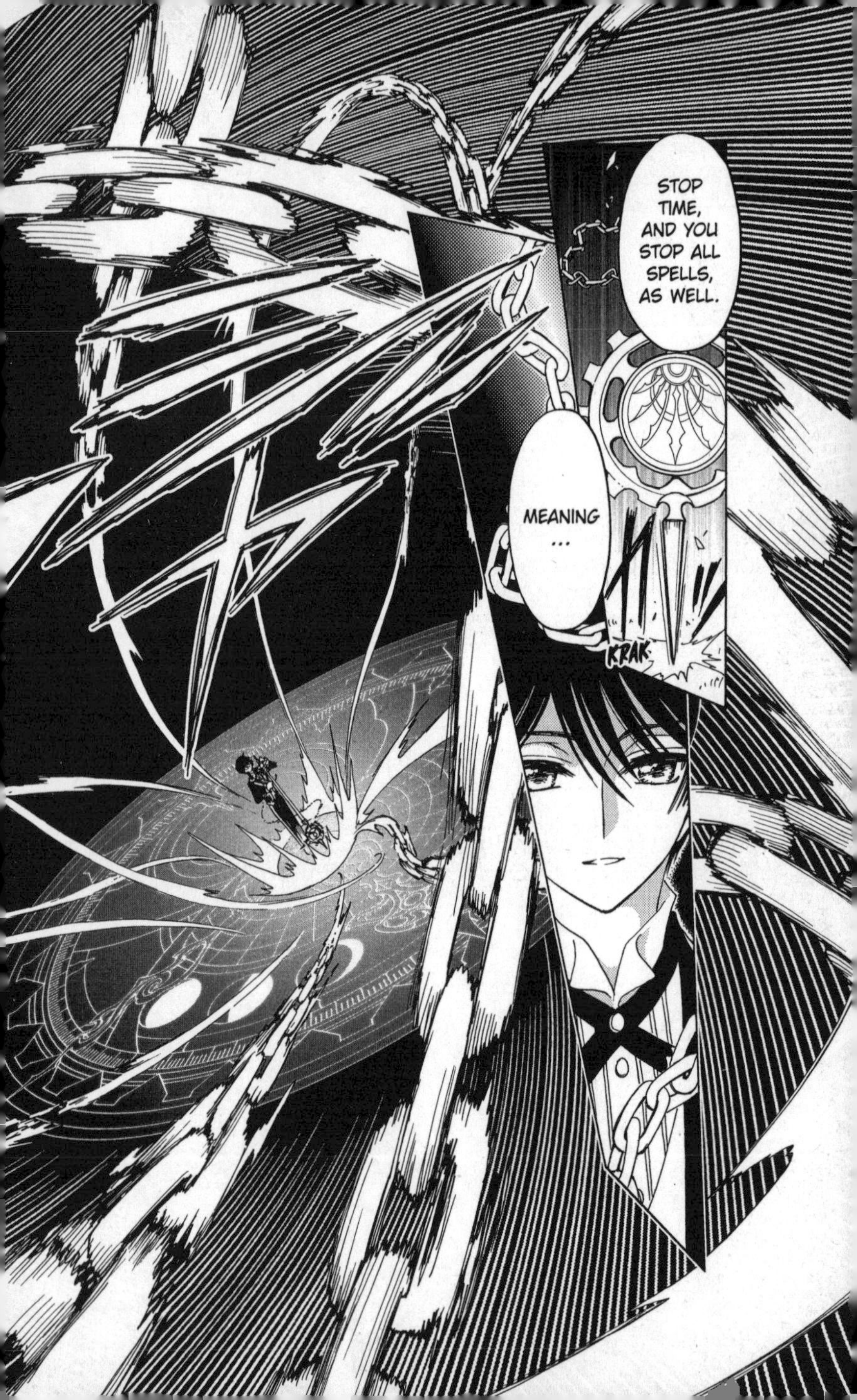
STOP TIME, AND YOU STOP ALL SPELLS, AS WELL.
MEANING ...
KRAK

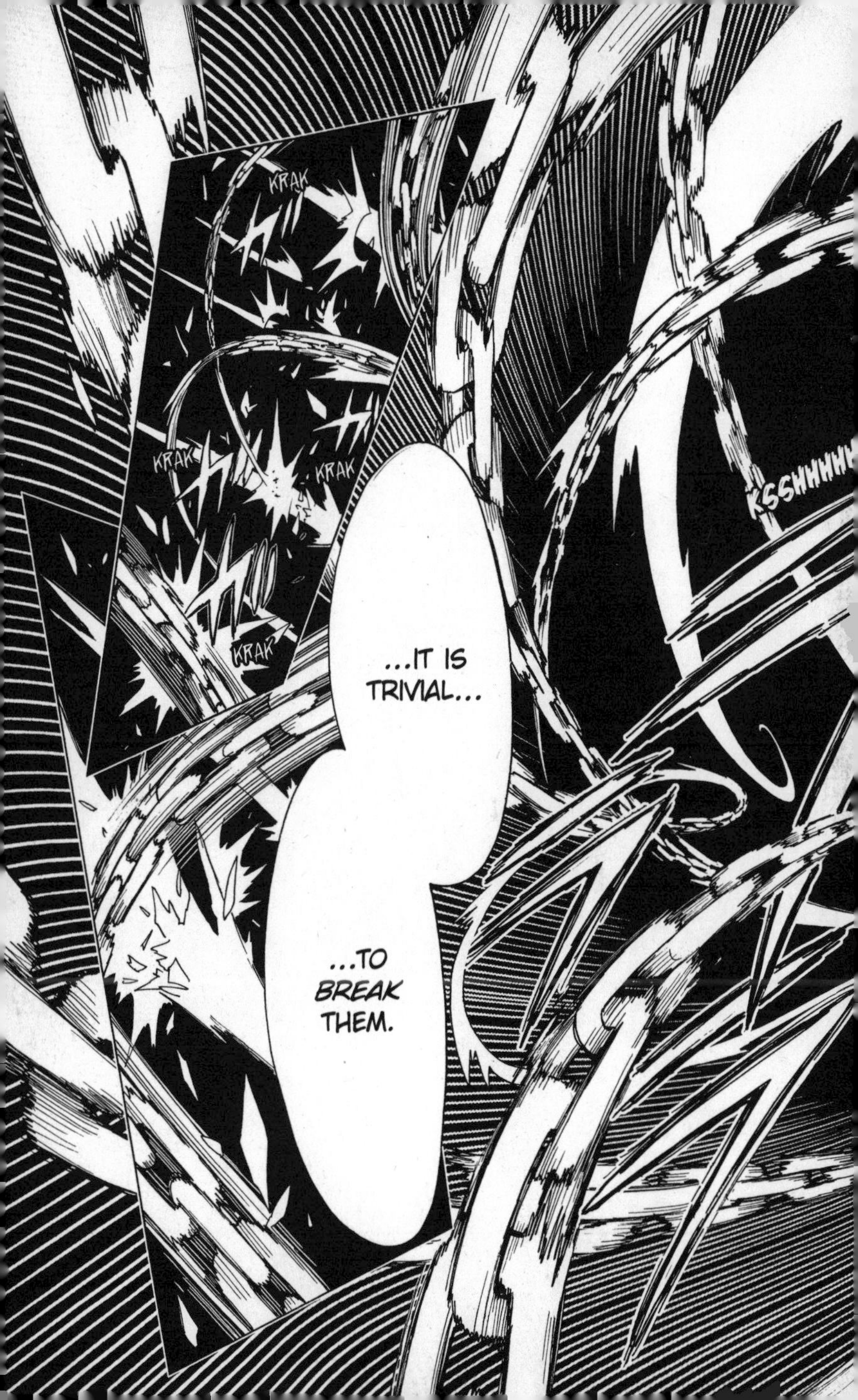
KSSHHHHH
...IT IS TRIVIAL...
...TO *BREAK* THEM.
KRAK
KRAK
KRAK
KRAK

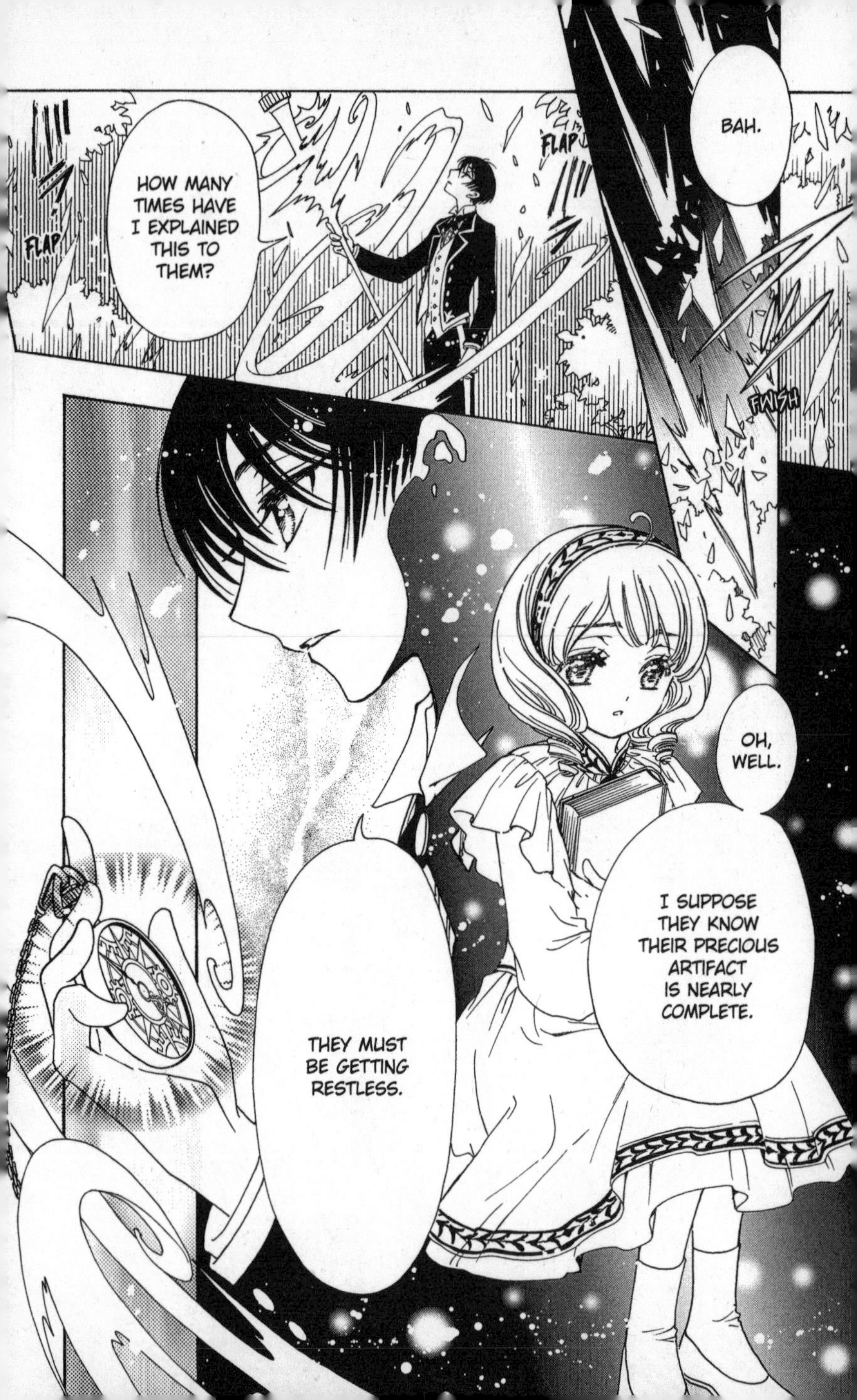
BAH.
FWISH
FLAP
HOW MANY TIMES HAVE I EXPLAINED THIS TO THEM?
FLAP
OH, WELL.
I SUPPOSE THEY KNOW THEIR PRECIOUS ARTIFACT IS NEARLY COMPLETE.
THEY MUST BE GETTING RESTLESS.

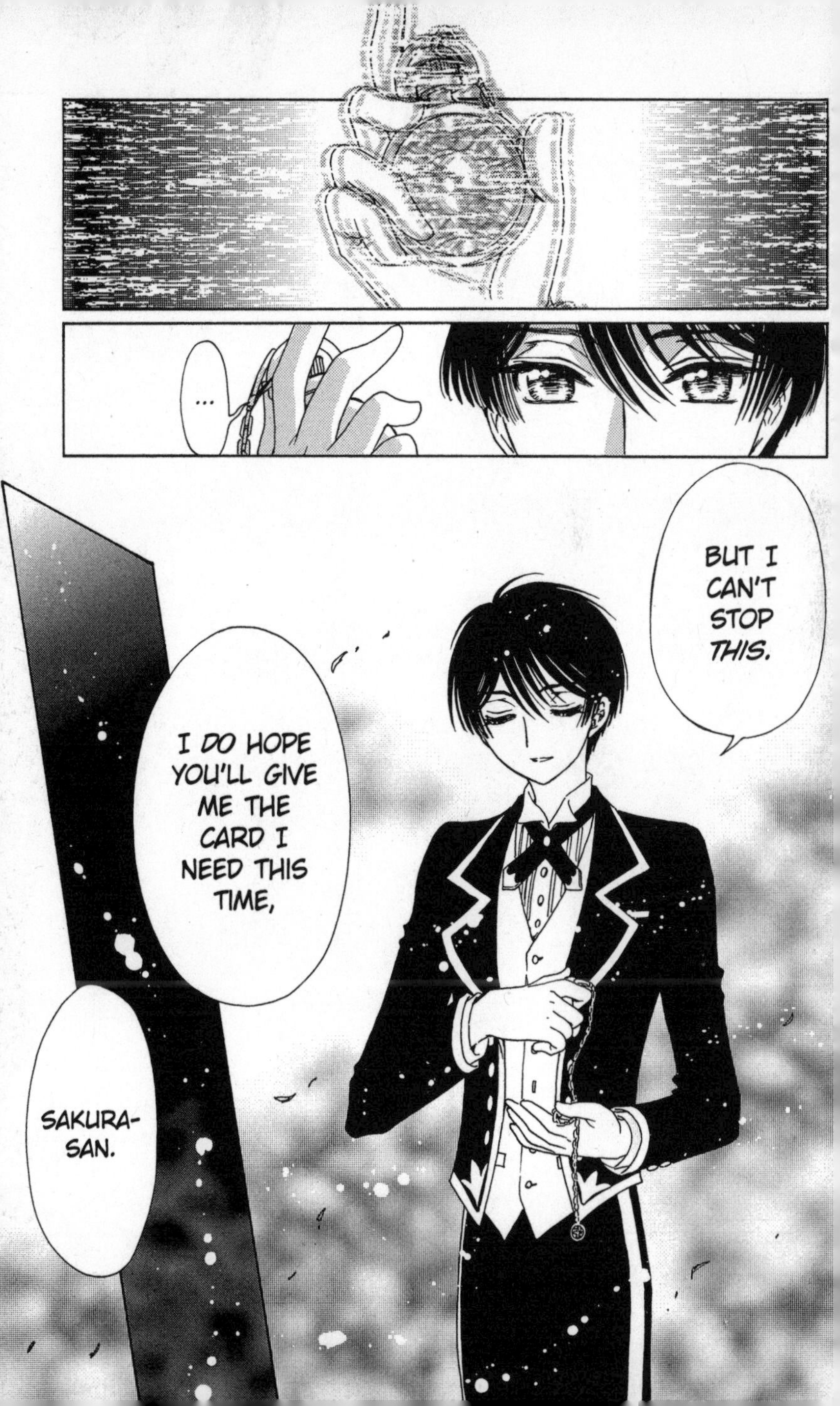
...
BUT I CAN'T STOP THIS.
I DO HOPE YOU'LL GIVE ME THE CARD I NEED THIS TIME,
SAKURA-SAN.

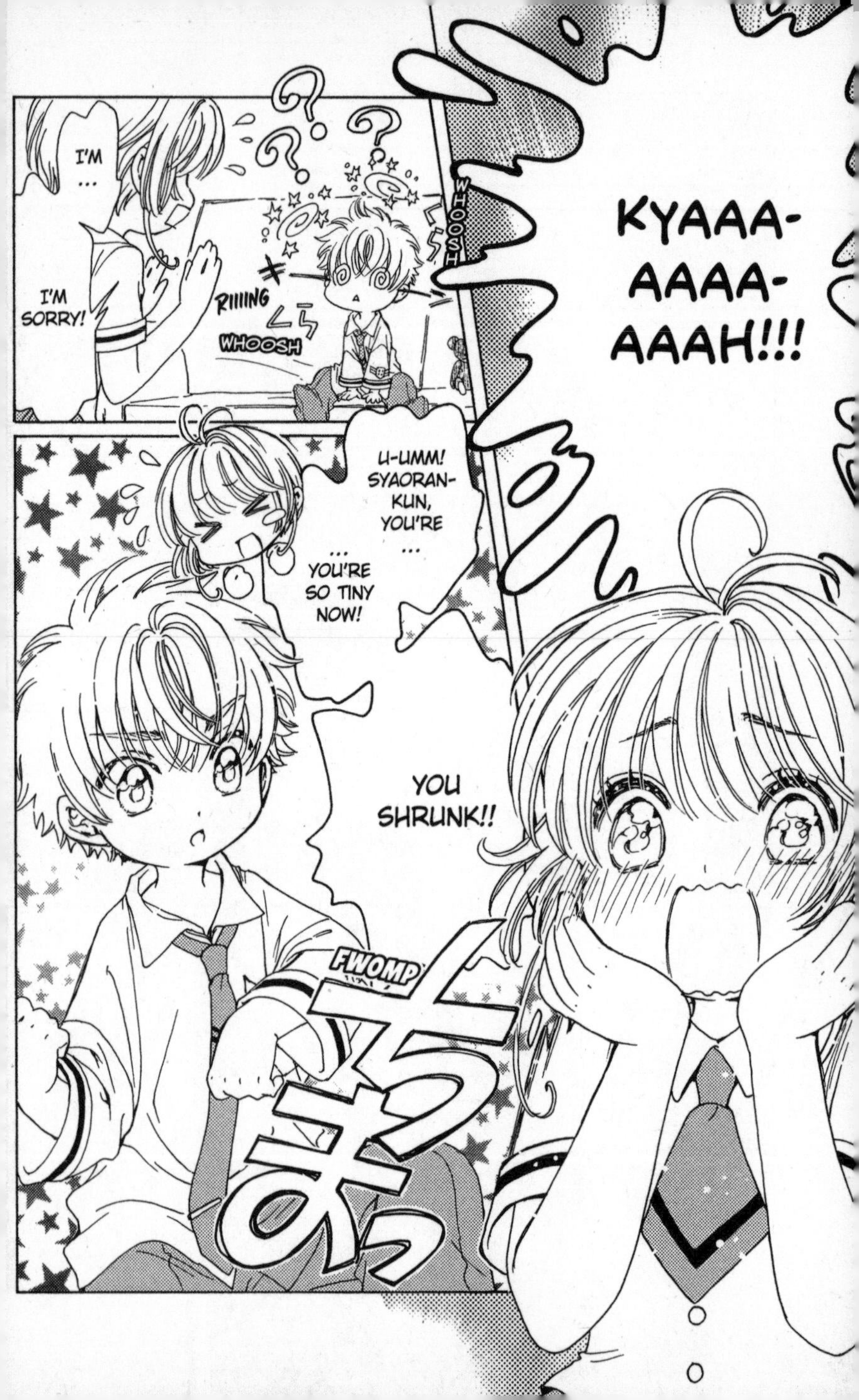
KYAAA-AAAA-AAAH!!!
WHOOSH
くら
RIIING
くら
WHOOSH
I'M ...
I'M SORRY!
U-UMM! SYAORAN-KUN, YOU'RE ...
... YOU'RE SO TINY NOW!
YOU SHRUNK!!
FWOMP
ちまっ

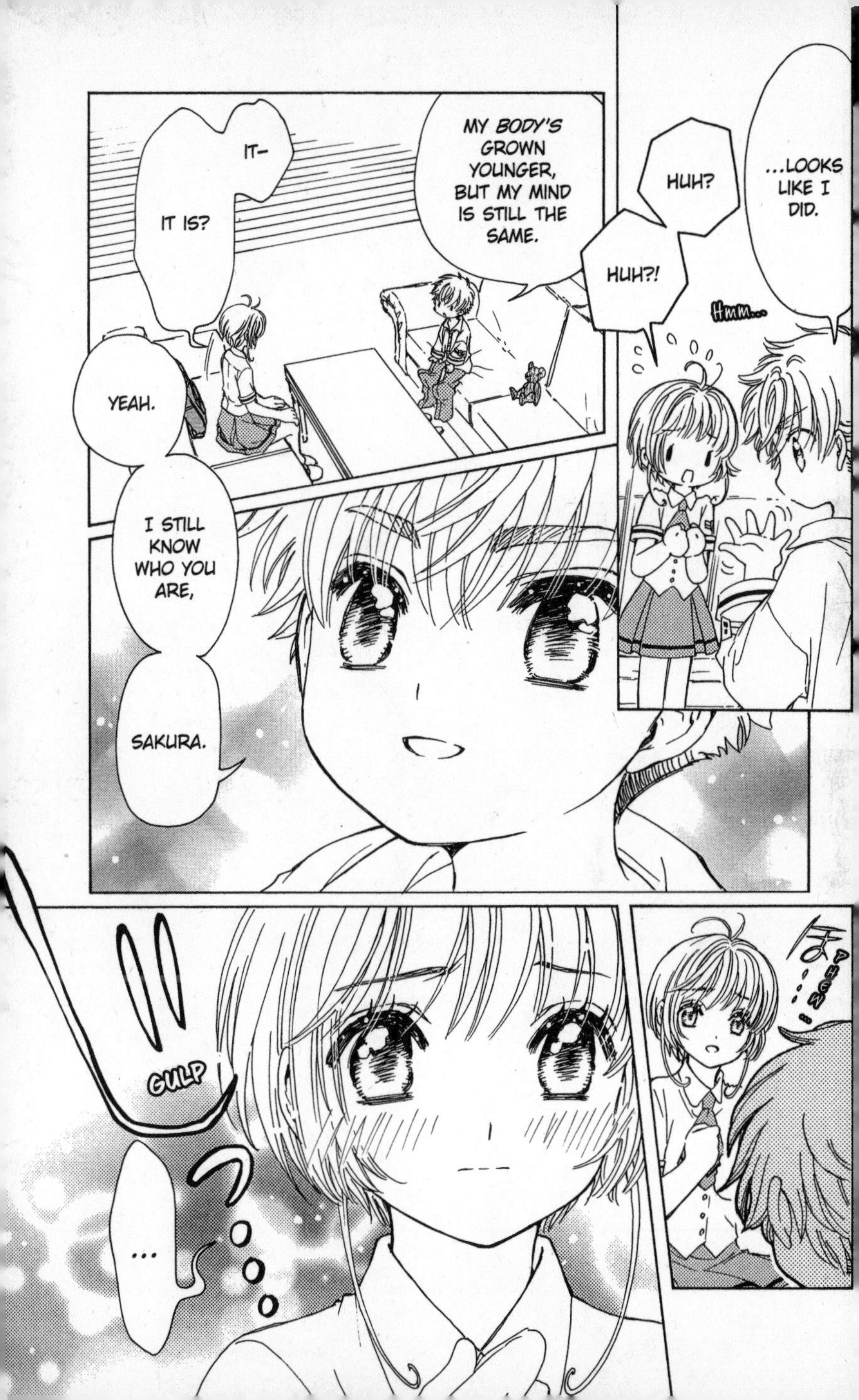
...LOOKS LIKE I DID.
HUH?
HUH?!
Hmm...
MY BODY'S GROWN YOUNGER, BUT MY MIND IS STILL THE SAME.
IT-
IT IS?
YEAH.
I STILL KNOW WHO YOU ARE,
SAKURA.
ほ PHEW...
GULP
...

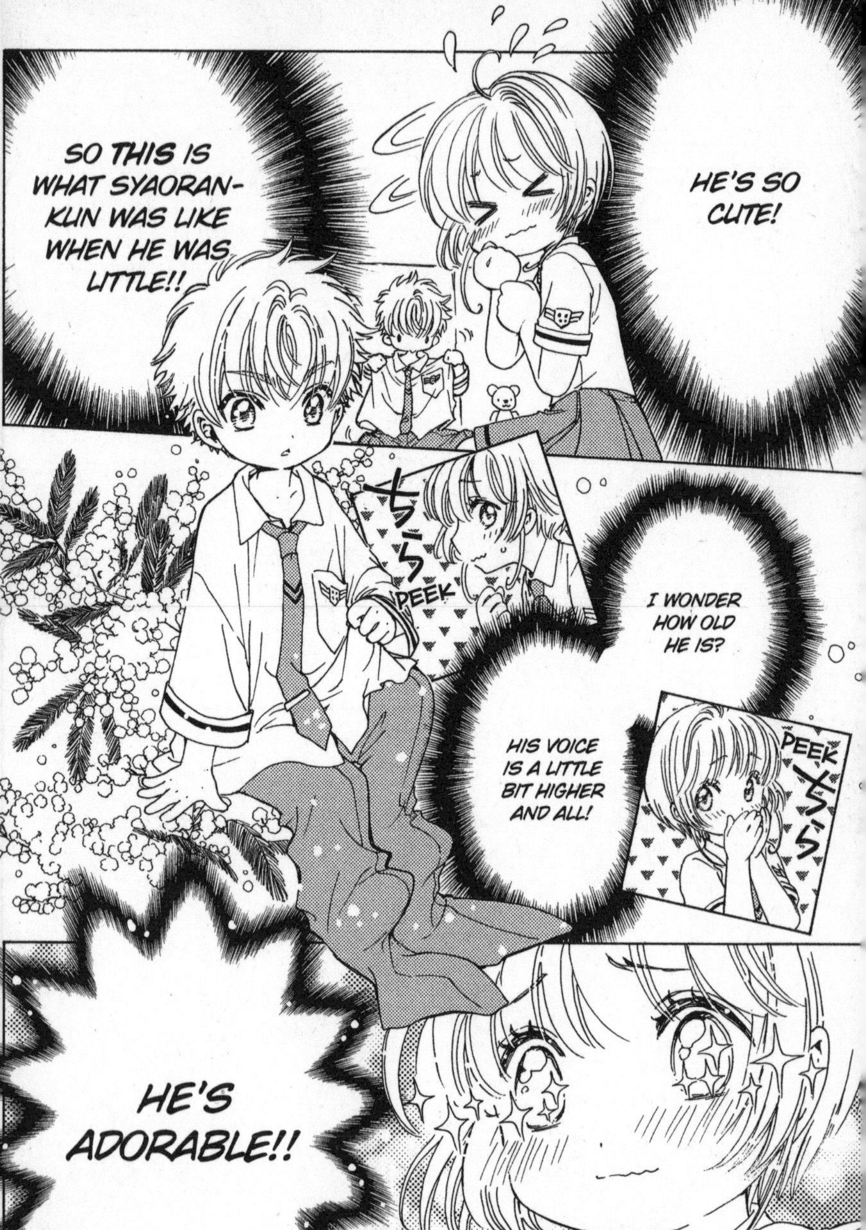
HE'S SO CUTE!
SO THIS IS WHAT SYAORAN-KUN WAS LIKE WHEN HE WAS LITTLE!!
ちら
PEEK
I WONDER HOW OLD HE IS?
HIS VOICE IS A LITTLE BIT HIGHER AND ALL!
PEEK
ちら
HE'S ADORABLE!!

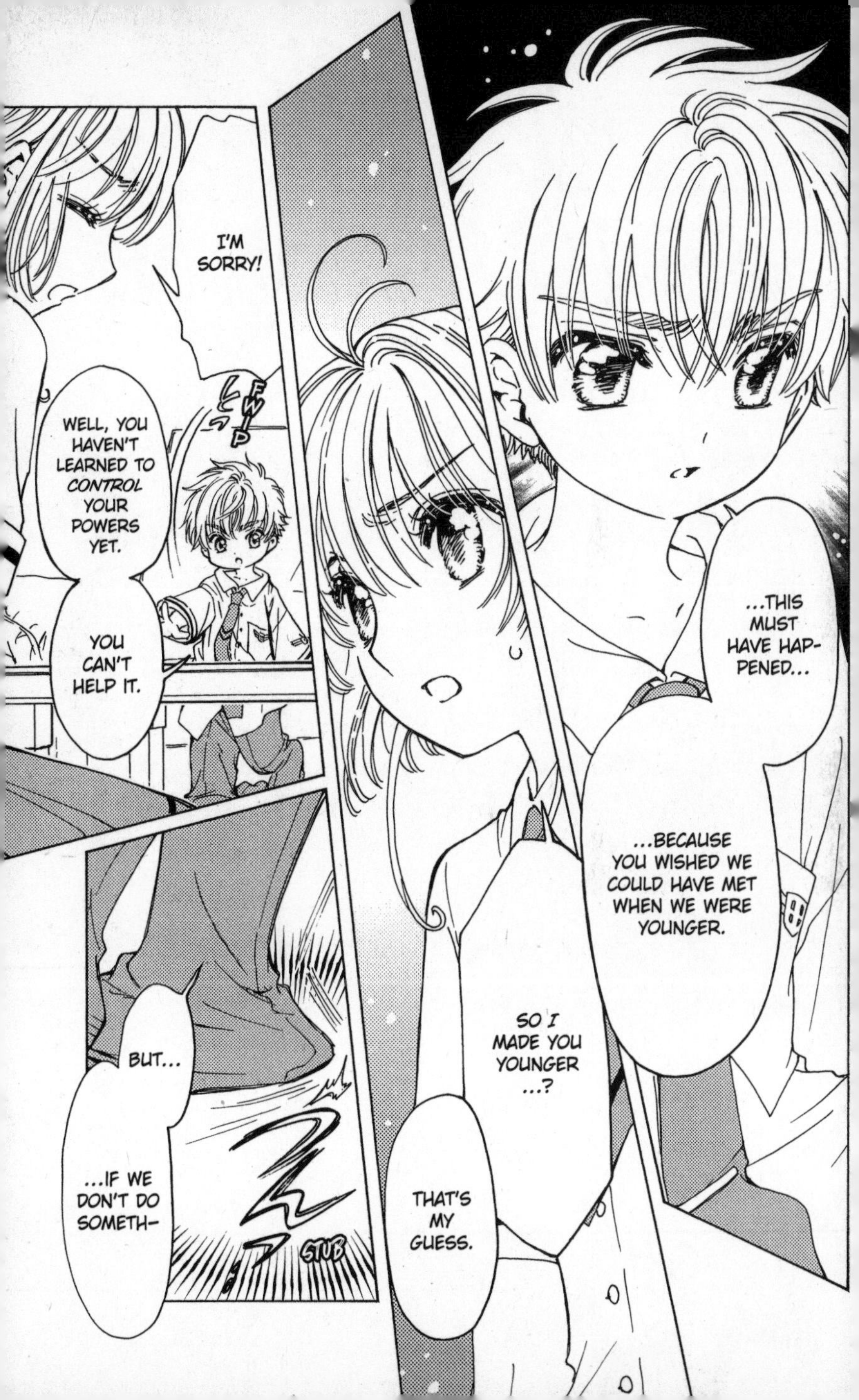
...THIS MUST HAVE HAP-PENED...
...BECAUSE YOU WISHED WE COULD HAVE MET WHEN WE WERE YOUNGER.
SO I MADE YOU YOUNGER ...?
THAT'S MY GUESS.
I'M SORRY!
FWIP
WELL, YOU HAVEN'T LEARNED TO CONTROL YOUR POWERS YET.
YOU CAN'T HELP IT.
BUT...
...IF WE DON'T DO SOMETH-
STUB

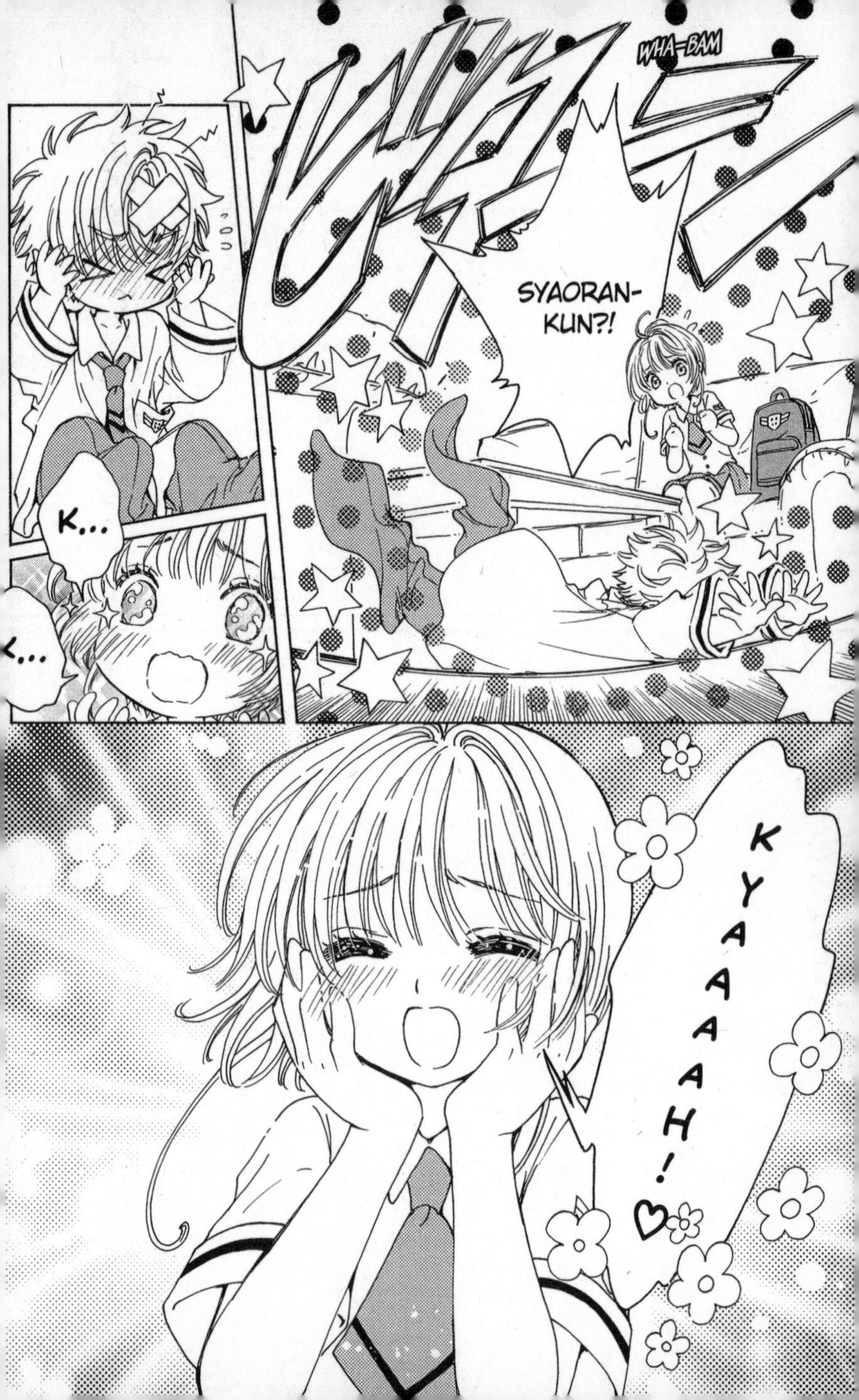
WHA-BAM
SYAORAN-KUN?!
K...
KYAAAAAH! ♥

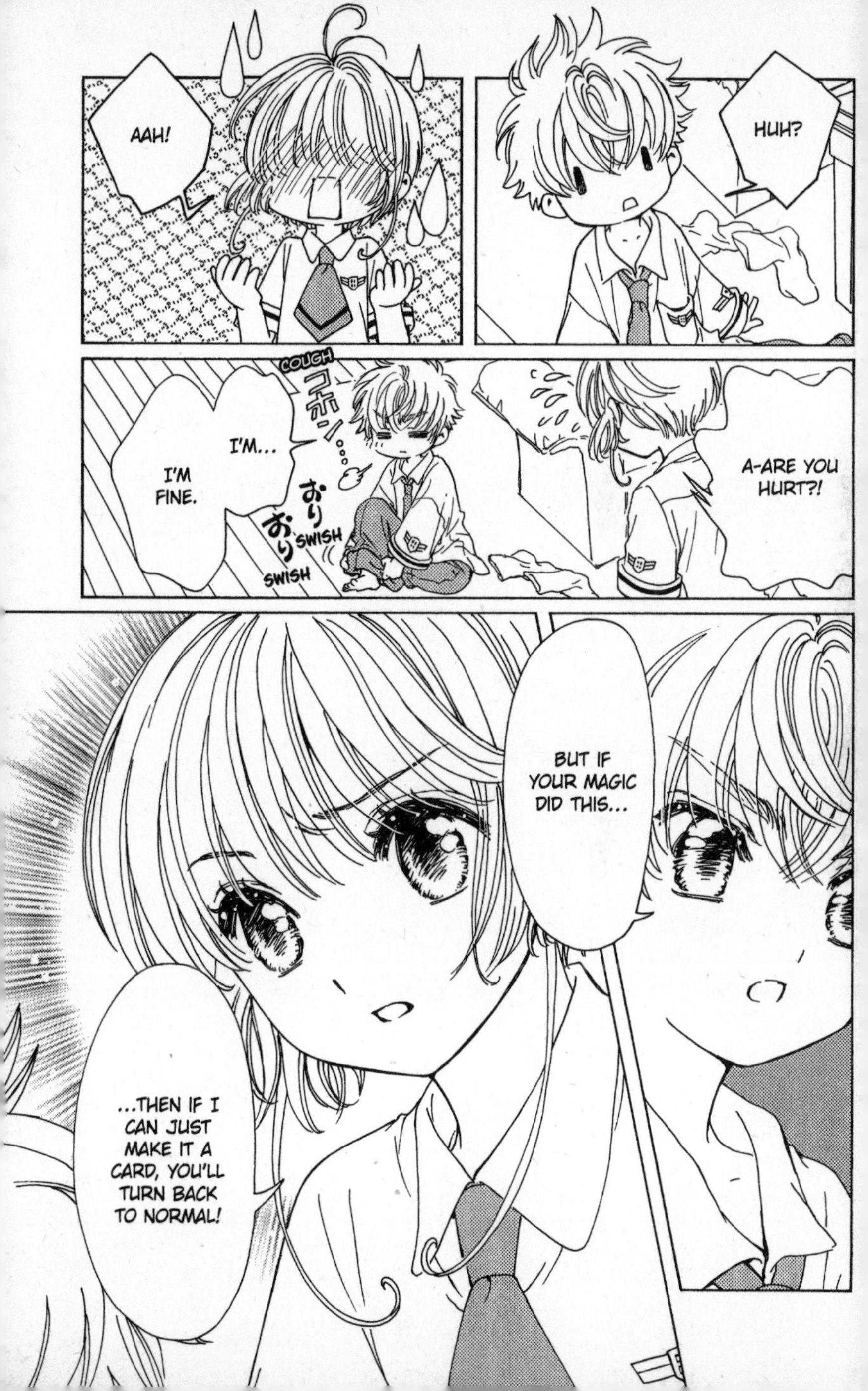
HUH?
AAH!
A-ARE YOU HURT?!
コホン
COUGH
I'M...
I'M FINE.
おり
SWISH
おり
SWISH
BUT IF YOUR MAGIC DID THIS...
...THEN IF I CAN JUST MAKE IT A CARD, YOU'LL TURN BACK TO NORMAL!

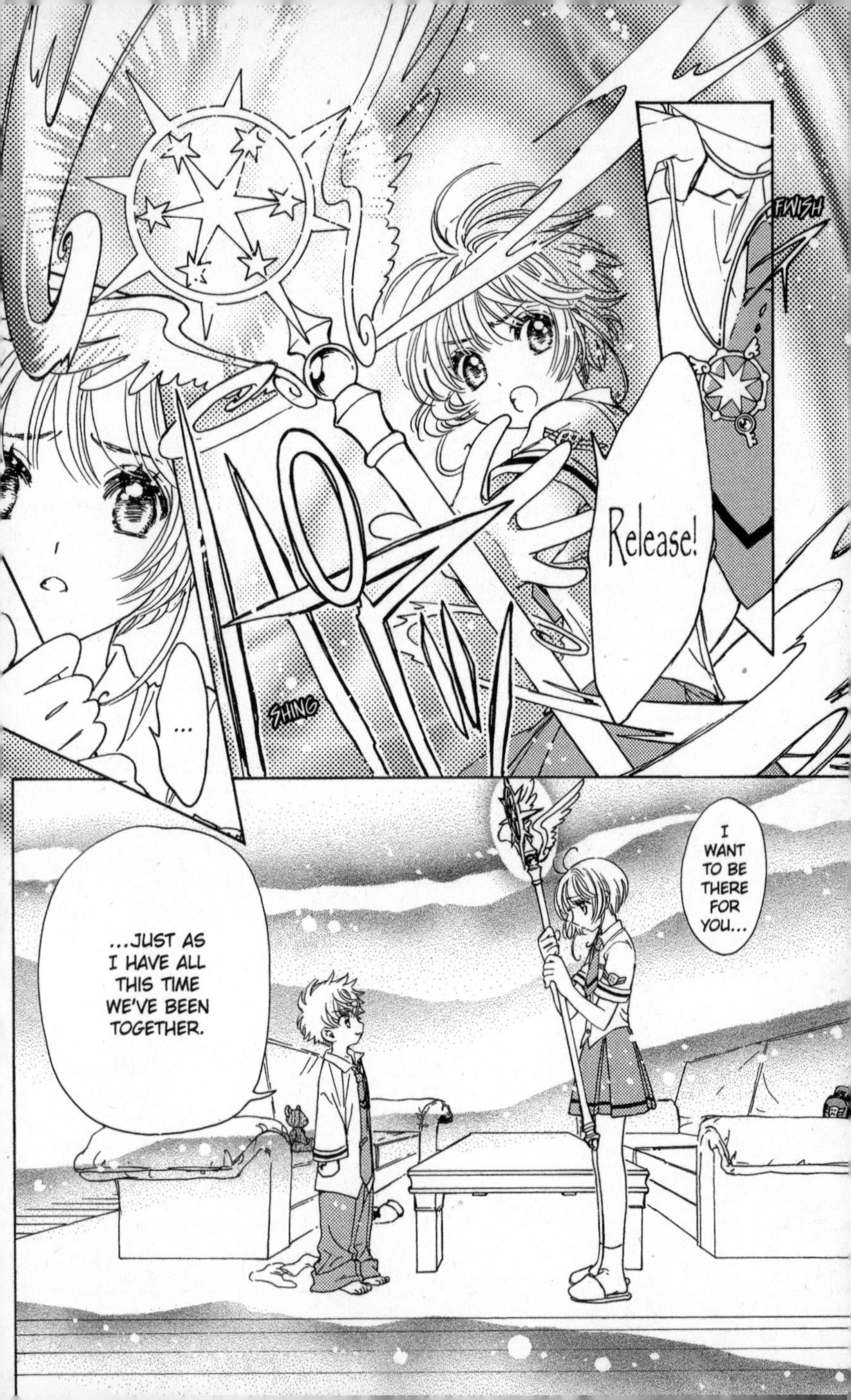
FWISH
Release!
SHING
...
I WANT TO BE THERE FOR YOU...
...JUST AS I HAVE ALL THIS TIME WE'VE BEEN TOGETHER.

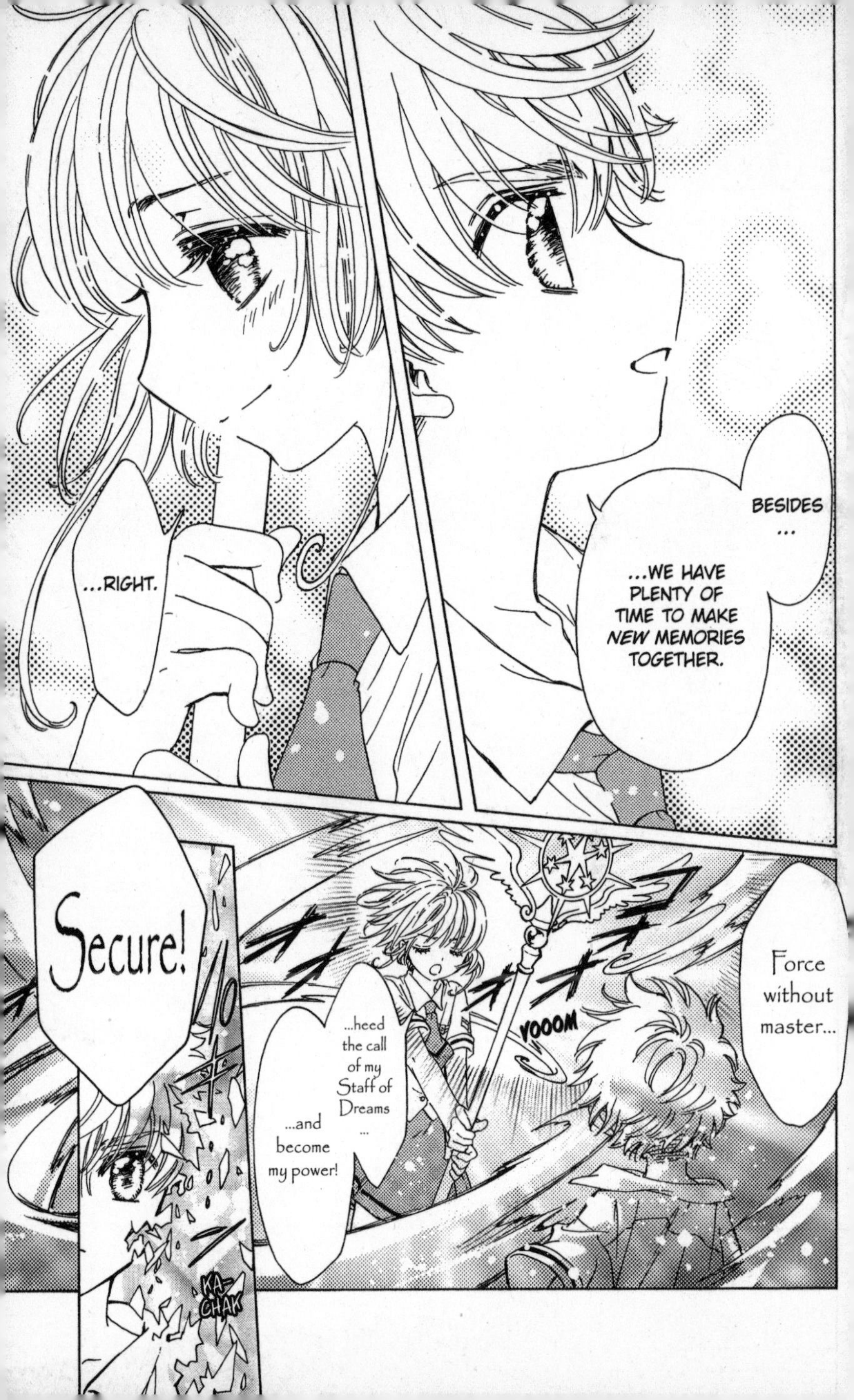
BESIDES...
...WE HAVE PLENTY OF TIME TO MAKE *NEW* MEMORIES TOGETHER.
...RIGHT.
Force without master...
...heed the call of my Staff of Dreams...
...and become my power!
YOOOM
Secure!
KA-CHAK

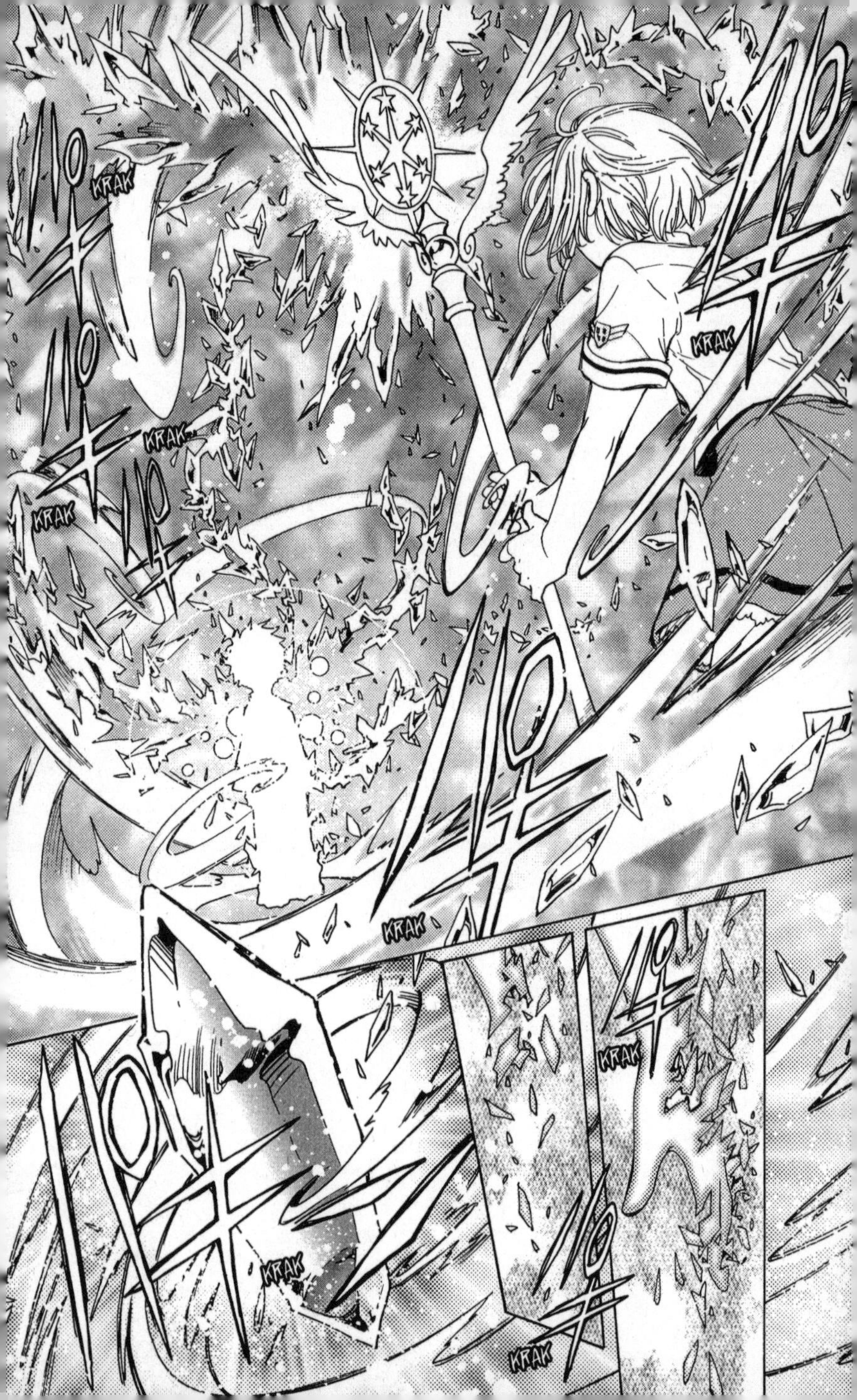
KRAK
KRAK
KRAK
KRAK
KRAK
KRAK
KRAK
KRAK

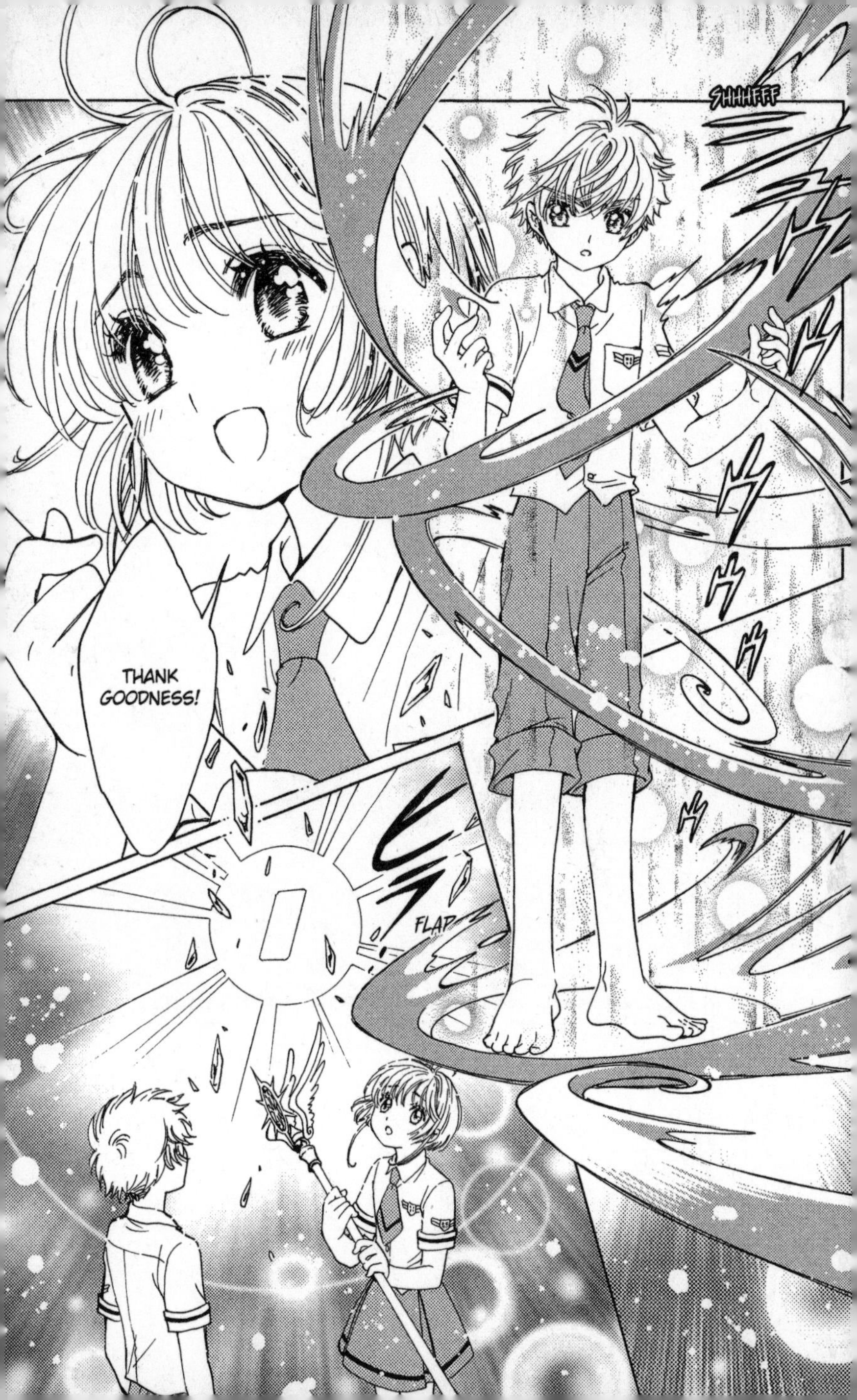
SHHHFFF
THANK GOODNESS!
FLAP

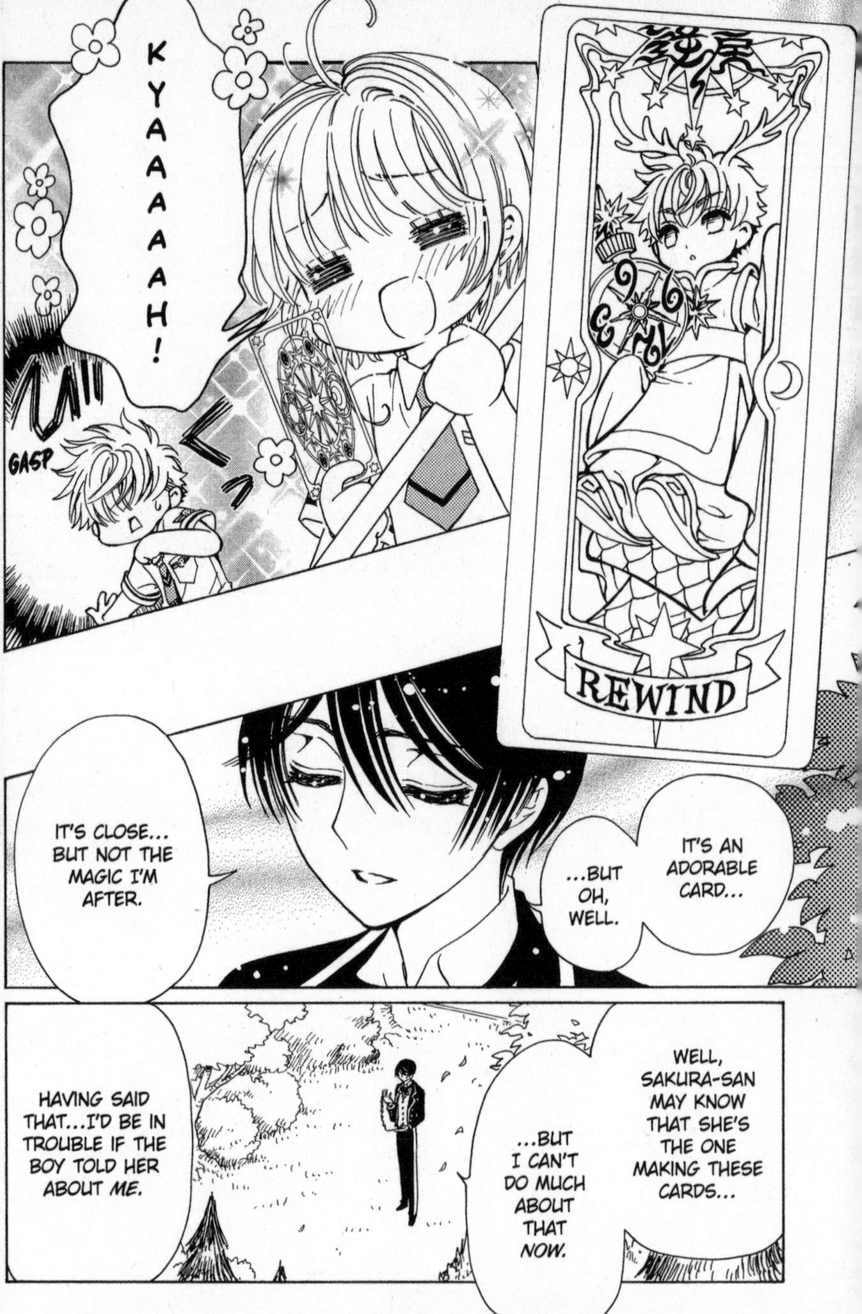
REWIND
KYAAAAAAH!
GASP
IT'S AN ADORABLE CARD...
...BUT OH, WELL.
IT'S CLOSE... BUT NOT THE MAGIC I'M AFTER.
WELL, SAKURA-SAN MAY KNOW THAT SHE'S THE ONE MAKING THESE CARDS...
...BUT I CAN'T DO MUCH ABOUT THAT NOW.
HAVING SAID THAT...I'D BE IN TROUBLE IF THE BOY TOLD HER ABOUT ME.

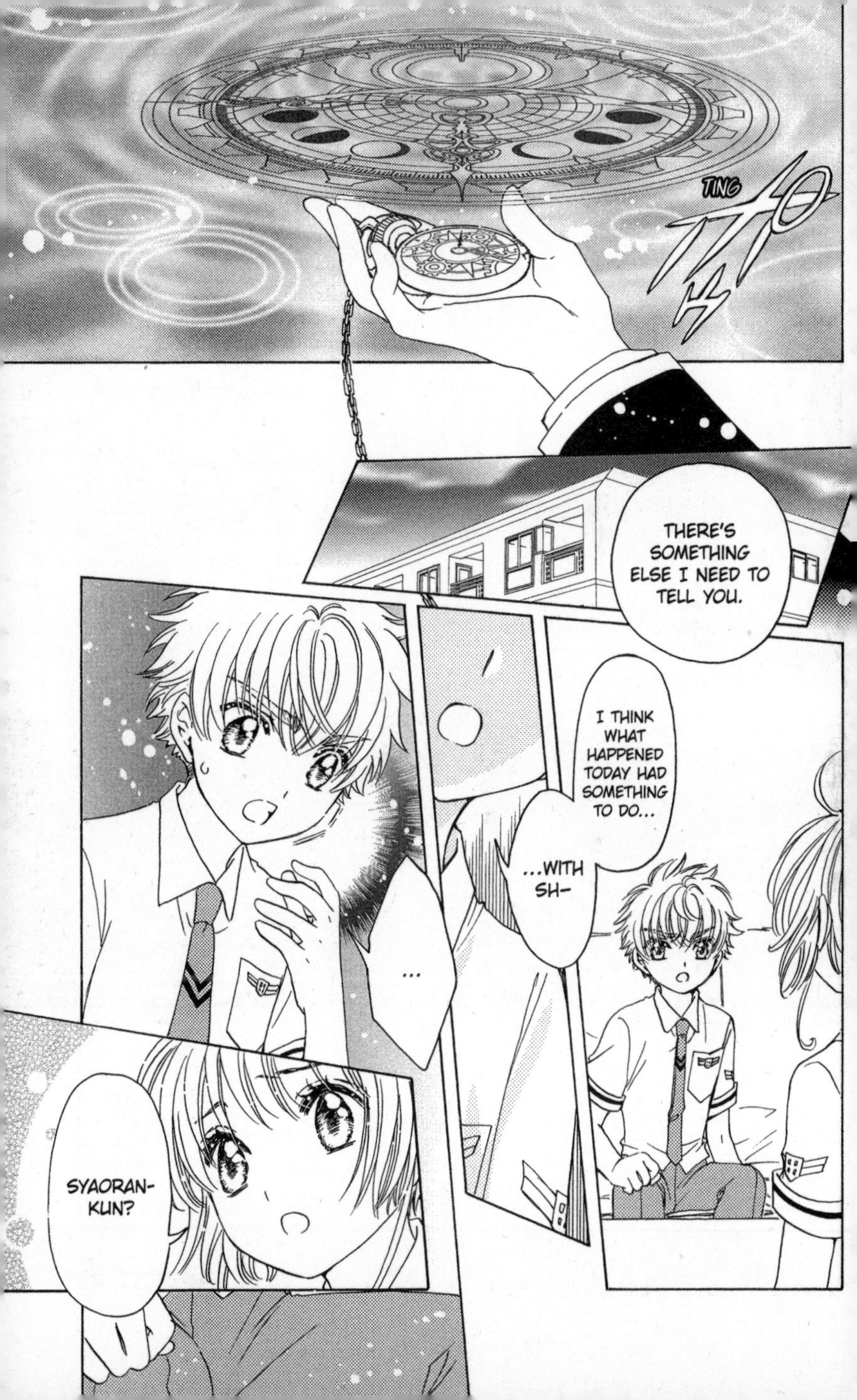
TING
THERE'S SOMETHING ELSE I NEED TO TELL YOU.
I THINK WHAT HAPPENED TODAY HAD SOMETHING TO DO...
...WITH SH-
...
SYAORAN-KUN?

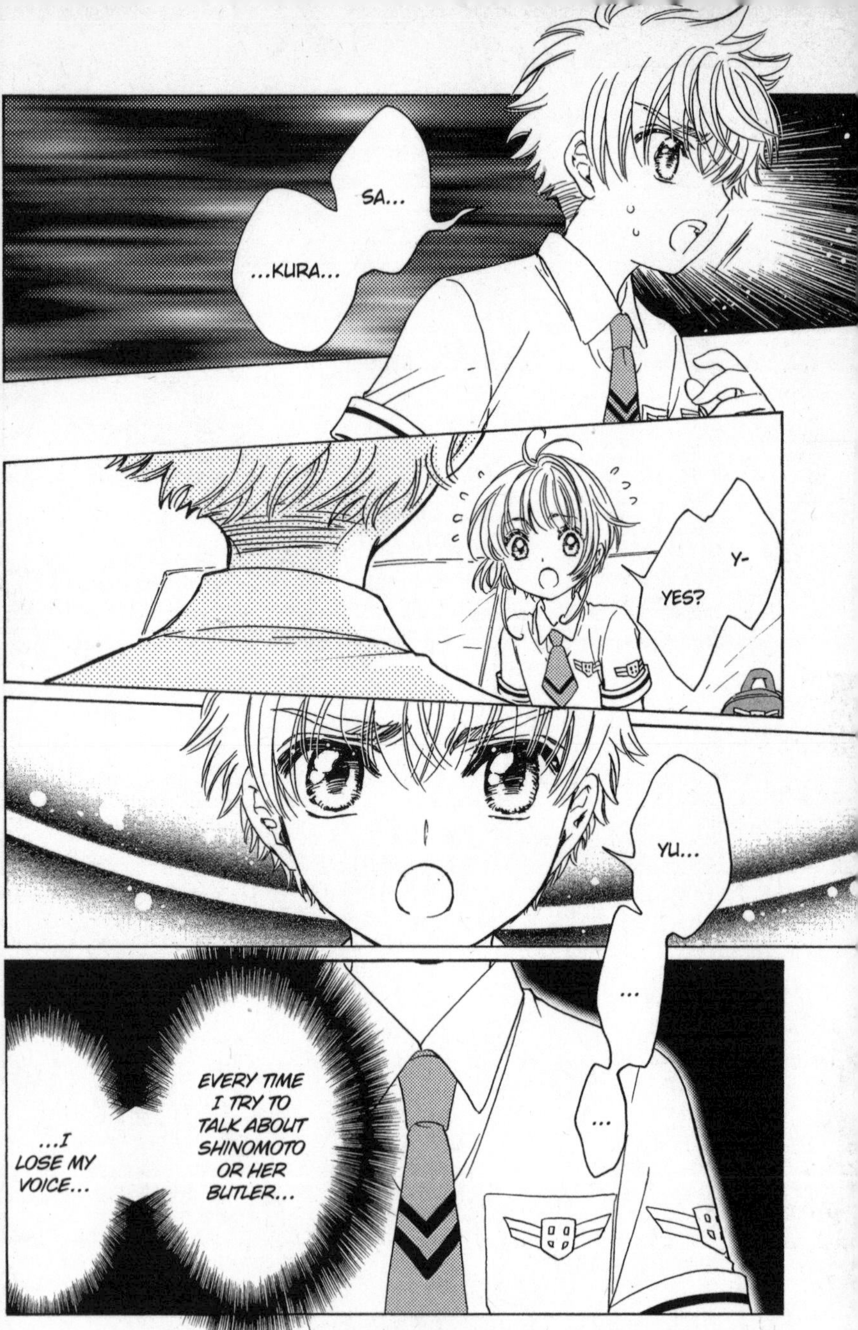
SA...
...KURA...
Y- YES?
YU...
...
...
EVERY TIME I TRY TO TALK ABOUT SHINOMOTO OR HER BUTLER...
...I LOSE MY VOICE...

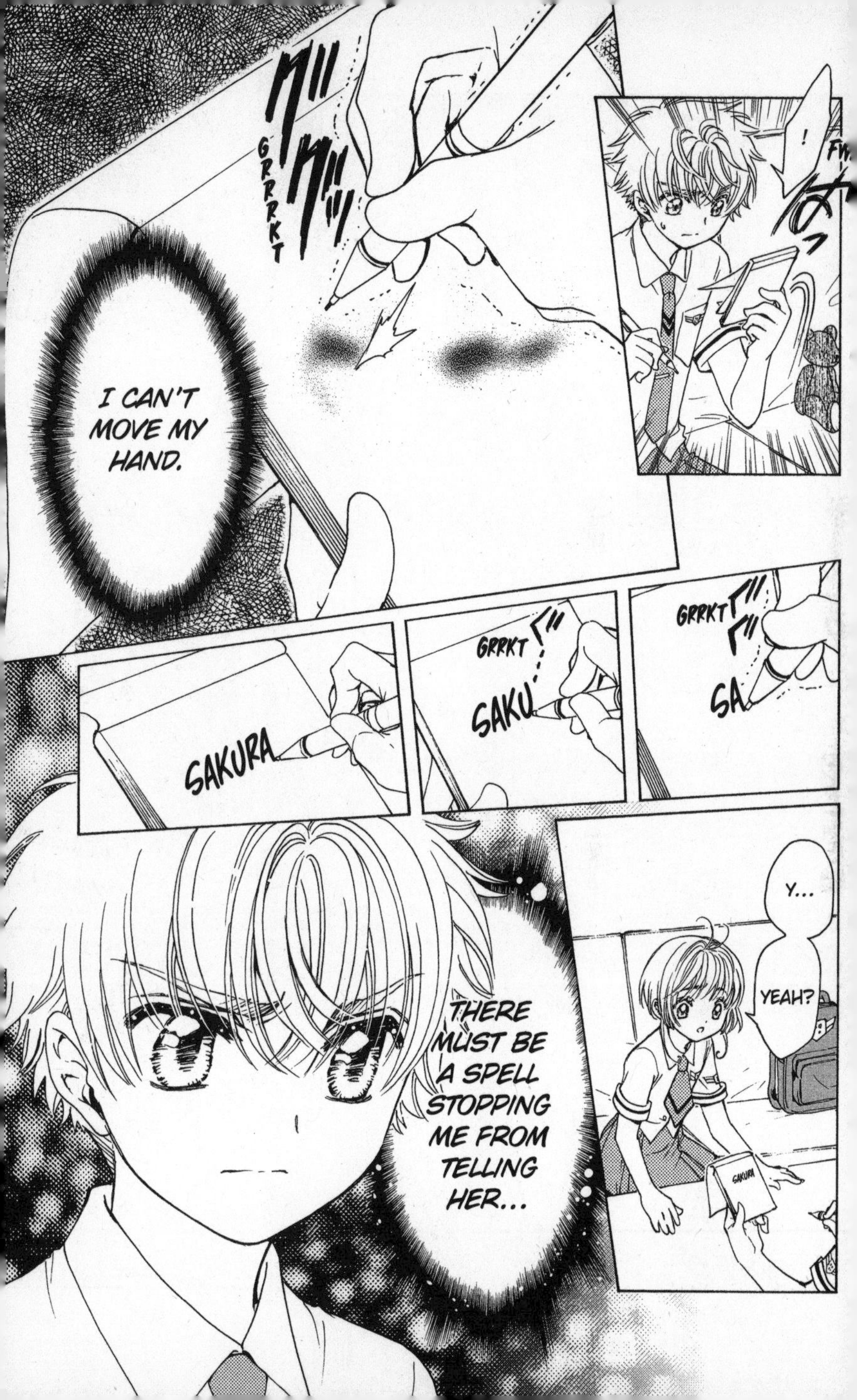
!
FW
GRRRKT
I CAN'T MOVE MY HAND.
GRRKT
SA
GRRKT
SAKU
SAKURA
Y...
YEAH?
SAKURA
THERE MUST BE A SPELL STOPPING ME FROM TELLING HER...

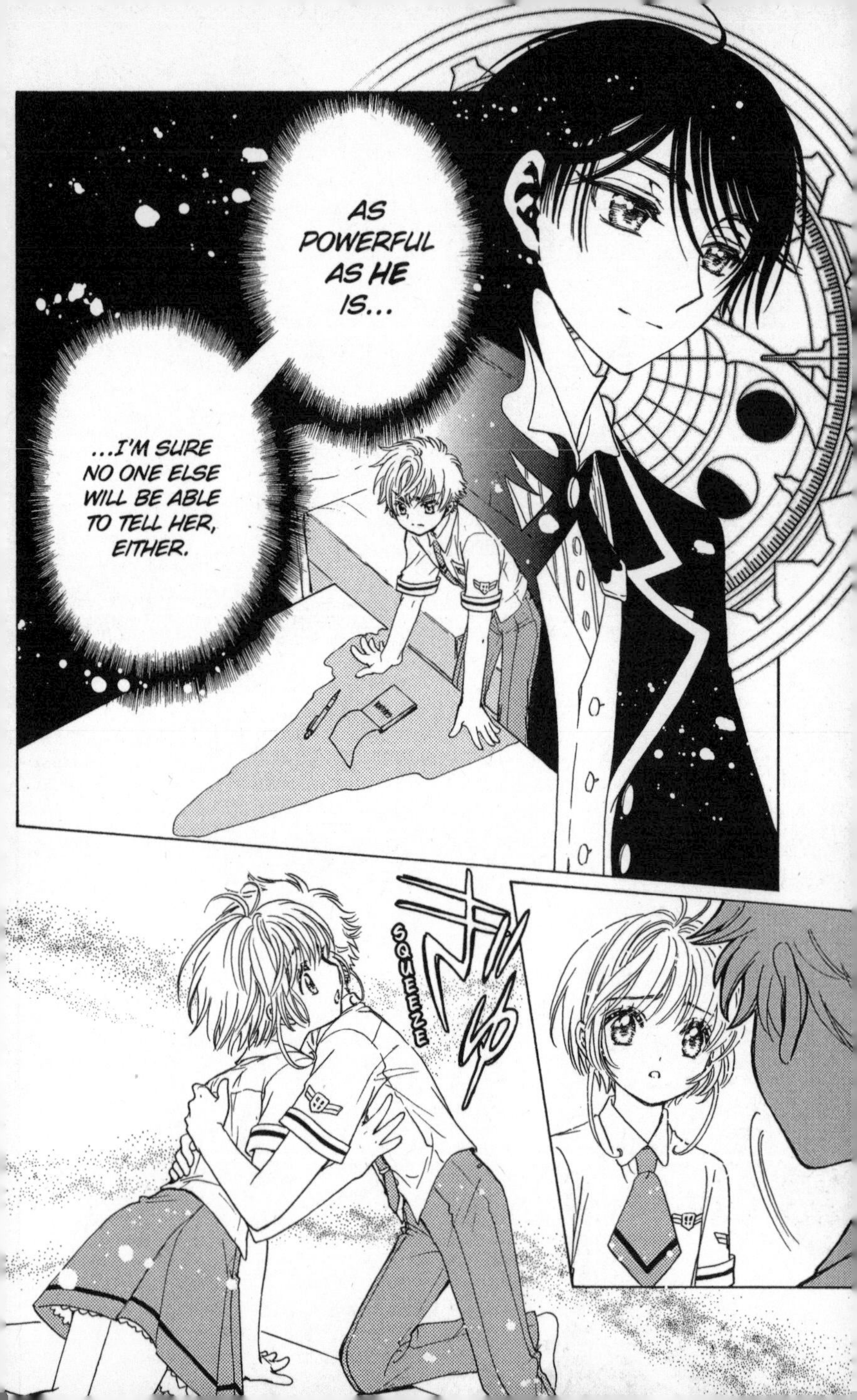
AS POWERFUL AS HE IS...
...I'M SURE NO ONE ELSE WILL BE ABLE TO TELL HER, EITHER.
SQUEEZE

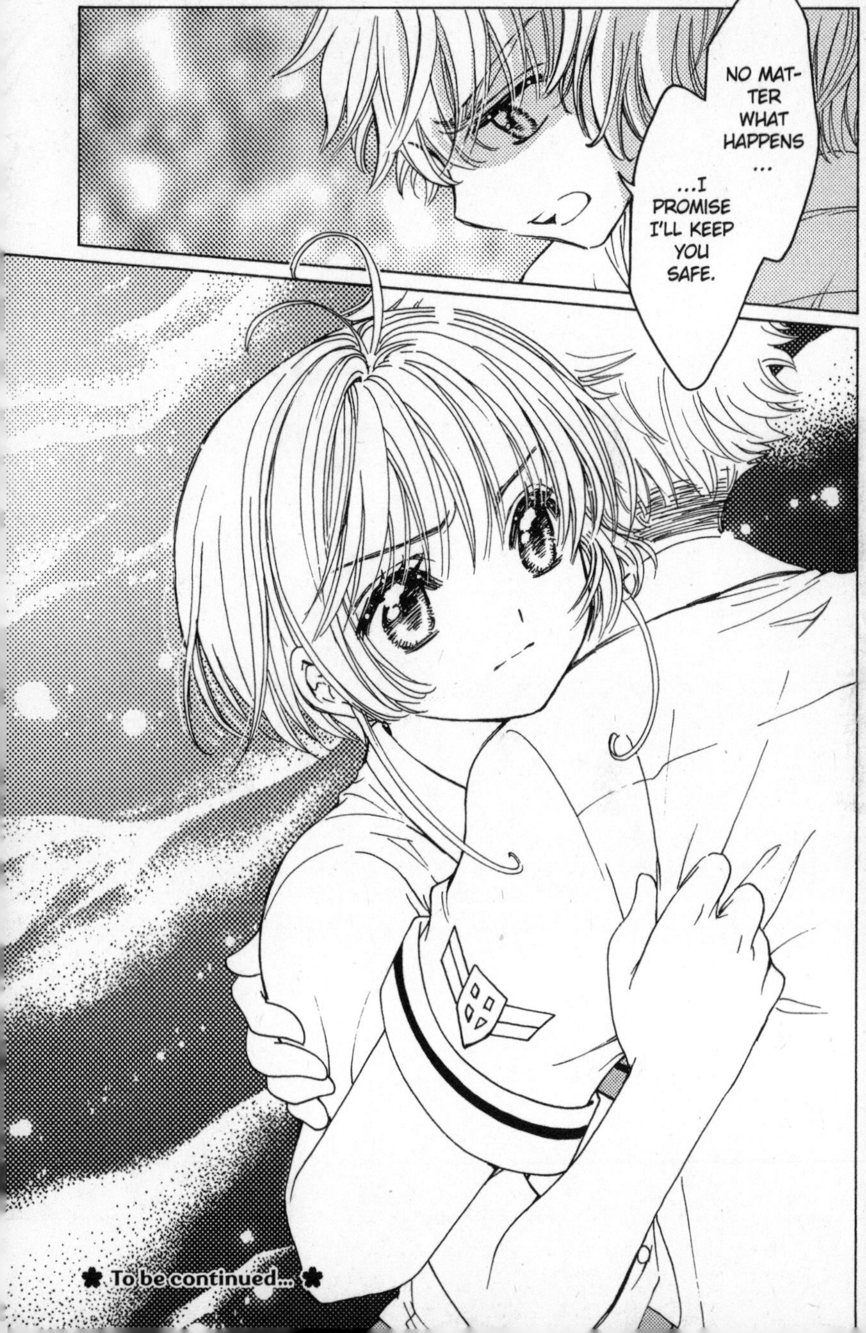
NO MATTER WHAT HAPPENS ...
...I PROMISE I'LL KEEP YOU SAFE.
To be continued...

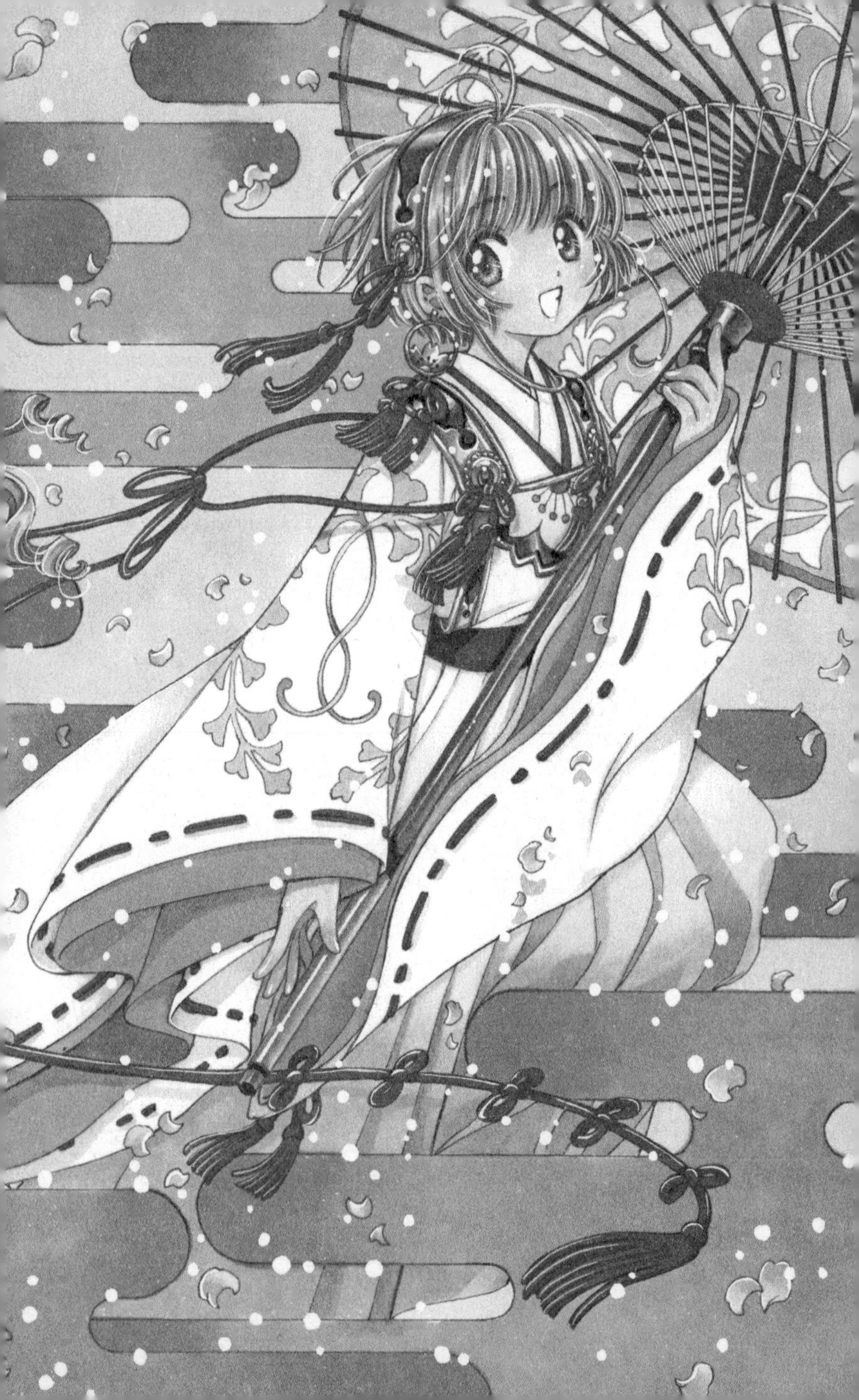

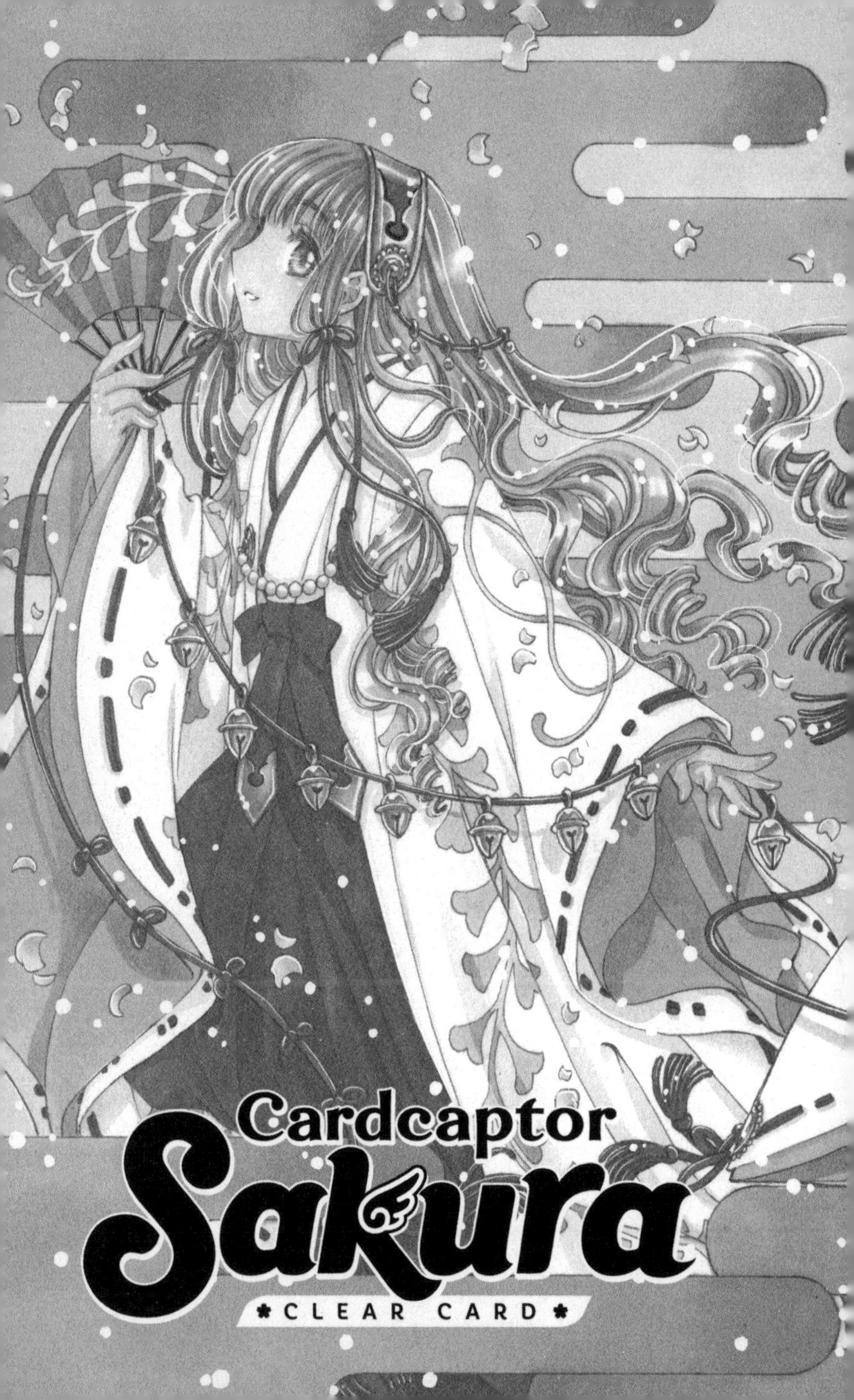
Cardcaptor
Sakura
CLEAR CARD

Cardcaptor Sakura
CLEAR CARD

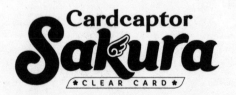

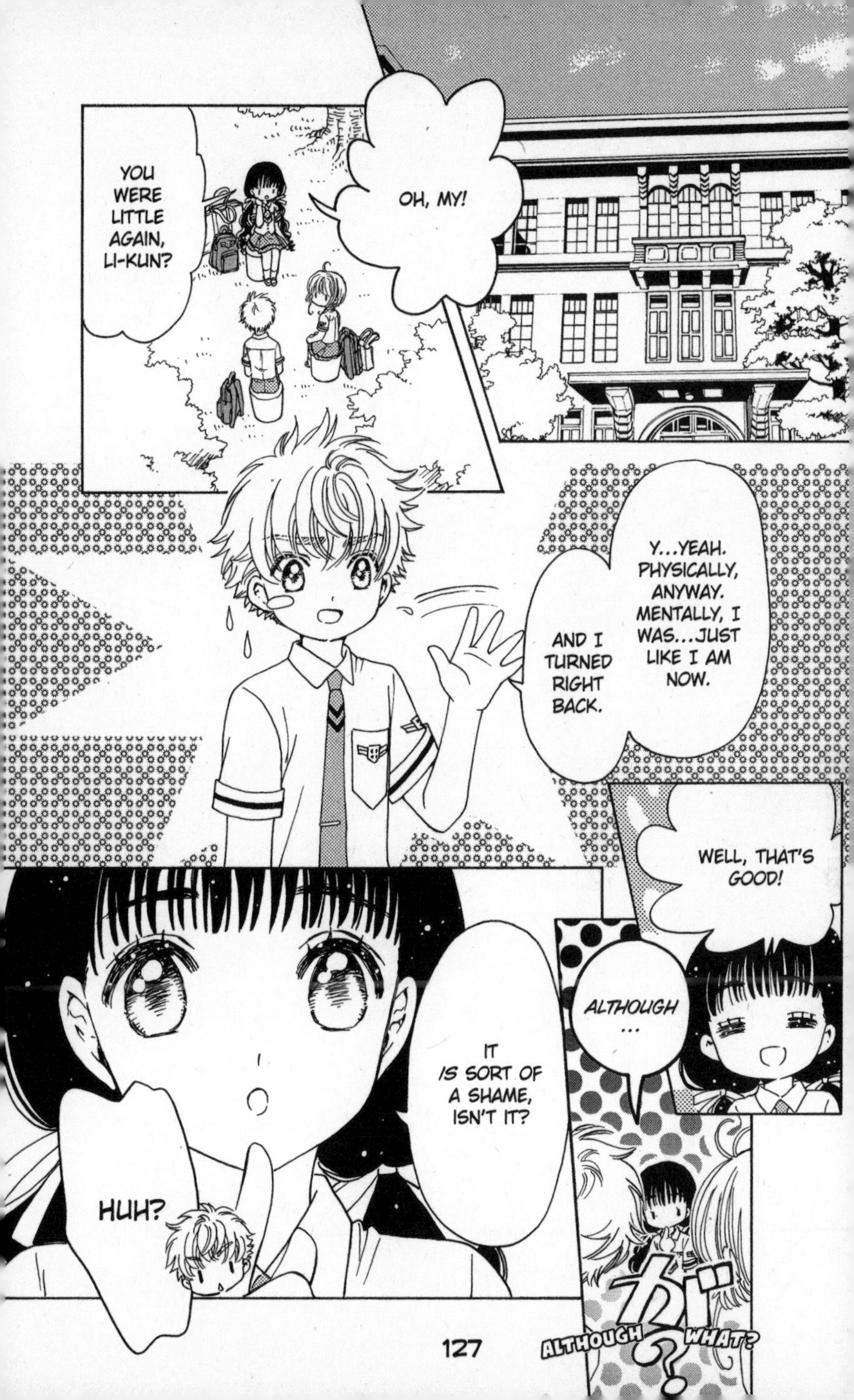
OH, MY!
YOU WERE LITTLE AGAIN, LI-KUN?
Y...YEAH. PHYSICALLY, ANYWAY. MENTALLY, I WAS...JUST LIKE I AM NOW.
AND I TURNED RIGHT BACK.
WELL, THAT'S GOOD!
ALTHOUGH ...
ALTHOUGH WHAT?
IT IS SORT OF A SHAME, ISN'T IT?
HUH?

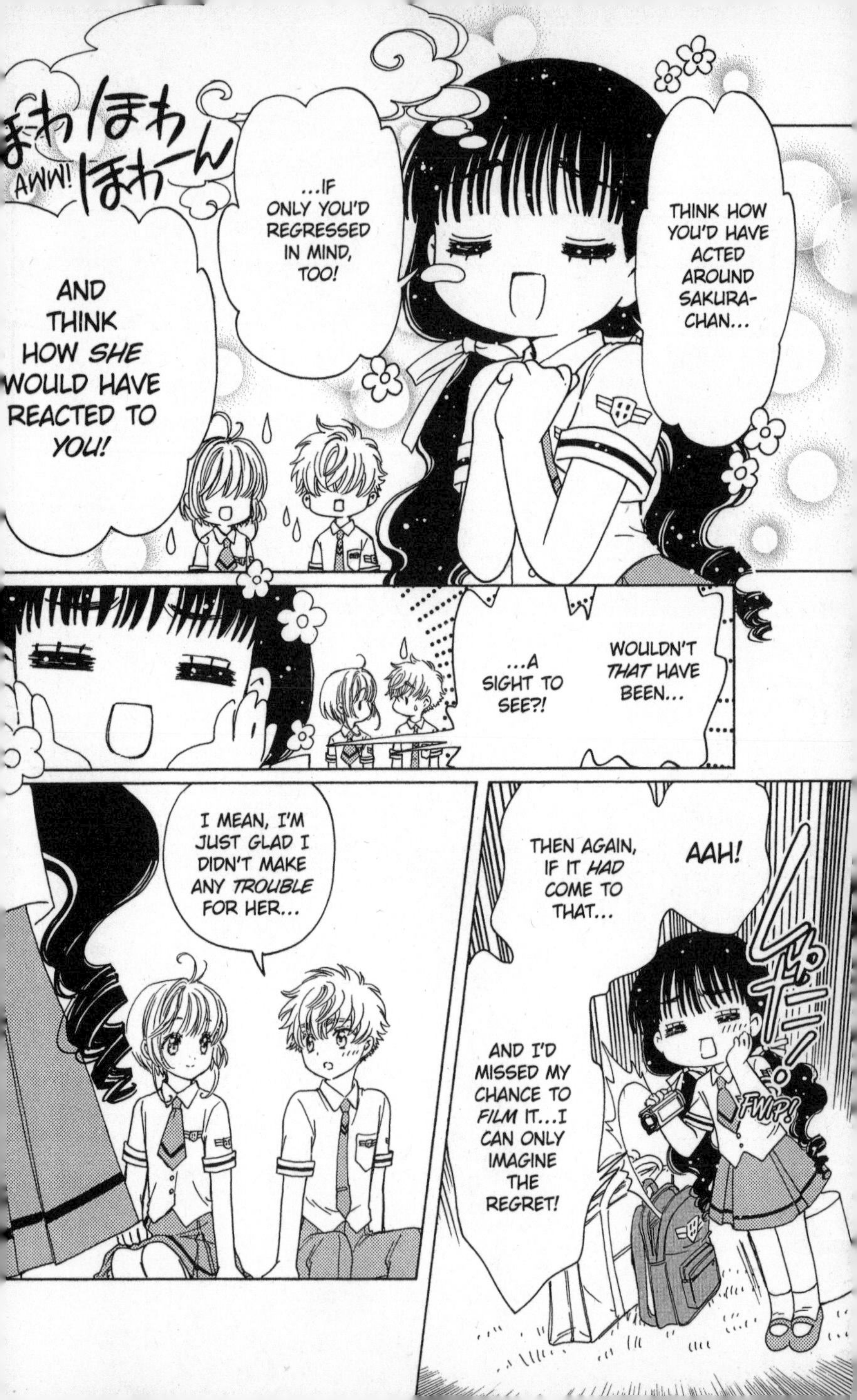
THINK HOW YOU'D HAVE ACTED AROUND SAKURA-CHAN...
...IF ONLY YOU'D REGRESSED IN MIND, TOO!
ほわほわほわーん
AWW!
AND THINK HOW *SHE* WOULD HAVE REACTED TO *YOU!*
WOULDN'T *THAT* HAVE BEEN...
...A SIGHT TO SEE?!
AAH!
THEN AGAIN, IF IT *HAD* COME TO THAT...
AND I'D MISSED MY CHANCE TO *FILM* IT...I CAN ONLY IMAGINE THE REGRET!
FWIP!
I MEAN, I'M JUST GLAD I DIDN'T MAKE ANY *TROUBLE* FOR HER...

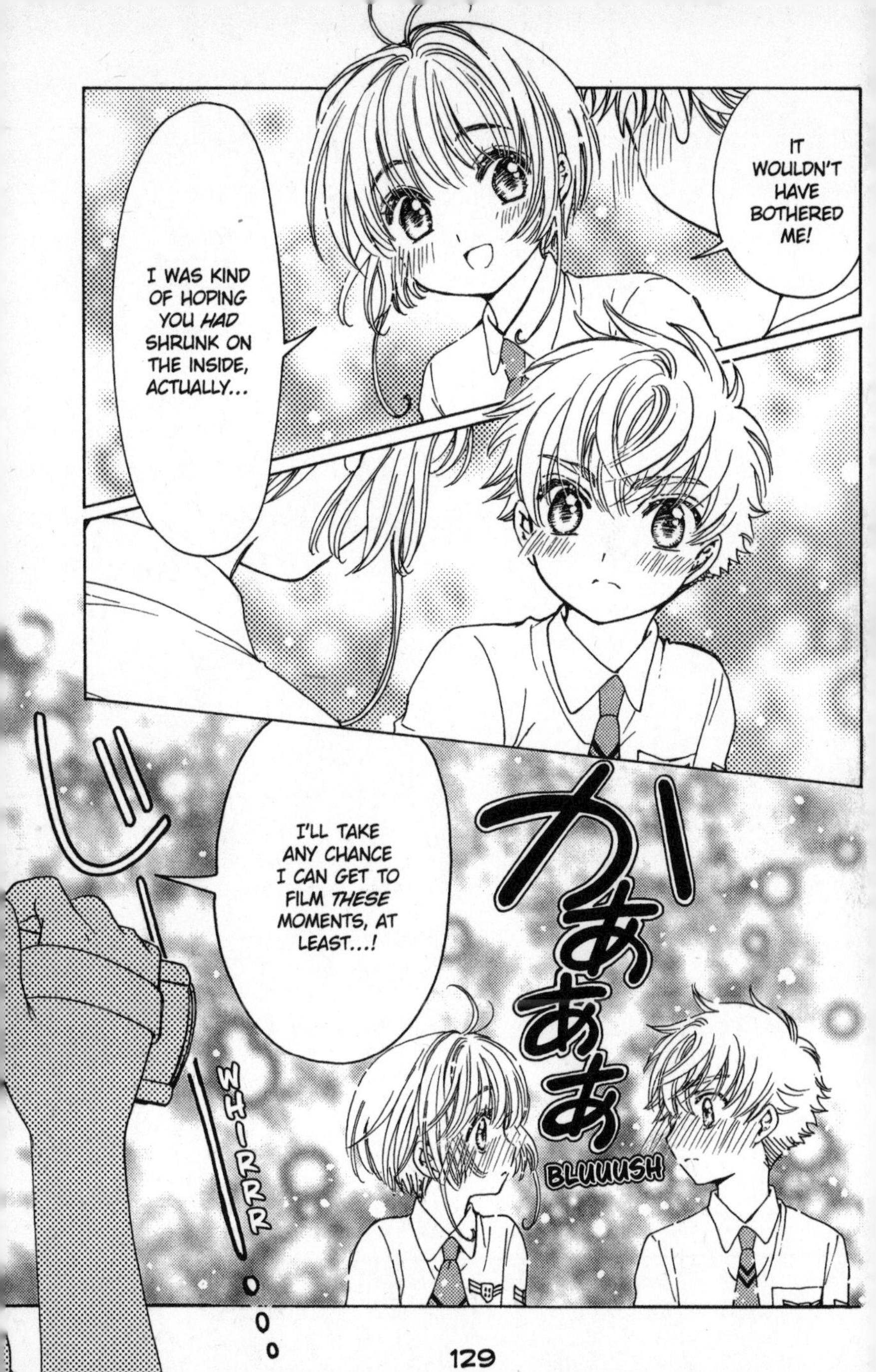
IT WOULDN'T HAVE BOTHERED ME!
I WAS KIND OF HOPING YOU *HAD* SHRUNK ON THE INSIDE, ACTUALLY...
かあああ
BLUUUSH
I'LL TAKE ANY CHANCE I CAN GET TO FILM *THESE* MOMENTS, AT LEAST...!
じー
WHIRRR

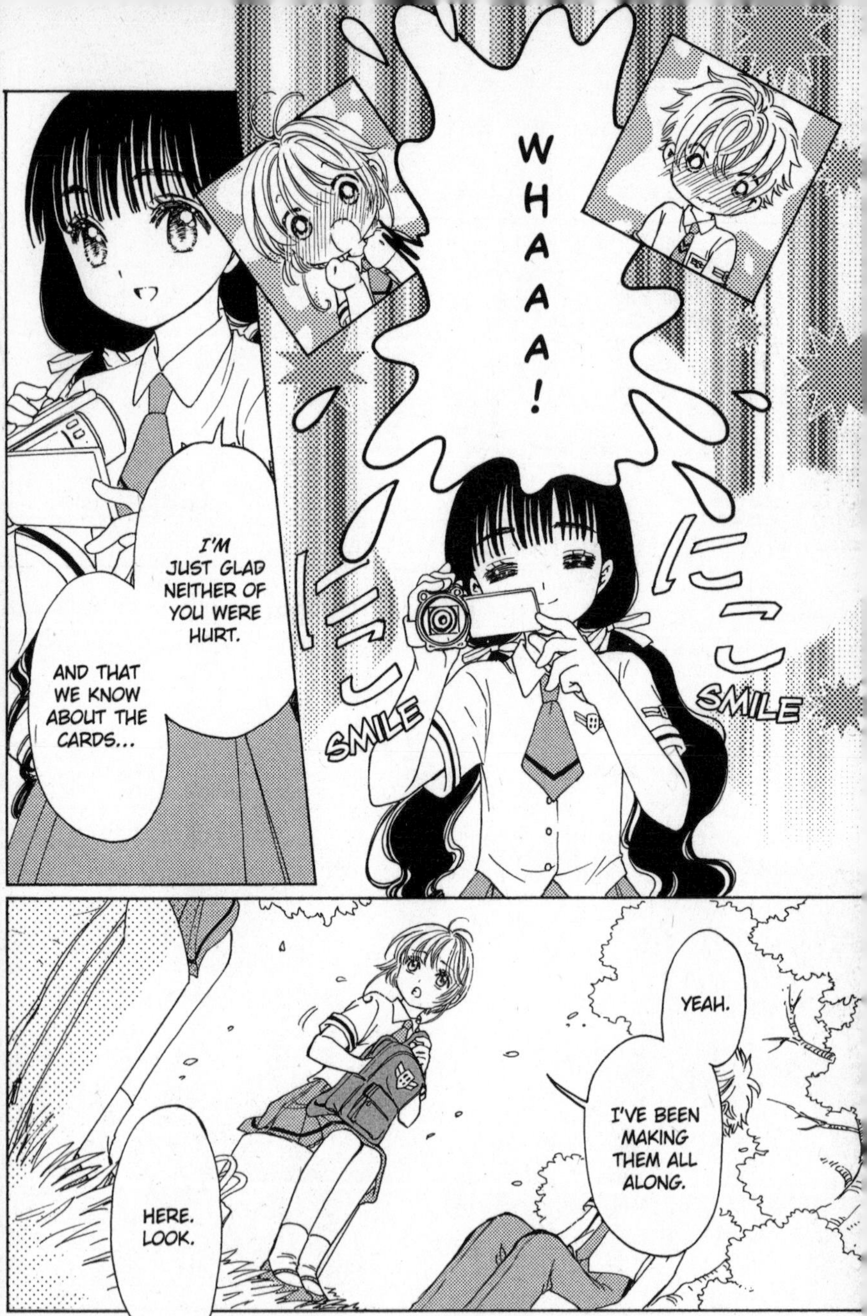
WHAAAA!
にこっ
SMILE
にこっ
SMILE
I'M JUST GLAD NEITHER OF YOU WERE HURT.
AND THAT WE KNOW ABOUT THE CARDS...
YEAH.
I'VE BEEN MAKING THEM ALL ALONG.
HERE. LOOK.

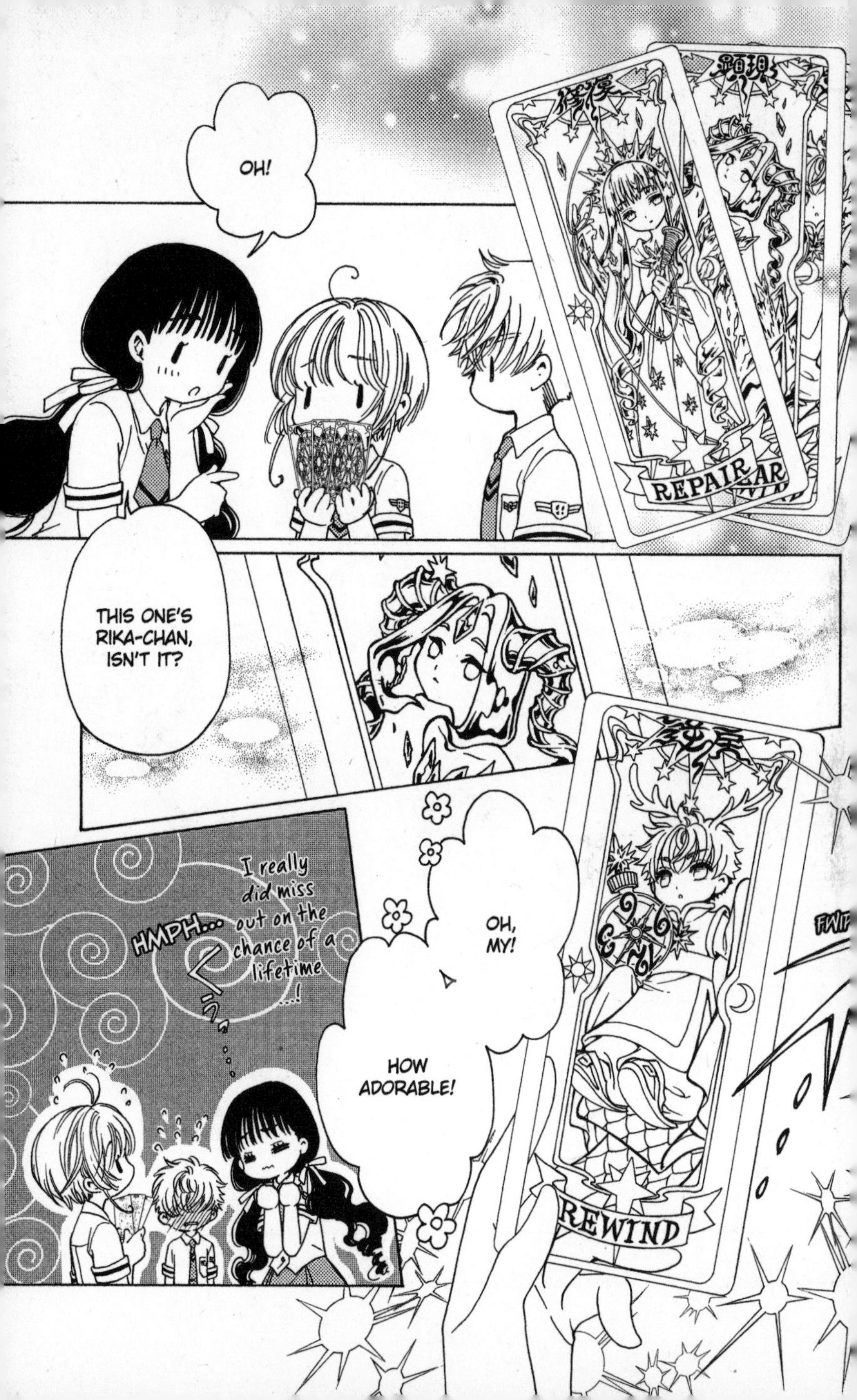
REPAIR
OH!
THIS ONE'S RIKA-CHAN, ISN'T IT?
FWIP
REWIND
OH, MY!
HOW ADORABLE!
I really did miss out on the chance of a lifetime...!
HMPH...

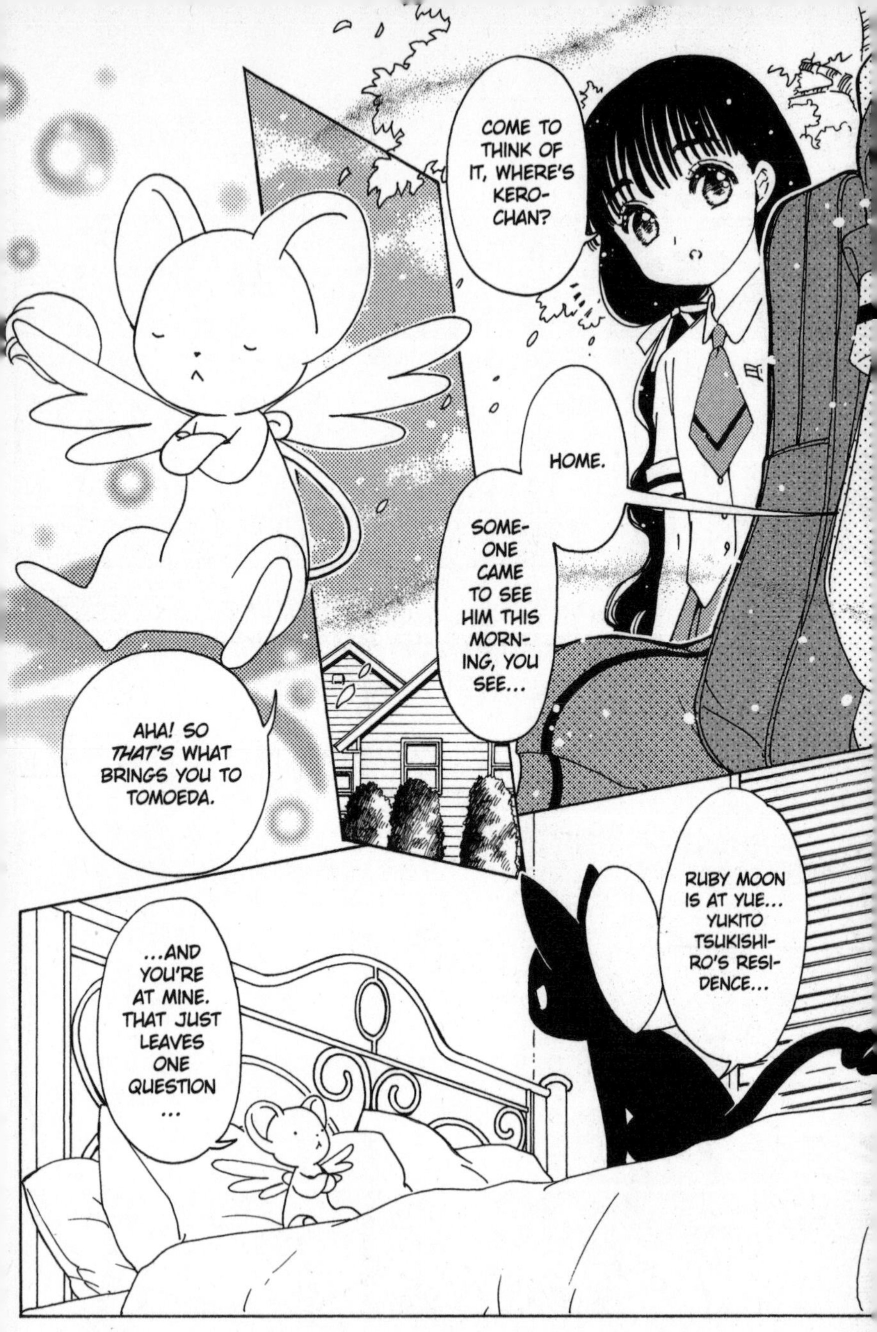
COME TO THINK OF IT, WHERE'S KERO-CHAN?
HOME.
SOME-ONE CAME TO SEE HIM THIS MORNING, YOU SEE...
AHA! SO *THAT'S* WHAT BRINGS YOU TO TOMOEDA.
RUBY MOON IS AT YUE... YUKITO TSUKISHIRO'S RESIDENCE...
...AND YOU'RE AT MINE. THAT JUST LEAVES ONE QUESTION...

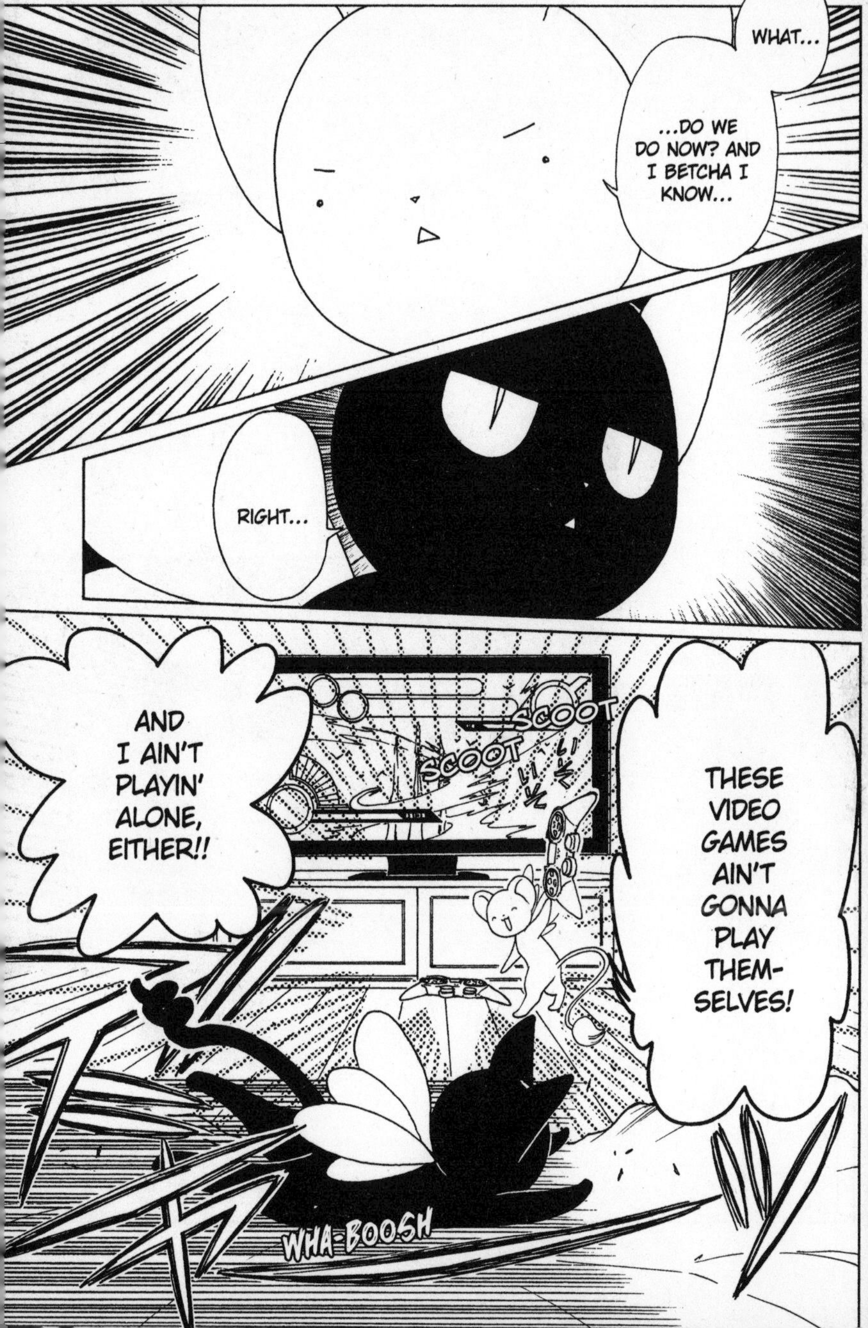
WHAT...
...DO WE DO NOW? AND I BETCHA I KNOW...
RIGHT...
THESE VIDEO GAMES AIN'T GONNA PLAY THEM-SELVES!
SCOOT
SCOOT
AND I AIN'T PLAYIN' ALONE, EITHER!!
WHA-BOOSH

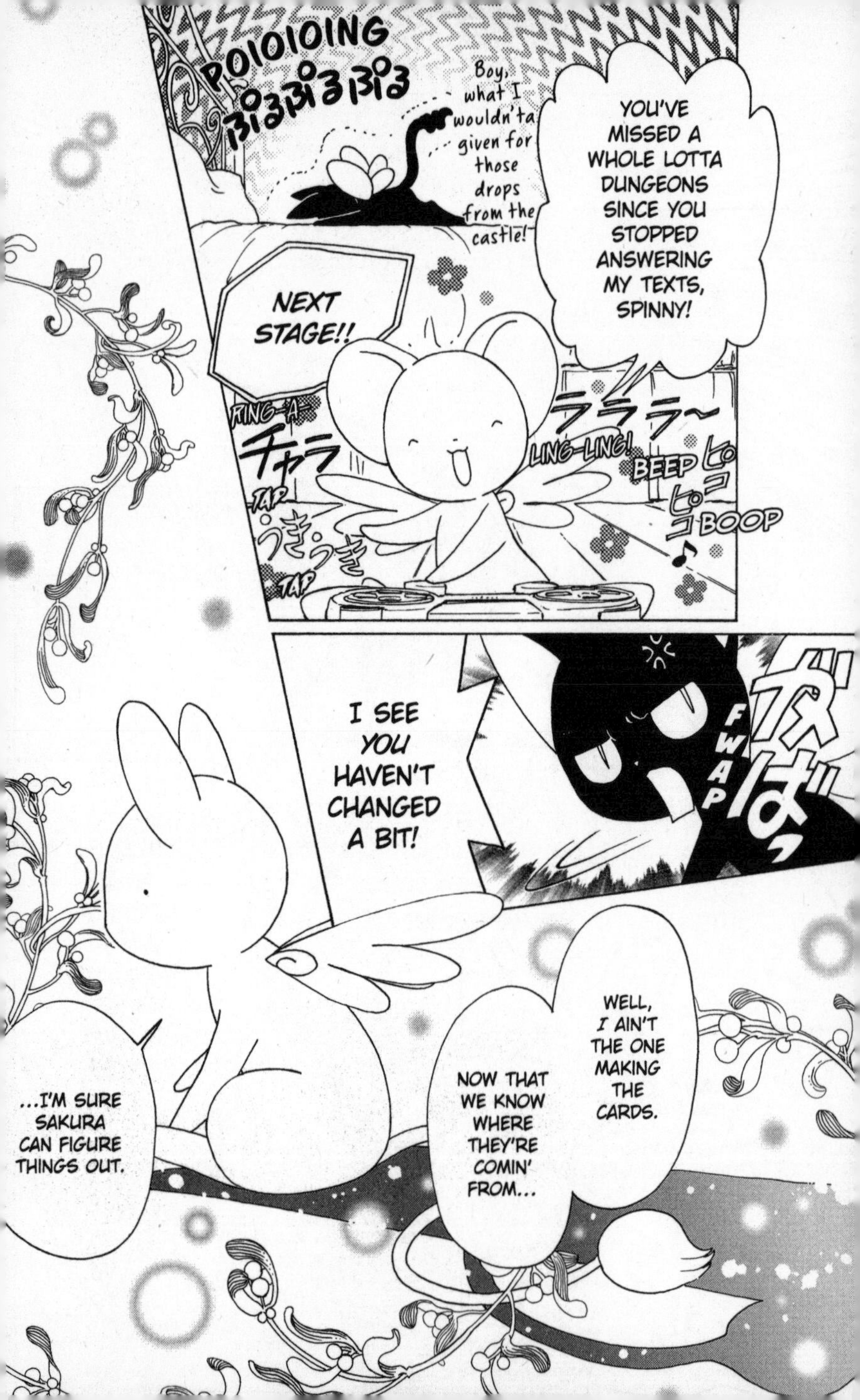
YOU'VE MISSED A WHOLE LOTTA DUNGEONS SINCE YOU STOPPED ANSWERING MY TEXTS, SPINNY!
Boy, what I wouldn'ta given for those drops from the castle!
POIOIOING ぷるぷるぷる
NEXT STAGE!!
ラララ～ LING-LING!
BEEP ピコピコ BOOP
RING-A チャラ
TAP うきうき TAP
FWAP ばっ
I SEE YOU HAVEN'T CHANGED A BIT!
WELL, I AIN'T THE ONE MAKING THE CARDS.
NOW THAT WE KNOW WHERE THEY'RE COMIN' FROM...
...I'M SURE SAKURA CAN FIGURE THINGS OUT.

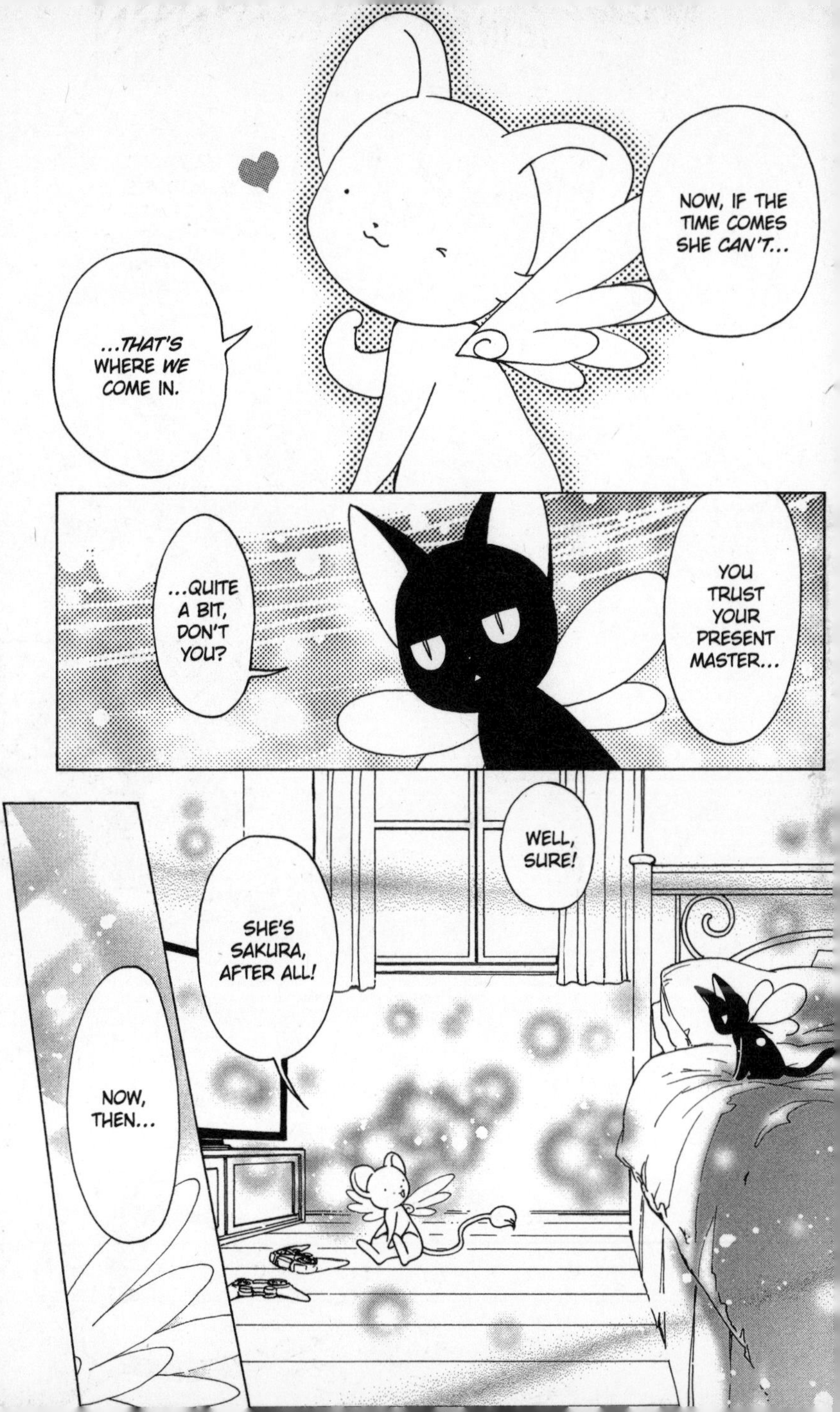
NOW, IF THE TIME COMES SHE CAN'T...
...THAT'S WHERE WE COME IN.
YOU TRUST YOUR PRESENT MASTER...
...QUITE A BIT, DON'T YOU?
WELL, SURE!
SHE'S SAKURA, AFTER ALL!
NOW, THEN...

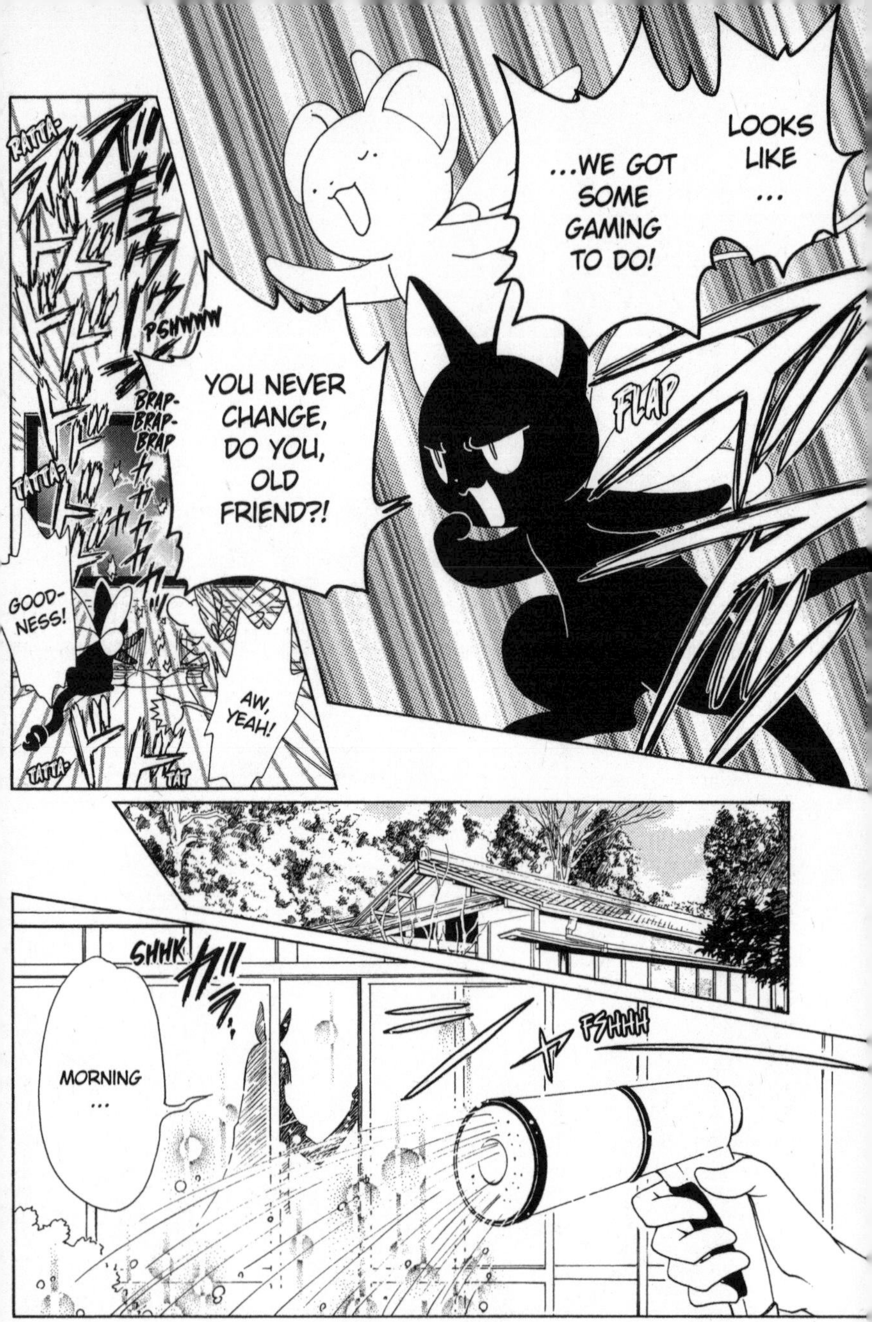
LOOKS LIKE ...
...WE GOT SOME GAMING TO DO!
FLAP
YOU NEVER CHANGE, DO YOU, OLD FRIEND?!
RATTA-
PSHWWW
BRAP-BRAP-BRAP
TATTA-
AW, YEAH!
GOODNESS!
TAT
TATTA-
FSHHH
SHHK
MORNING ...

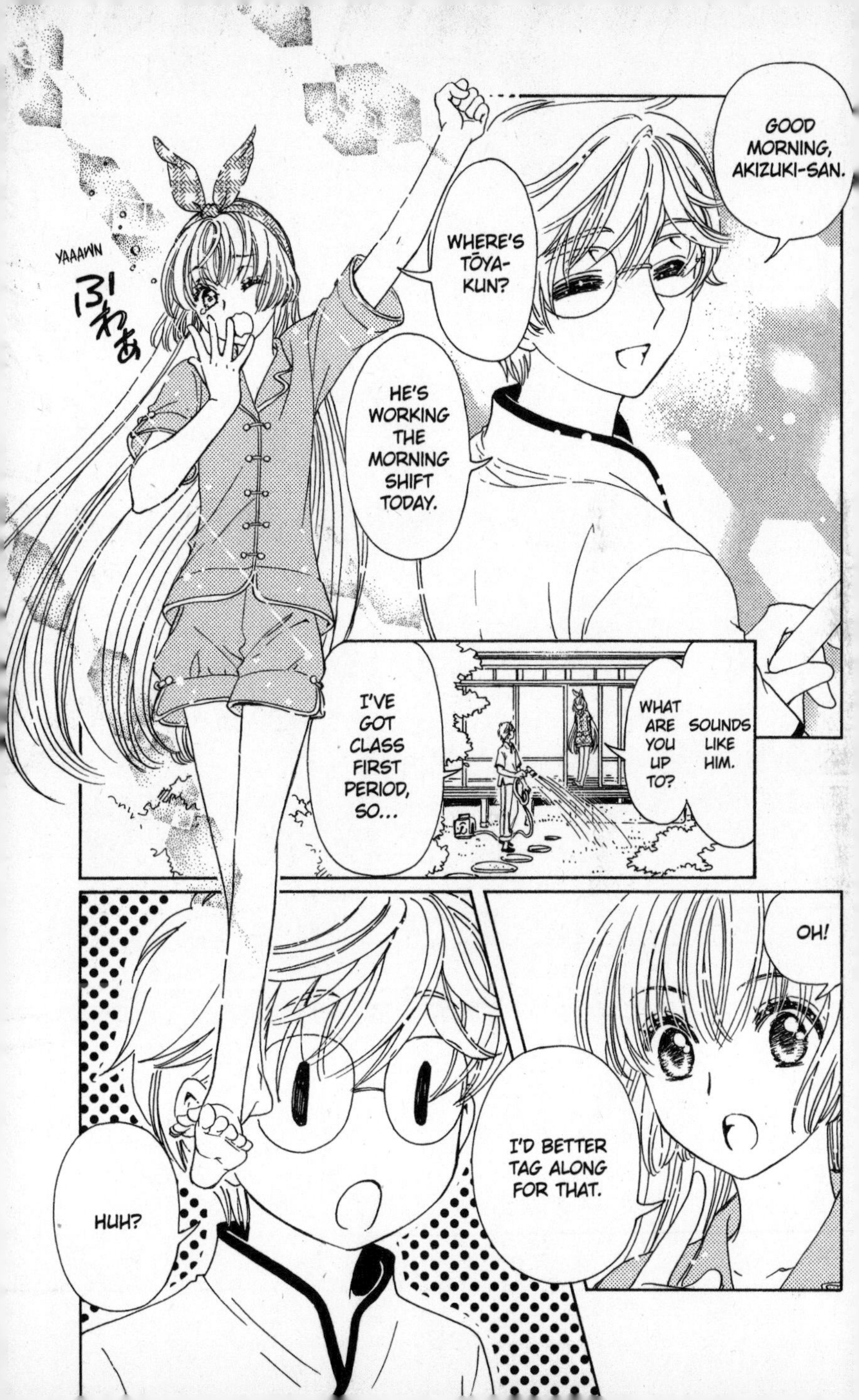
GOOD MORNING, AKIZUKI-SAN.
YAAAWN
ふわあ
WHERE'S TŌYA-KUN?
HE'S WORKING THE MORNING SHIFT TODAY.
SOUNDS LIKE HIM.
WHAT ARE YOU UP TO?
I'VE GOT CLASS FIRST PERIOD, SO...
OH!
I'D BETTER TAG ALONG FOR THAT.
HUH?

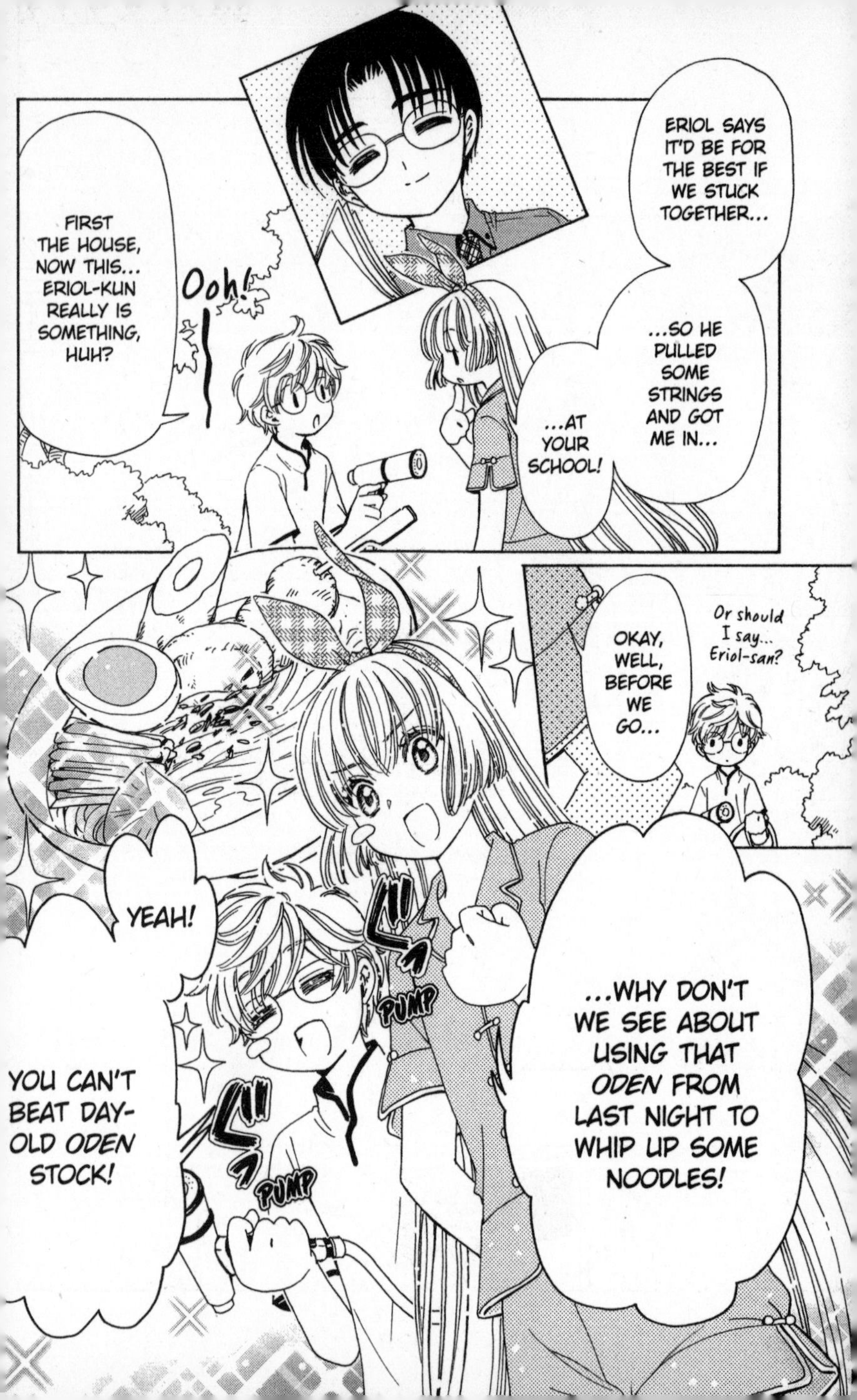
ERIOL SAYS IT'D BE FOR THE BEST IF WE STUCK TOGETHER...
...SO HE PULLED SOME STRINGS AND GOT ME IN...
...AT YOUR SCHOOL!
Ooh!
FIRST THE HOUSE, NOW THIS... ERIOL-KUN REALLY IS SOMETHING, HUH?
Or should I say... Eriol-san?
OKAY, WELL, BEFORE WE GO...
...WHY DON'T WE SEE ABOUT USING THAT *ODEN* FROM LAST NIGHT TO WHIP UP SOME NOODLES!
PUMP
PUMP
YEAH!
YOU CAN'T BEAT DAY-OLD *ODEN* STOCK!

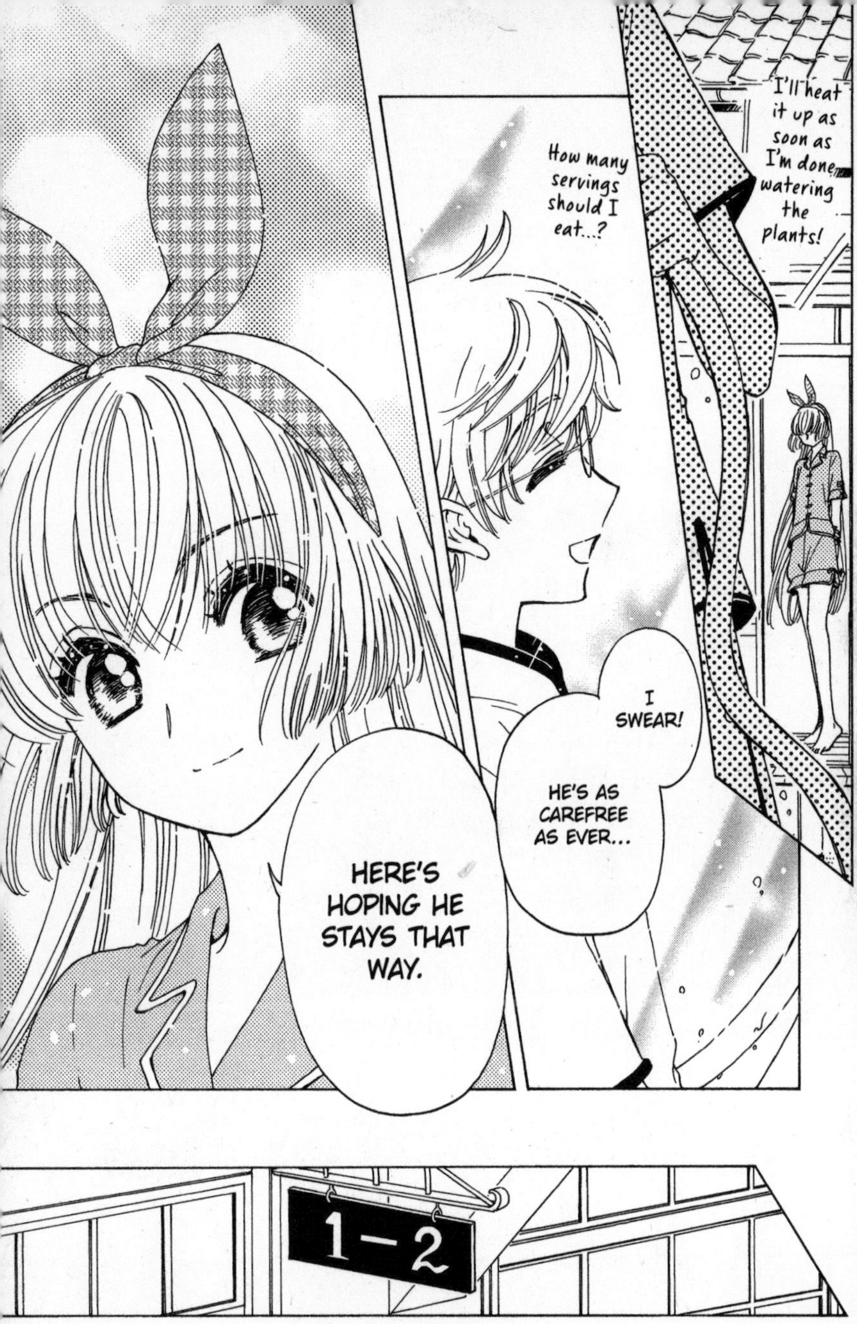
I'll heat it up as soon as I'm done watering the plants!
How many servings should I eat...?
I SWEAR!
HE'S AS CAREFREE AS EVER...
HERE'S HOPING HE STAYS THAT WAY.
1-2

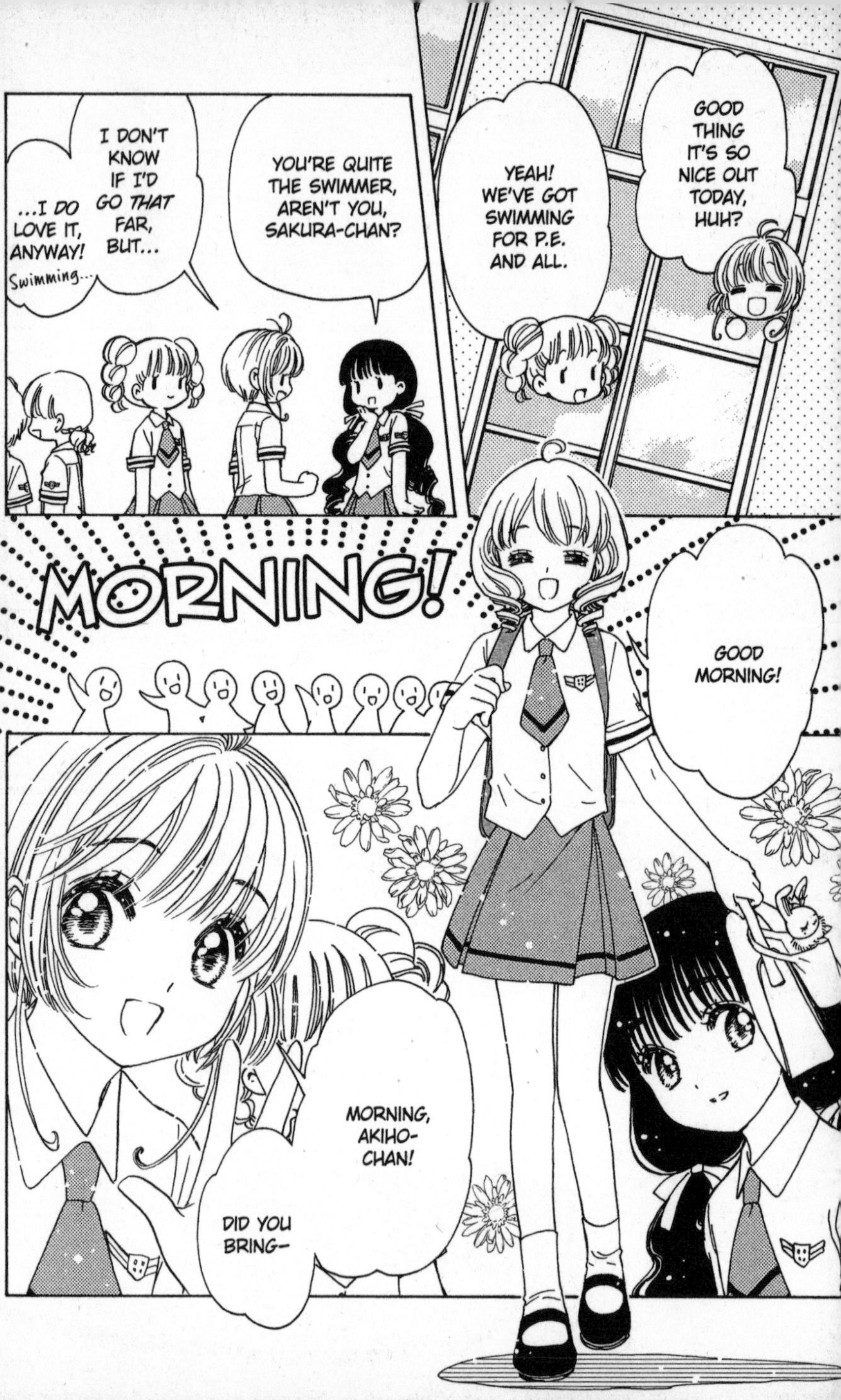
GOOD THING IT'S SO NICE OUT TODAY, HUH?
YEAH! WE'VE GOT SWIMMING FOR P.E. AND ALL.
YOU'RE QUITE THE SWIMMER, AREN'T YOU, SAKURA-CHAN?
I DON'T KNOW IF I'D GO *THAT* FAR, BUT...
...I DO LOVE IT, ANYWAY!
Swimming...
GOOD MORNING!
MORNING!
MORNING, AKIHO-CHAN!
DID YOU BRING-

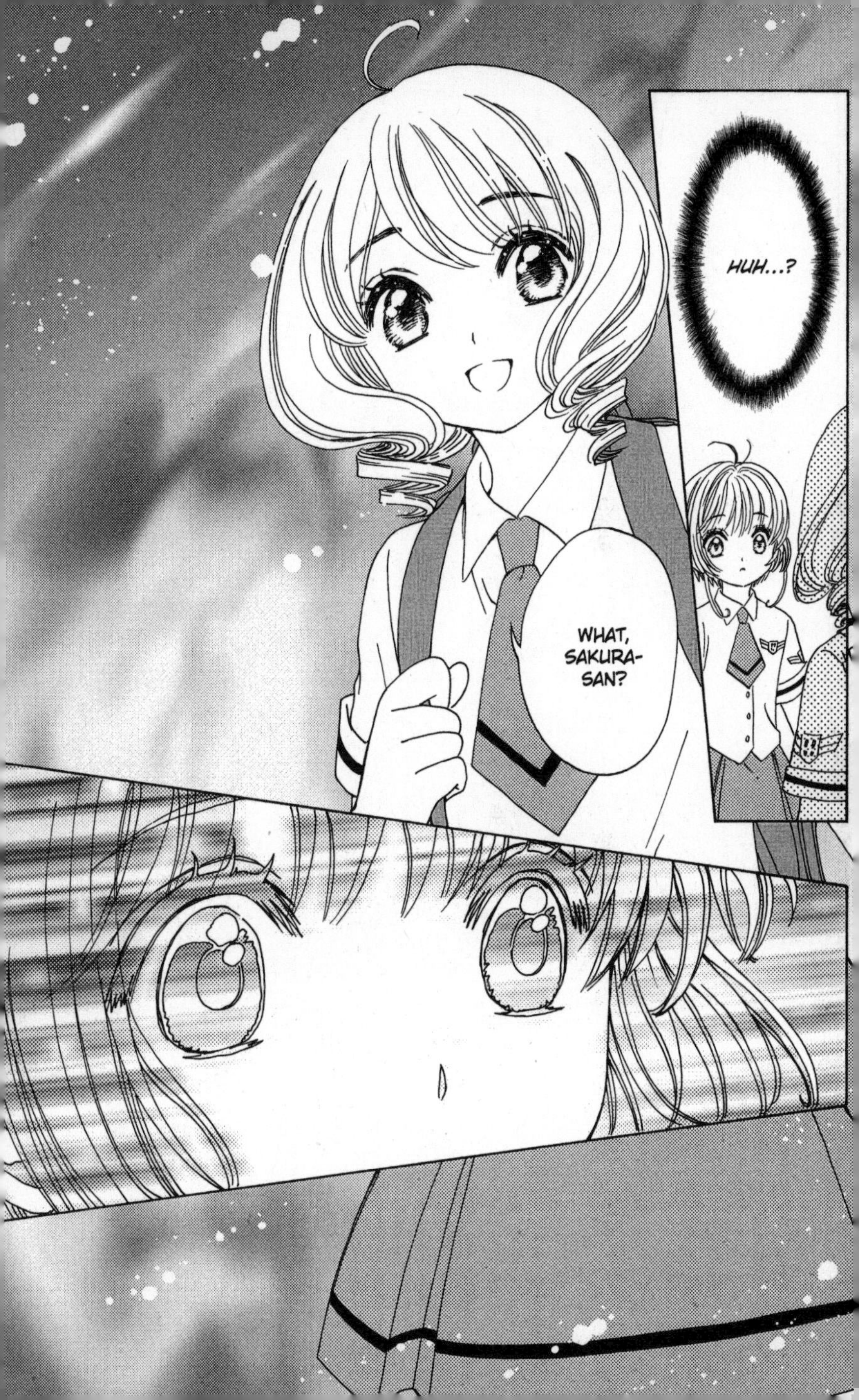
HUH...?
WHAT, SAKURA-SAN?

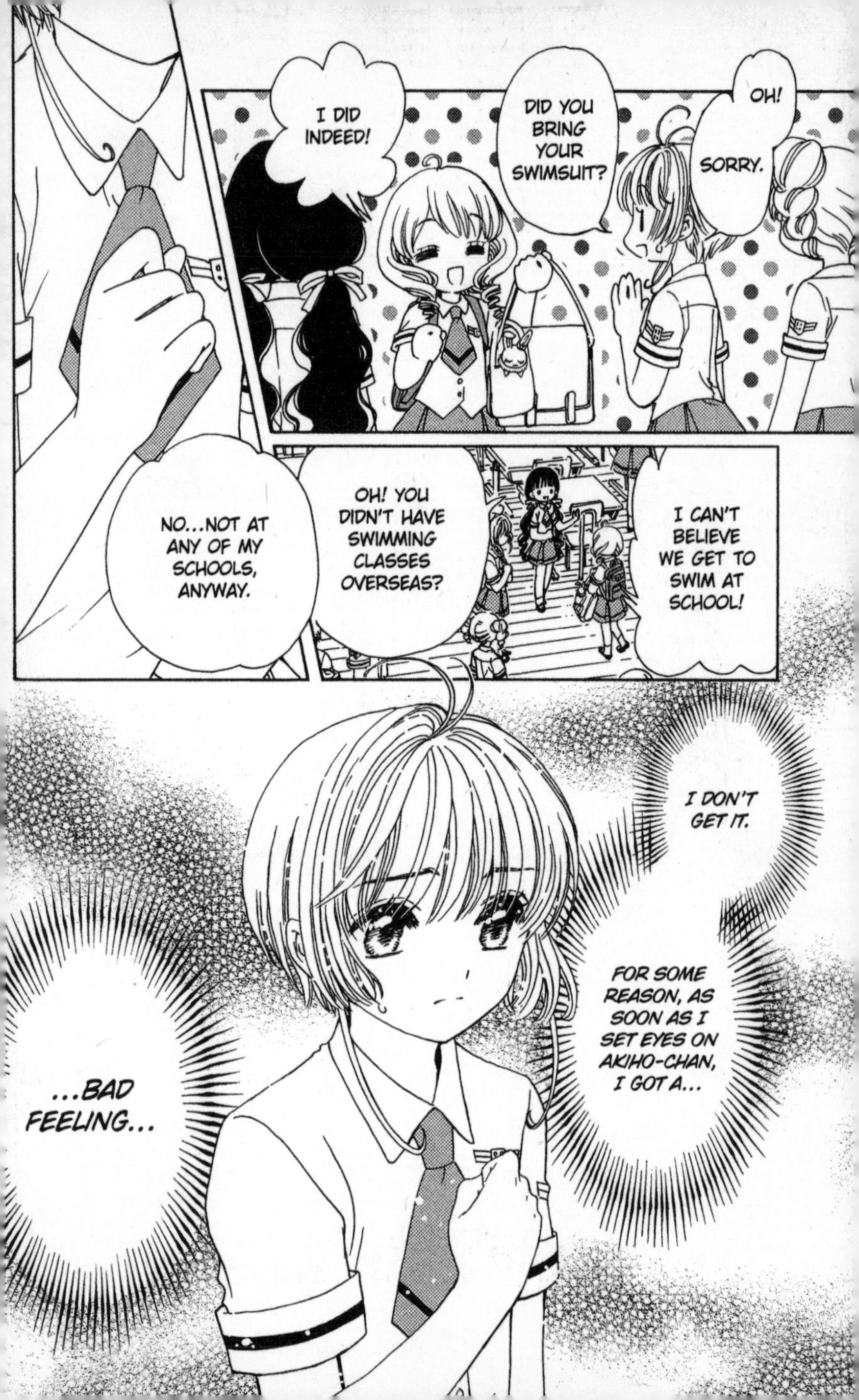
OH! SORRY.
DID YOU BRING YOUR SWIMSUIT?
I DID INDEED!
I CAN'T BELIEVE WE GET TO SWIM AT SCHOOL!
OH! YOU DIDN'T HAVE SWIMMING CLASSES OVERSEAS?
NO...NOT AT ANY OF MY SCHOOLS, ANYWAY.
I DON'T GET IT.
FOR SOME REASON, AS SOON AS I SET EYES ON AKIHO-CHAN, I GOT A...
...BAD FEELING...

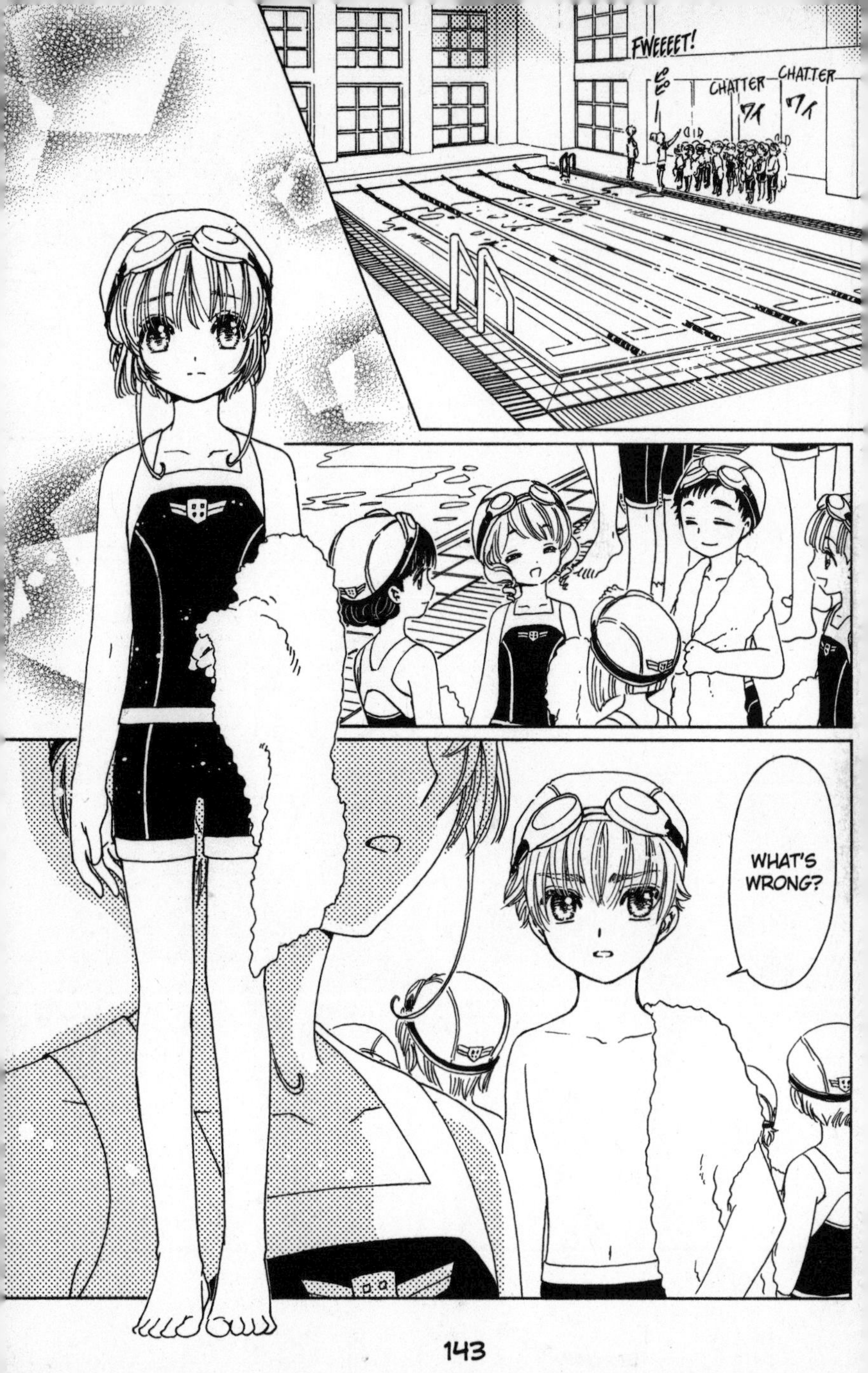
FWEEEET!
ピピー
CHATTER CHATTER
ワイ ワイ
WHAT'S WRONG?

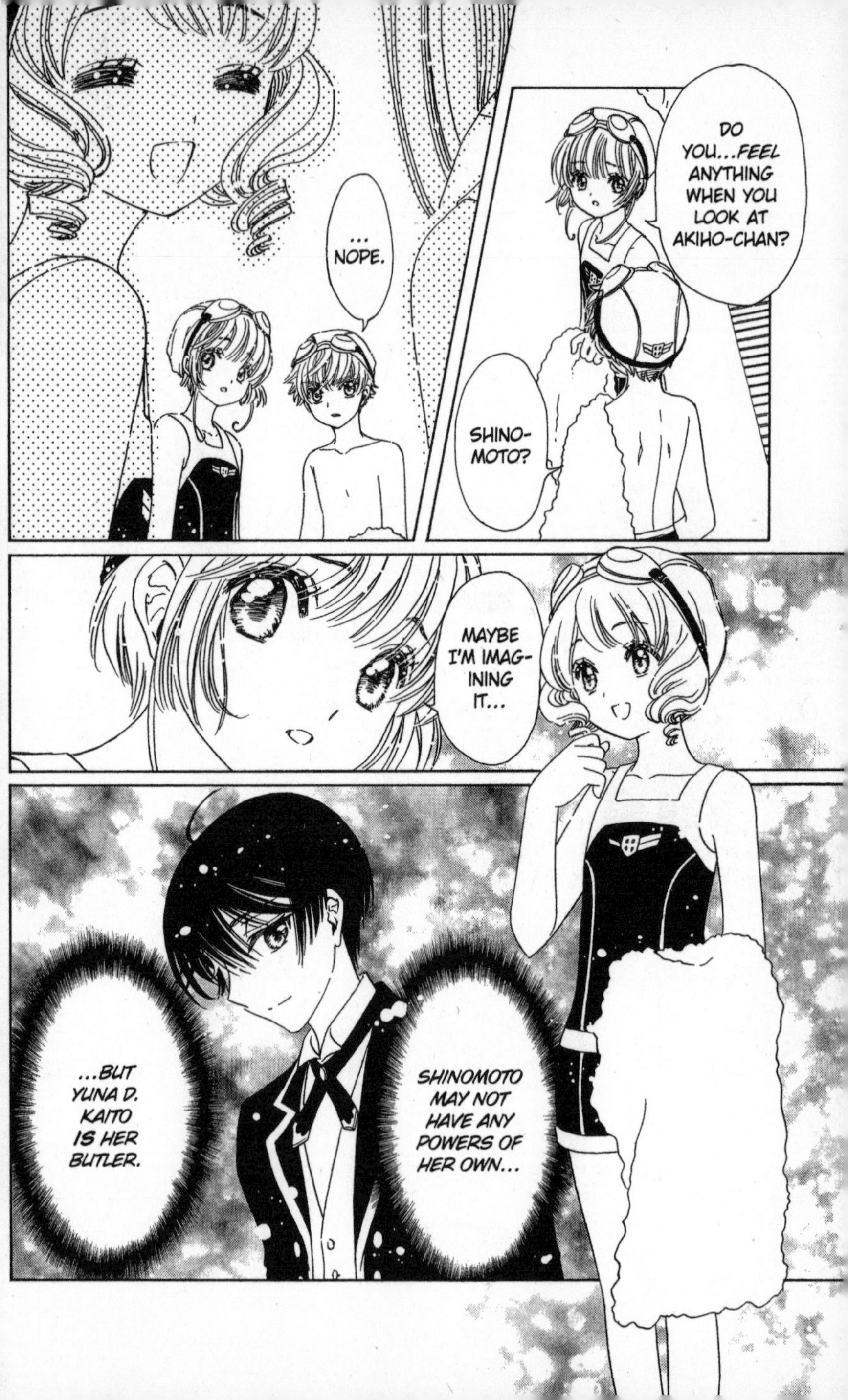
DO YOU...FEEL ANYTHING WHEN YOU LOOK AT AKIHO-CHAN?
SHINO-MOTO?
...NOPE.
MAYBE I'M IMAG-INING IT...
SHINOMOTO MAY NOT HAVE ANY POWERS OF HER OWN...
...BUT YUNA D. KAITO IS HER BUTLER.

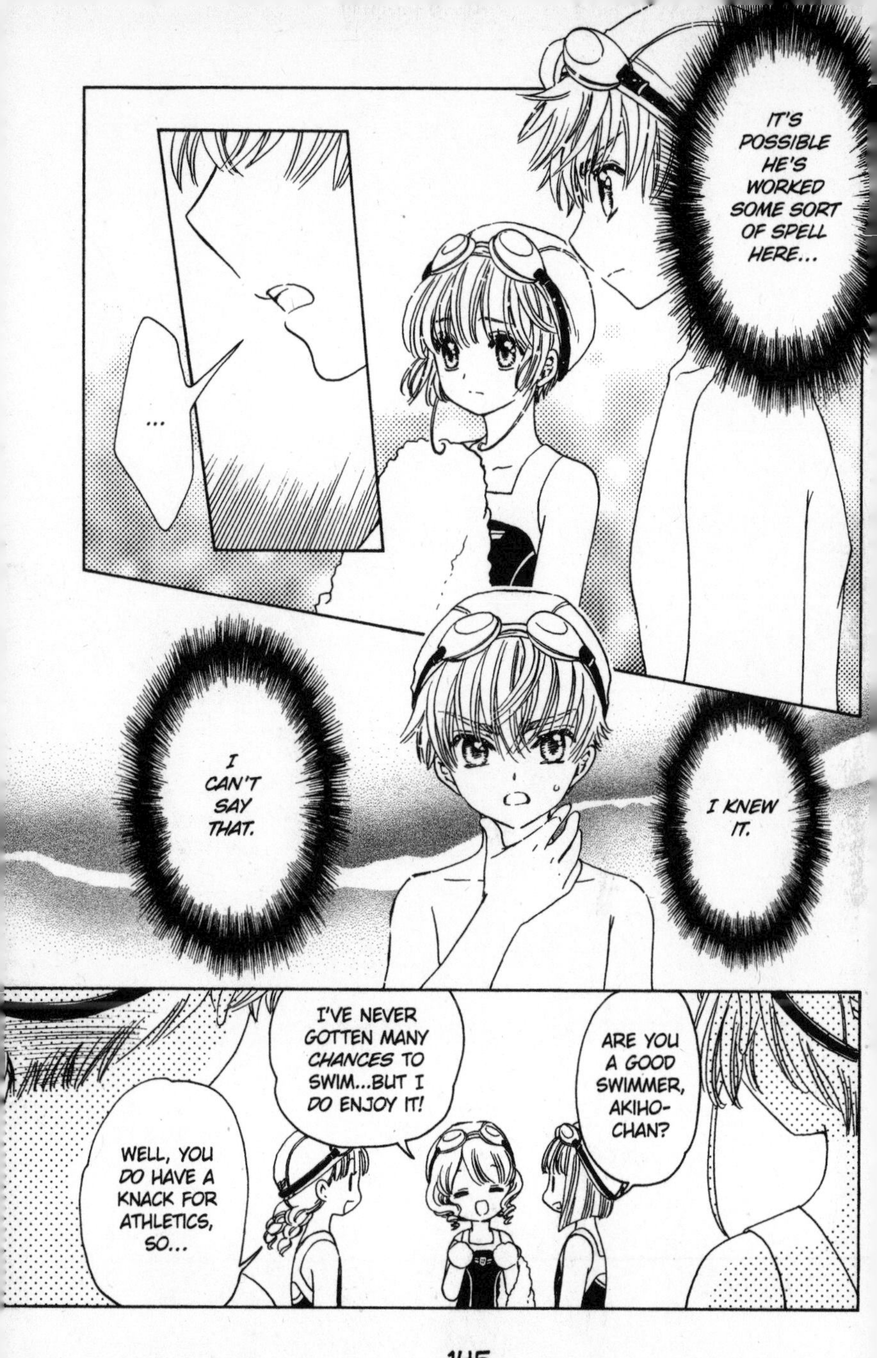
IT'S POSSIBLE HE'S WORKED SOME SORT OF SPELL HERE...
...
I KNEW IT.
I CAN'T SAY THAT.
ARE YOU A GOOD SWIMMER, AKIHO-CHAN?
I'VE NEVER GOTTEN MANY CHANCES TO SWIM...BUT I DO ENJOY IT!
WELL, YOU DO HAVE A KNACK FOR ATHLETICS, SO...

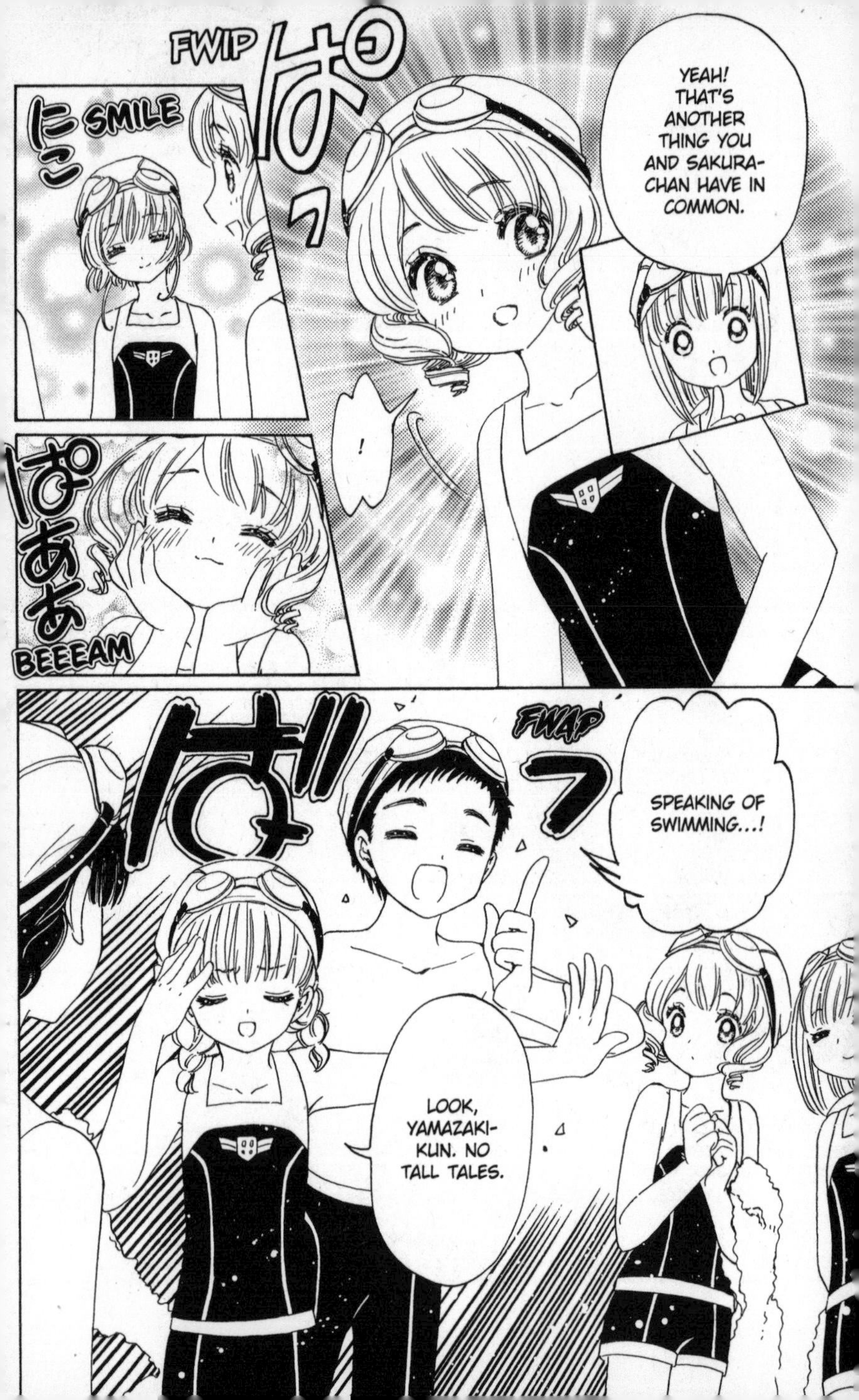
YEAH! THAT'S ANOTHER THING YOU AND SAKURA-CHAN HAVE IN COMMON.
!
ぱっ
FWIP
にこ
SMILE
ぱあぁ
BEEEAM
ばっ
FWAP
SPEAKING OF SWIMMING...!
LOOK, YAMAZAKI-KUN. NO TALL TALES.

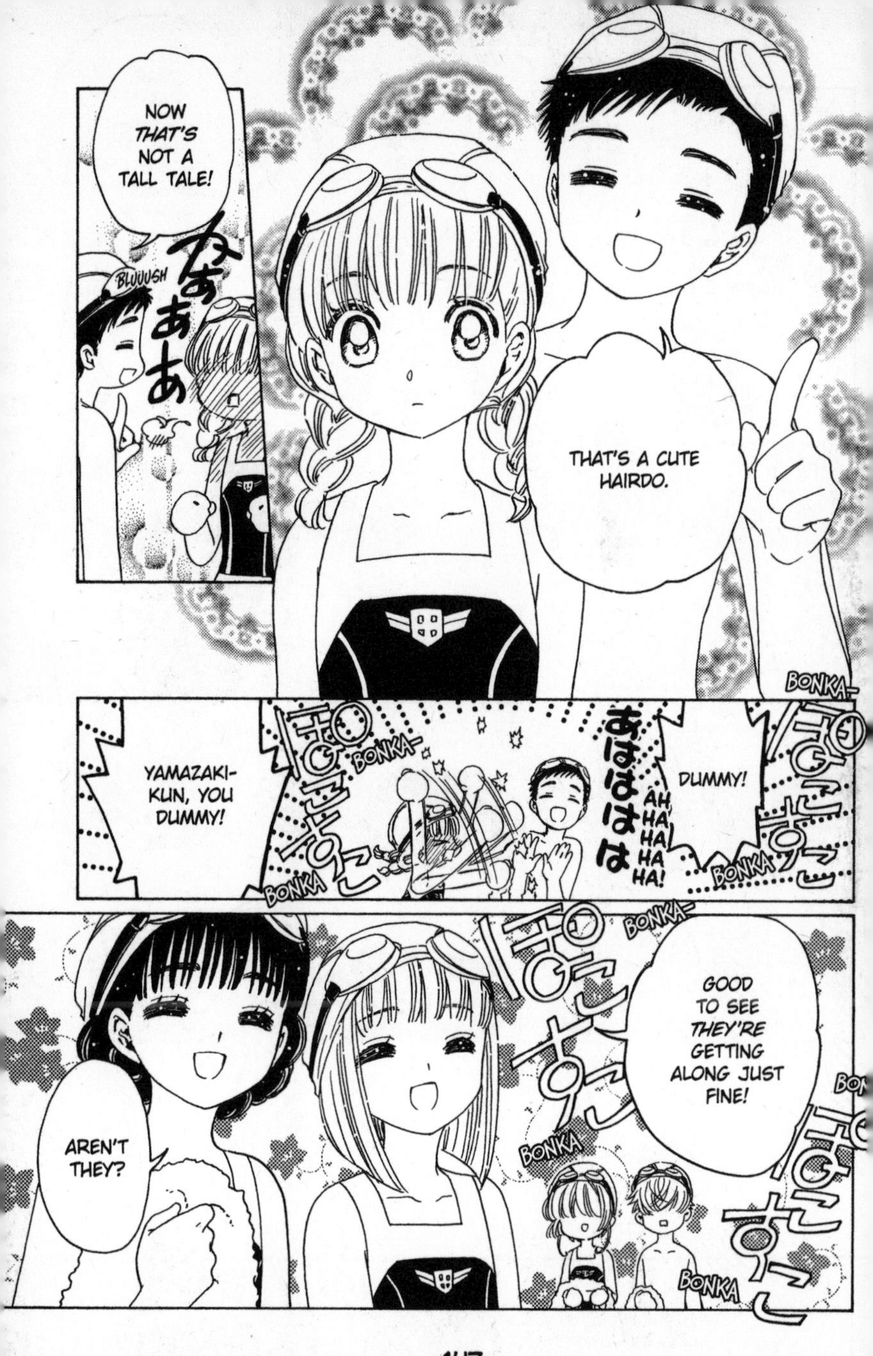

THAT'S A CUTE HAIRDO.
NOW *THAT'S* NOT A TALL TALE!
BLUUUSH
なあああ
BONKA-
DUMMY!
BONKA
あははは
AH HA HA HA HA!
BONKA-
BONKA
YAMAZAKI-KUN, YOU DUMMY!
BONKA-
GOOD TO SEE *THEY'RE* GETTING ALONG JUST FINE!
BONKA
BONKA
AREN'T THEY?

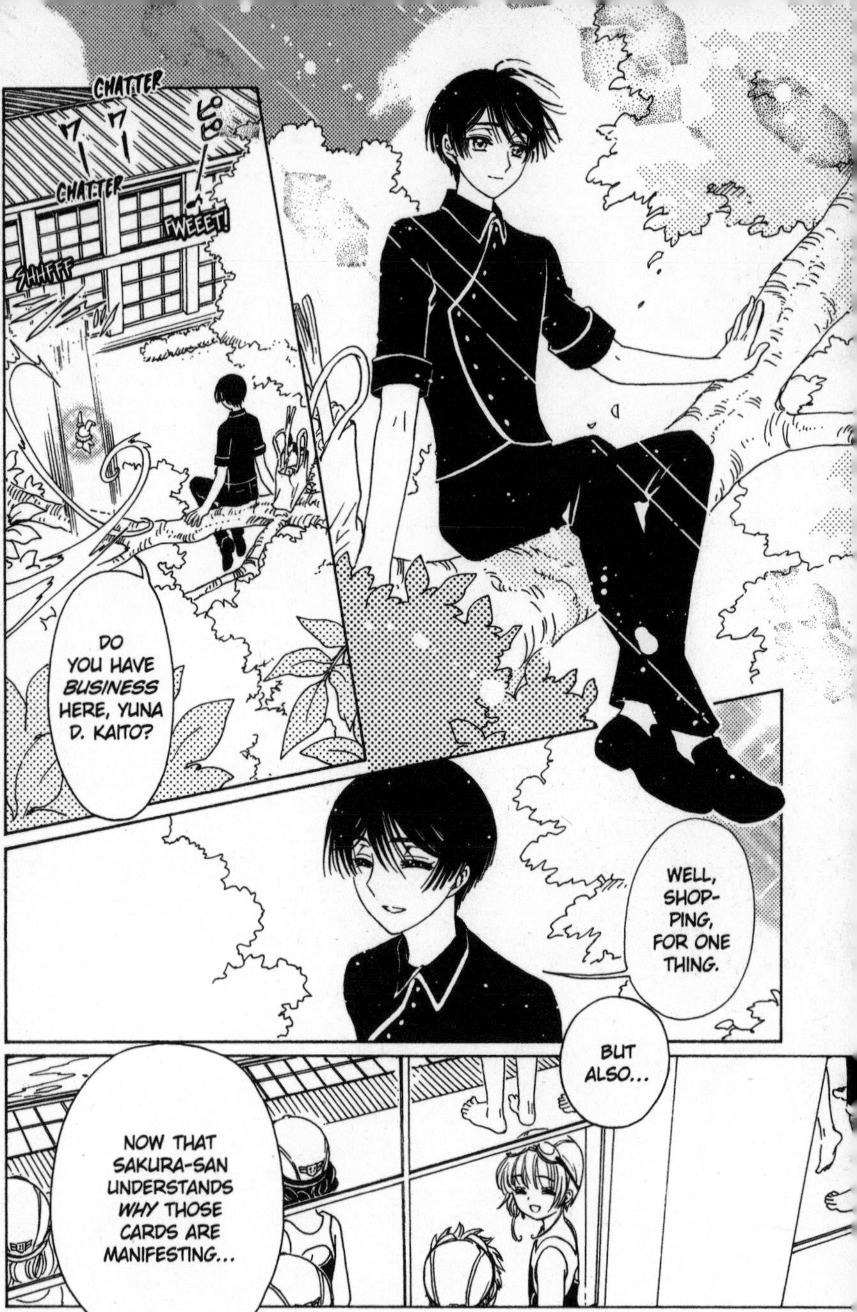

ピピー！
FWEEET!
ワー
CHATTER
ワー
CHATTER
SHHFFF
DO YOU HAVE *BUSINESS* HERE, YUNA D. KAITO?
WELL, SHOP-PING, FOR ONE THING.
BUT ALSO...
NOW THAT SAKURA-SAN UNDERSTANDS *WHY* THOSE CARDS ARE MANIFESTING...

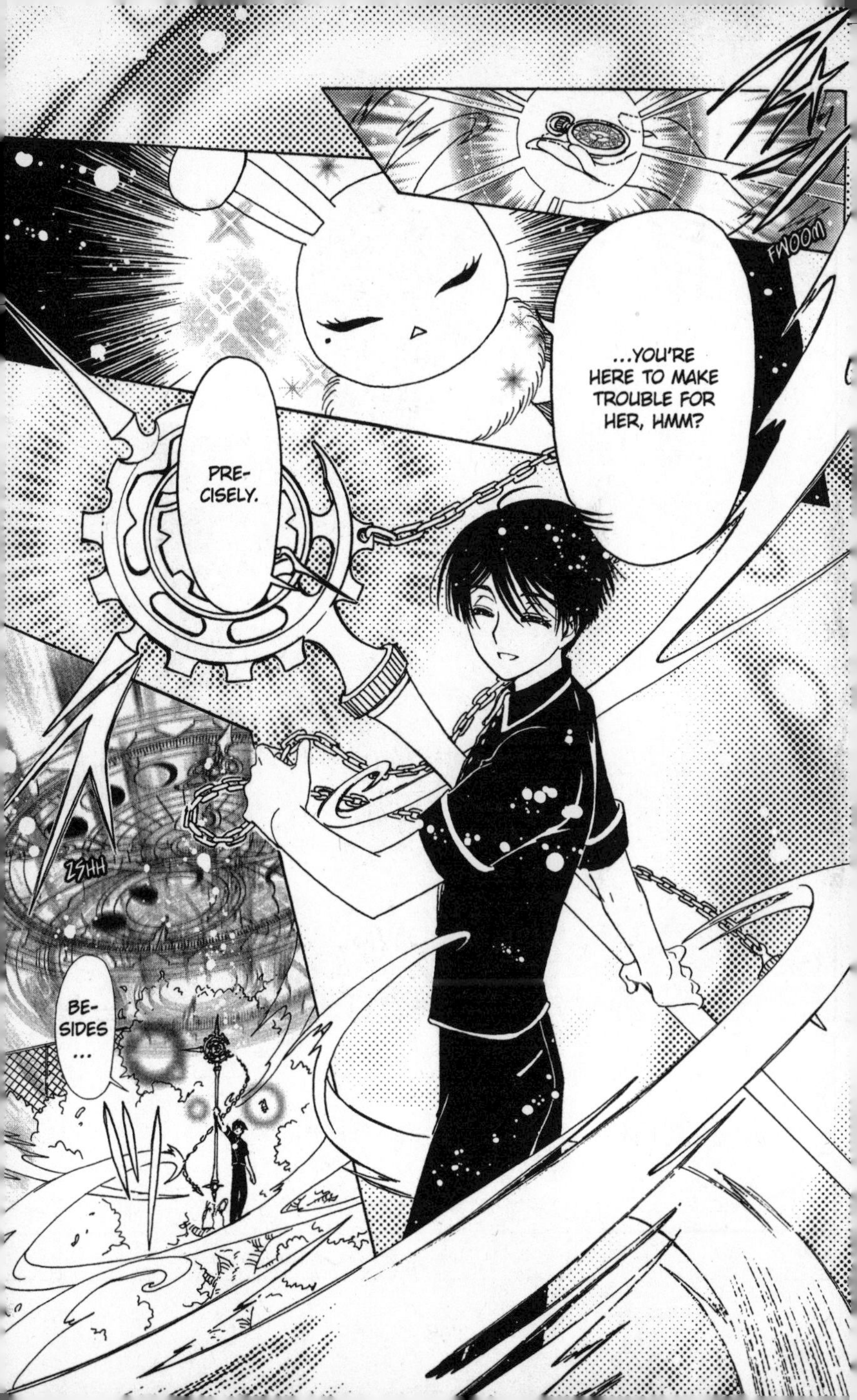
FWOOM
...YOU'RE HERE TO MAKE TROUBLE FOR HER, HMM?
PRE-CISELY.
ZSHH
BE-SIDES ...

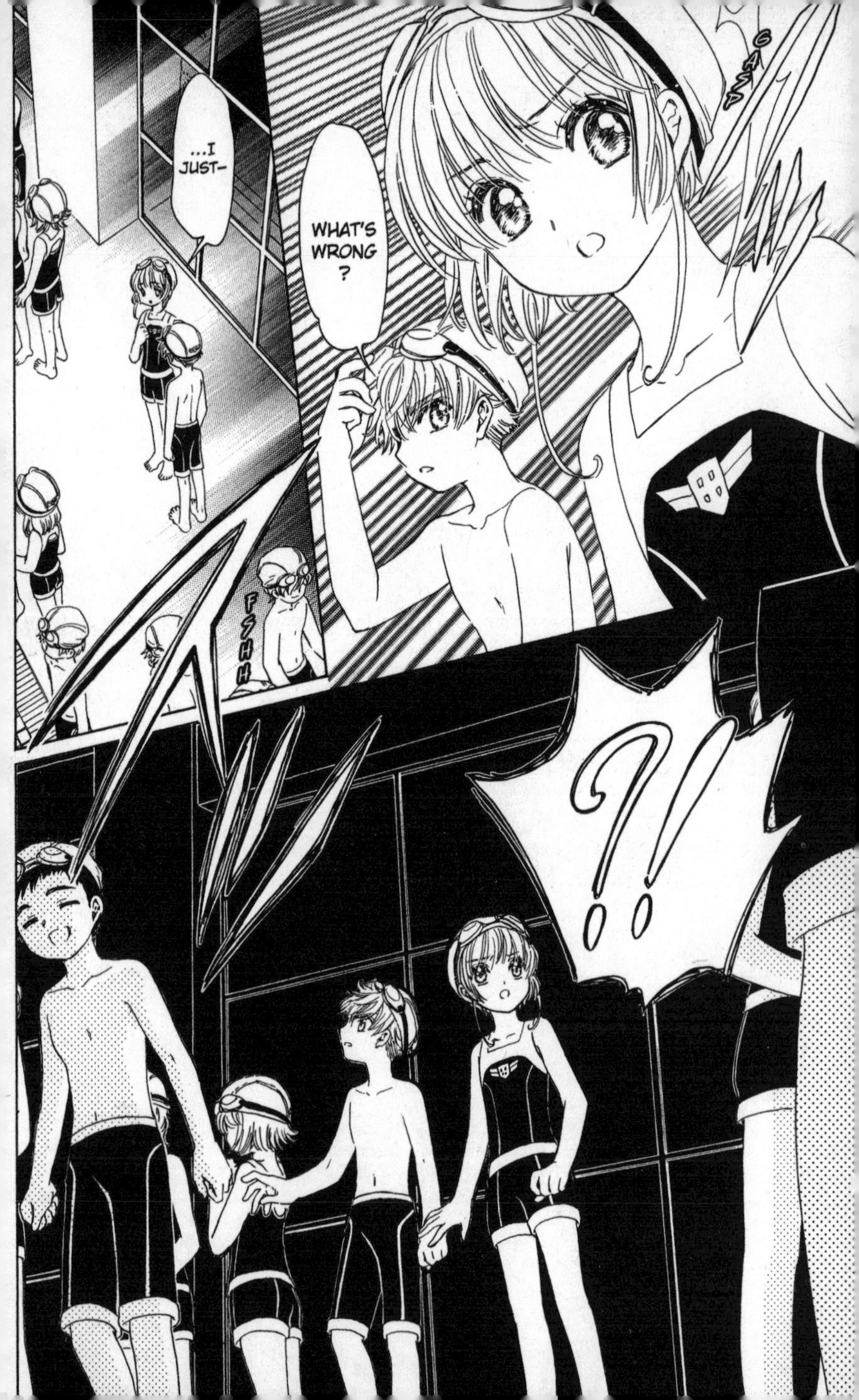
GASP
WHAT'S WRONG ?
...I JUST-
FSHH
?!!

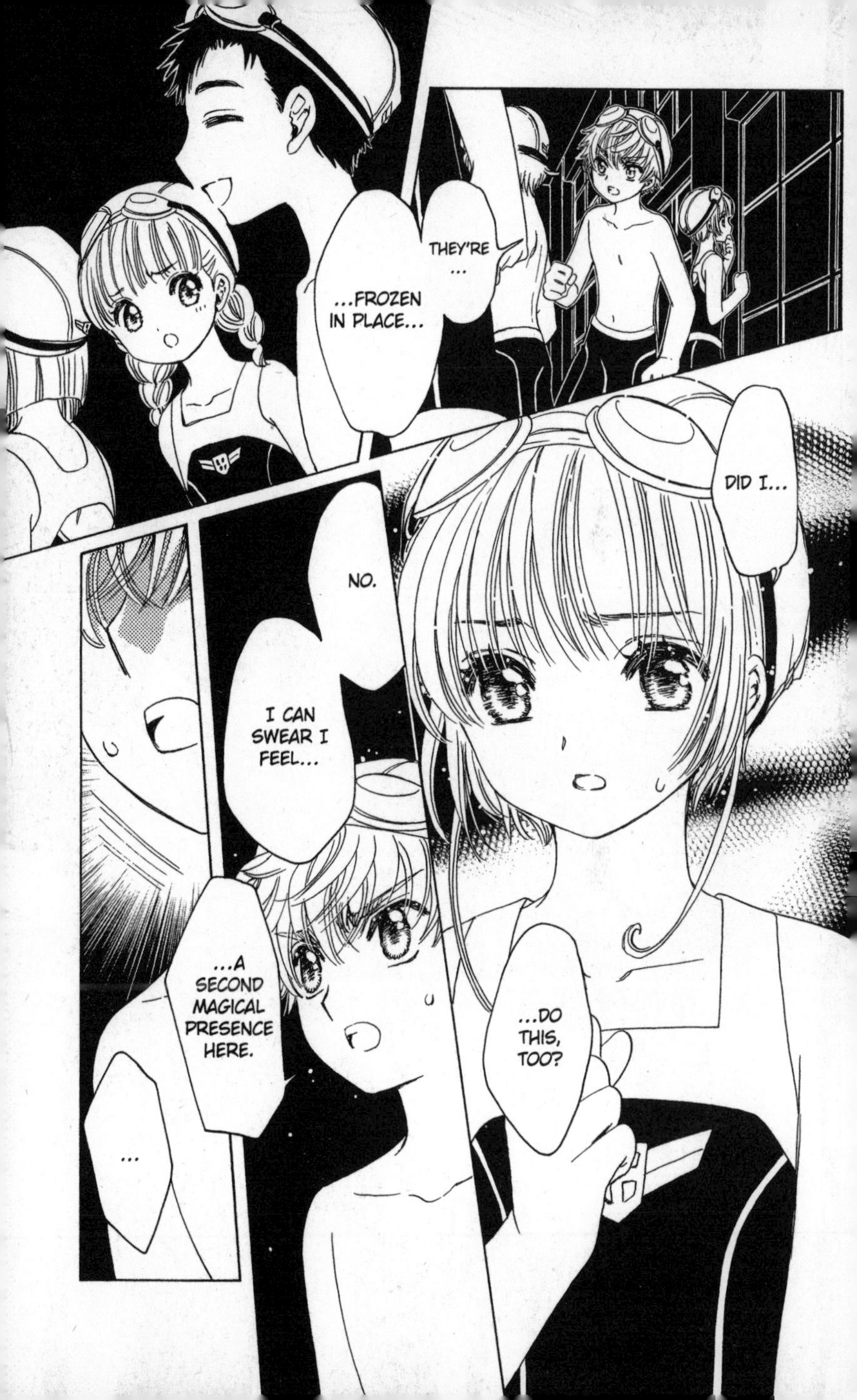
THEY'RE ...
...FROZEN IN PLACE...
DID I...
...DO THIS, TOO?
NO.
I CAN SWEAR I FEEL...
...A SECOND MAGICAL PRESENCE HERE.
...

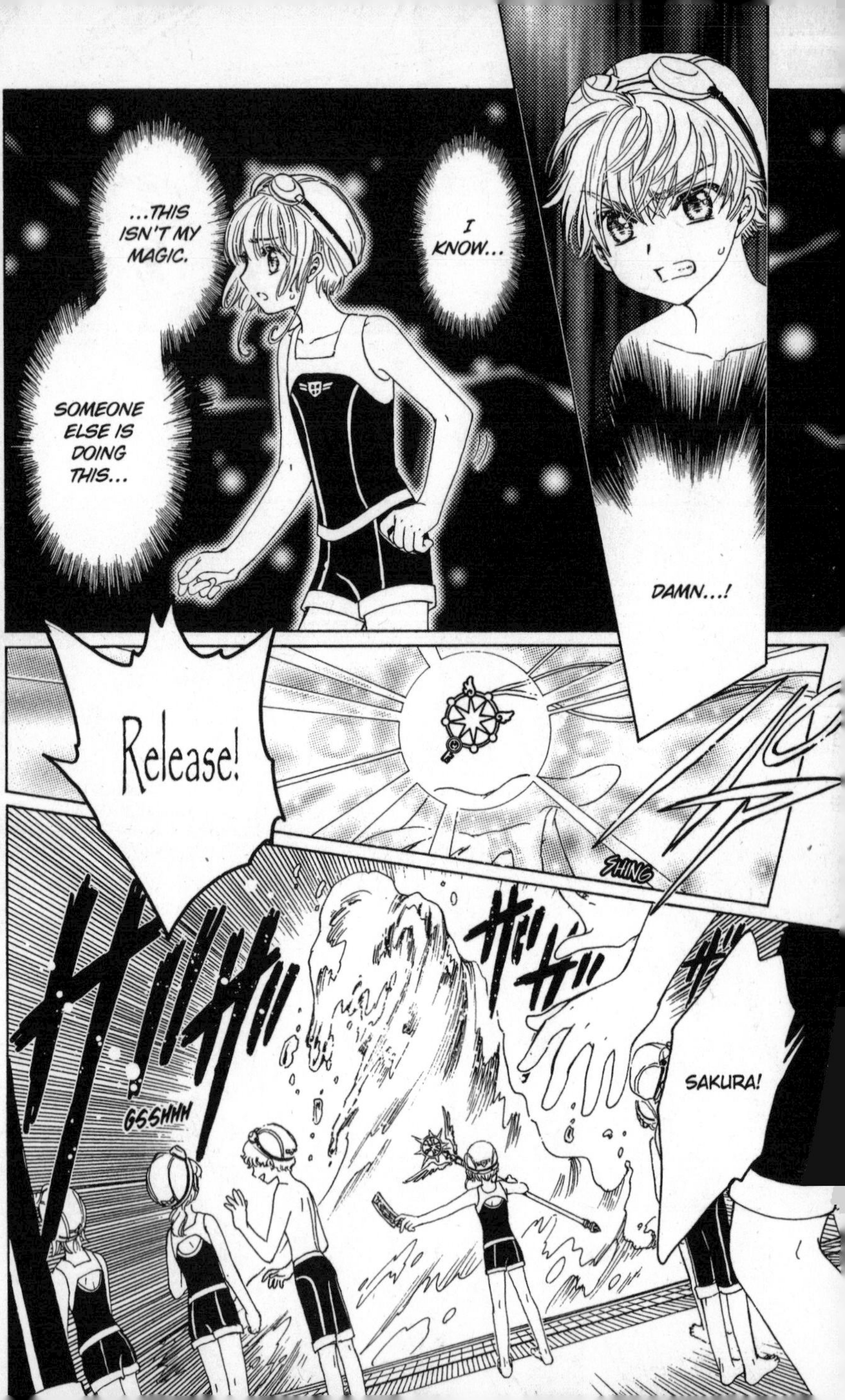
...THIS ISN'T MY MAGIC.
I KNOW...
SOMEONE ELSE IS DOING THIS...
DAMN...!
Release!
SHING
SAKURA!
GSSHHH

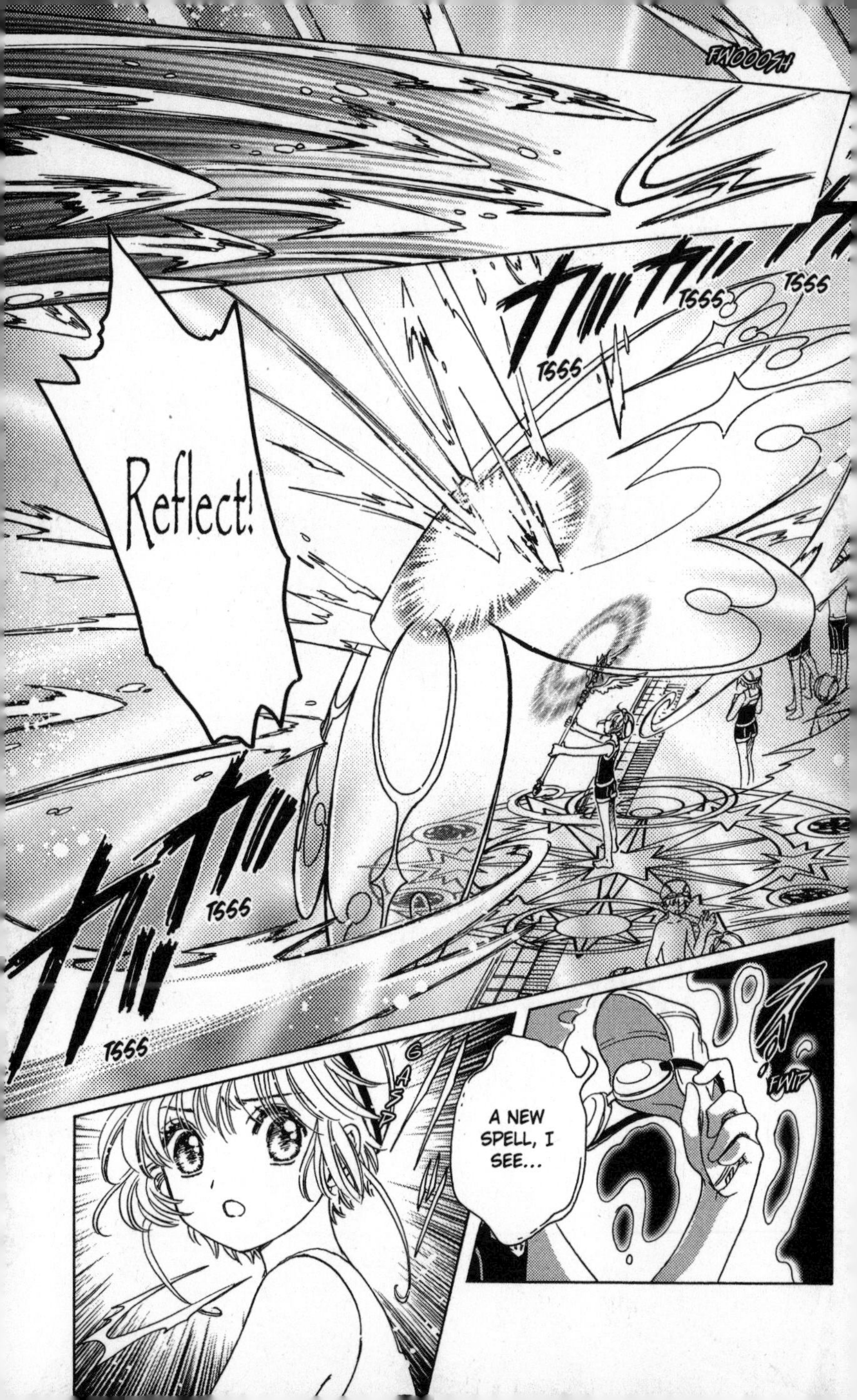
FWOOOSH
TSSS
TSSS
TSSS
Reflect!
TSSS
TSSS
FWIP
A NEW SPELL, I SEE...
GASA

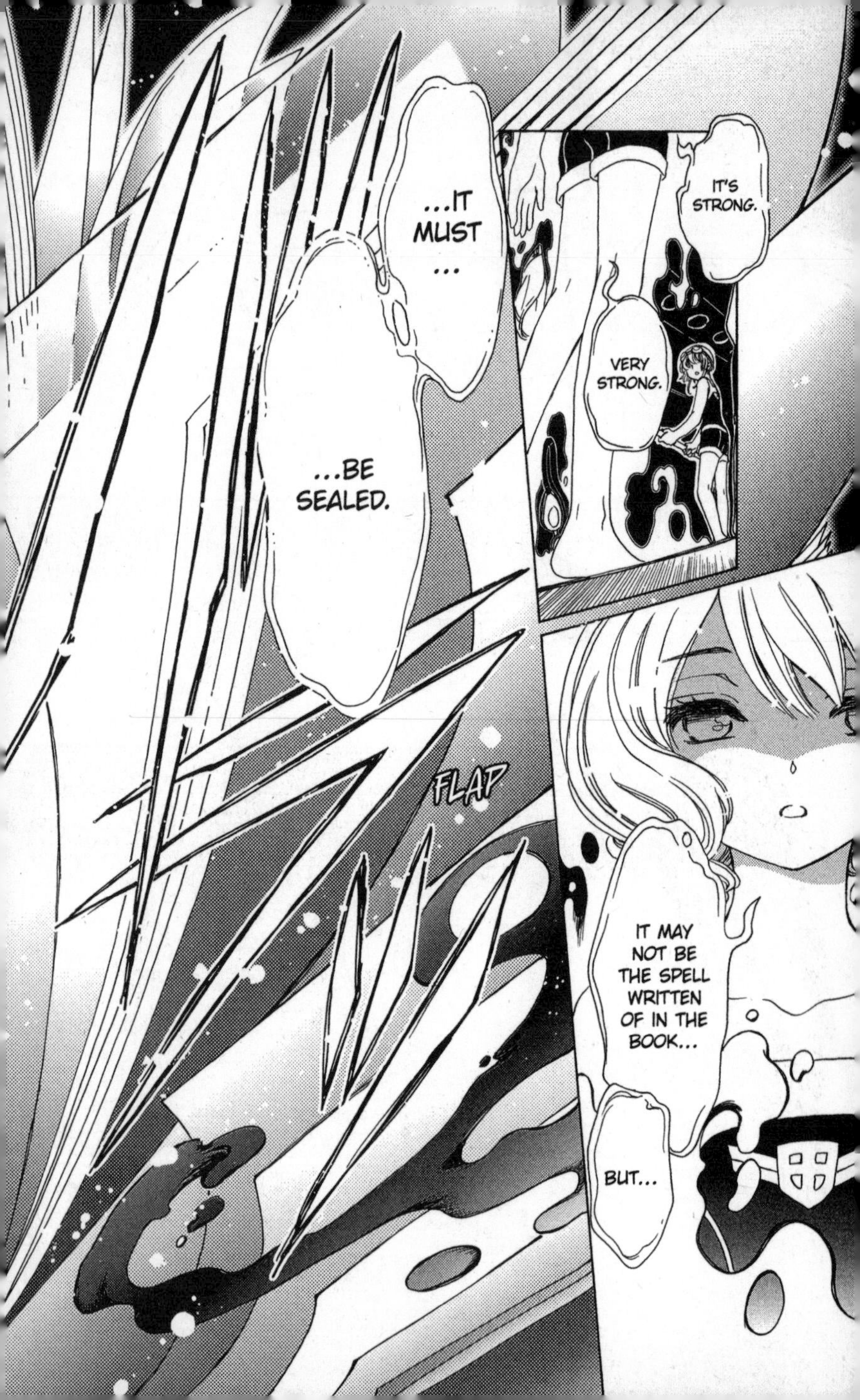
IT'S STRONG.
VERY STRONG.
IT MAY NOT BE THE SPELL WRITTEN OF IN THE BOOK...
BUT...
...IT MUST ...
...BE SEALED.
FLAP

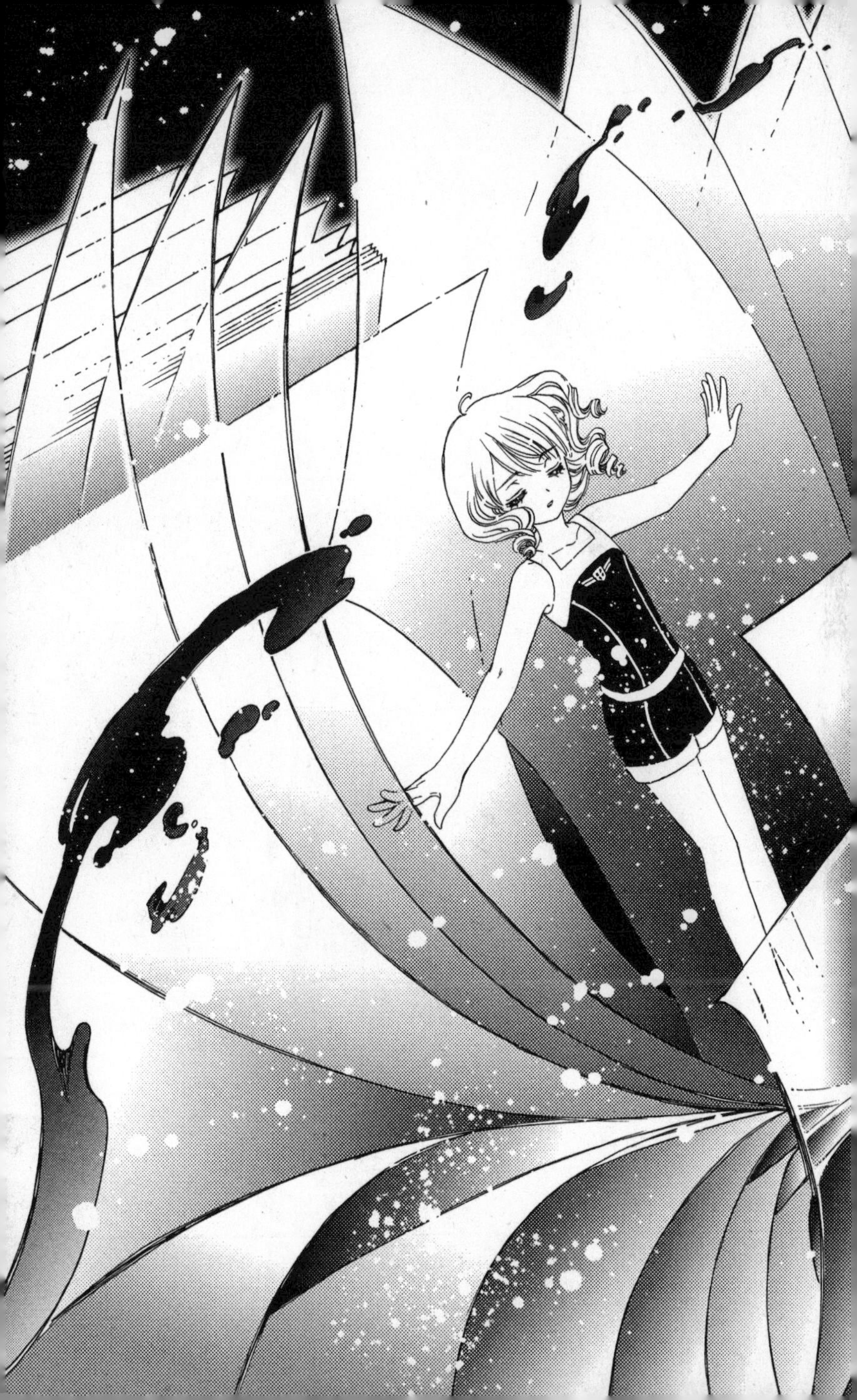

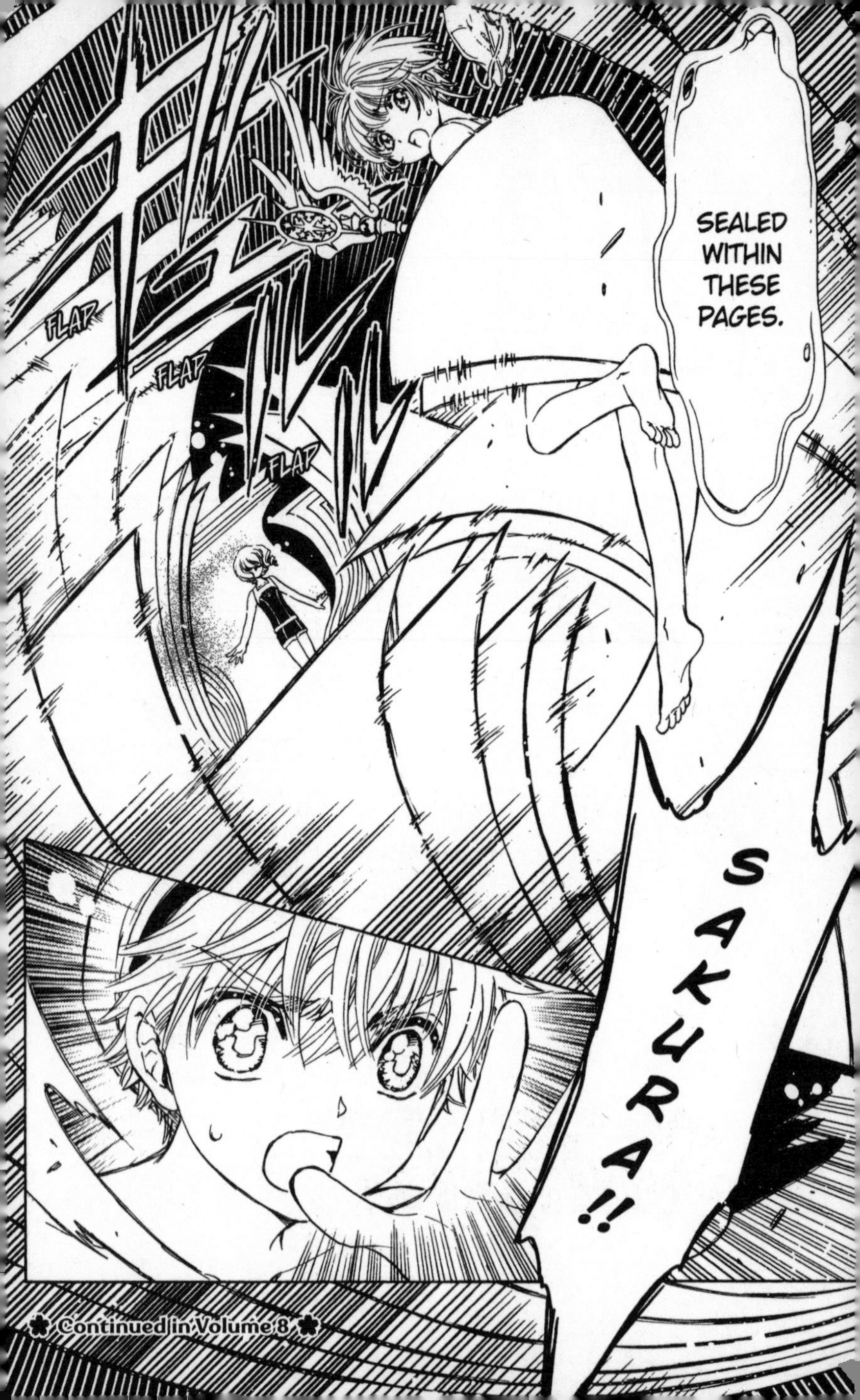
SEALED WITHIN THESE PAGES.
FLAP
FLAP
FLAP
SAKURA!!
Continued in Volume 8

Cardcaptor Sakura

CLEAR CARD

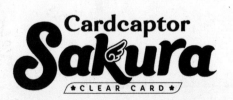

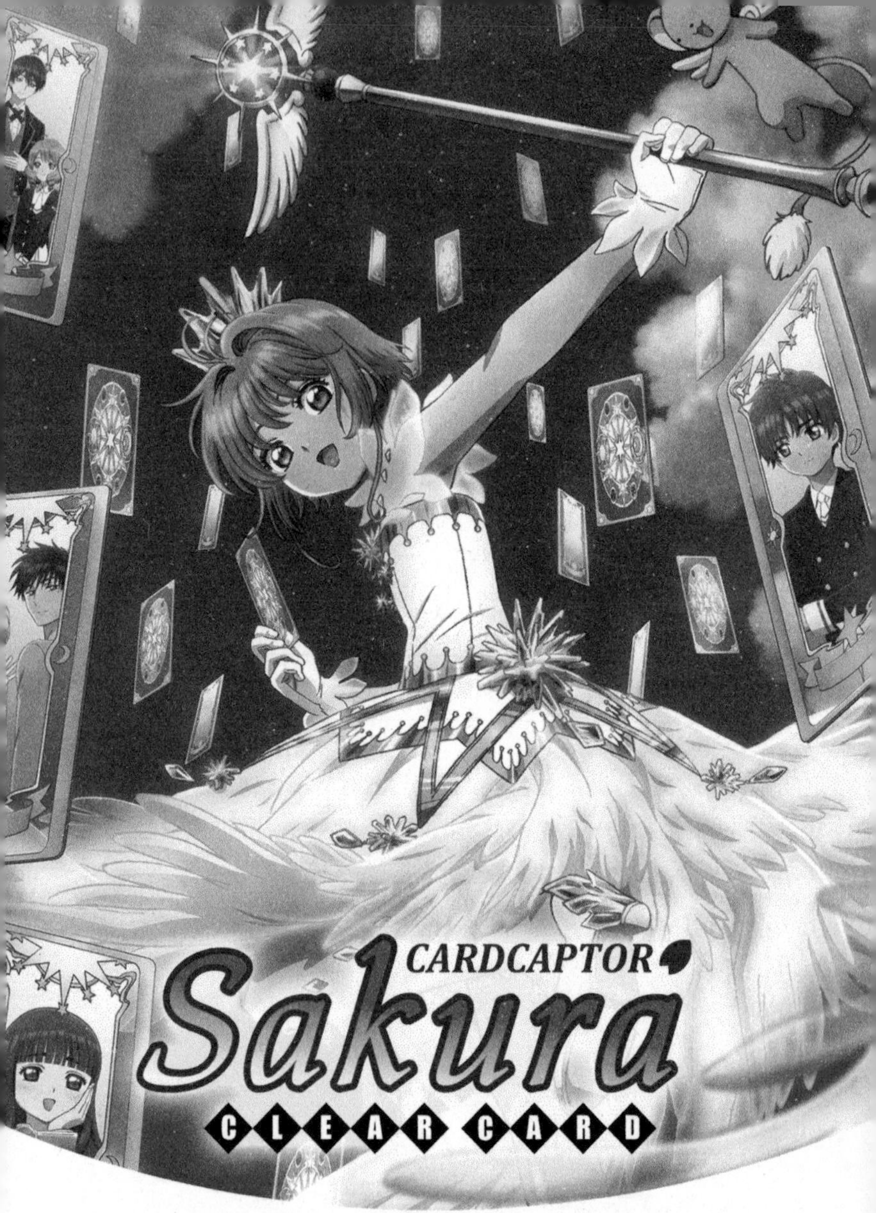
CARDCAPTOR
Sakura
CLEAR CARD

Cardcaptor Sakura: Clear Card volume 7 is a work of fiction. Names, characters, places, and incidents are the products of the author's imagination or are used fictitiously. Any resemblance to actual events, locales, or persons, living or dead, is entirely coincidental.

A Kodansha Comics Trade Paperback Original
Cardcaptor Sakura: Clear Card volume 7
copyright © 2019 CLAMP · Shigatsu Tsuitachi Co., Ltd. / Kodansha Ltd.
English translation copyright © 2020 CLAMP · Shigatsu Tsuitachi Co., Ltd. / Kodansha Ltd.

Published in the United States by Kodansha Comics, an imprint of
Kodansha USA Publishing, LLC, New York.

Publication rights for this English edition arranged through Kodansha Ltd.,
Tokyo.

First published in Japan in 2019 by Kodansha Ltd., Tokyo, as
Kaadokyaputaa Sakura Kuriakaado Hen volume 7.

ISBN 978-1-63236-832-4

Printed in the United States of America.

www.kodanshacomics.com

9 8 7 6 5 4 3 2 1
Translation: Erin Procter
Lettering: Erika Terriquez
Editing: Tiff Ferentini and Alexandra Swanson
Kodansha Comics edition cover design: Phil Balsman

Publisher: Kiichiro Sugawara
Vice president of marketing & publicity: Naho Yamada

Director of publishing services: Ben Applegate
Associate director of operations: Stephen Pakula
Publishing services managing editor: Noelle Webster
Assistant production managers: Emi Lotto, Angela Zurlo